SEEKING A
BETTER
COUNTRY

SEEKING A BETTER COUNTRY

300 Years of American Presbyterianism

D. G. HART AND JOHN R. MUETHER

P&R PUBLISHING

P.O. BOX 817 • PHILLIPSBURG • NEW JERSEY 08865-0817

Unless otherwise indicated, Scripture quotations are from The Holy Bible, English Standard Version, copyright © 2001 by Crossway Bibles, a division of Good News Publishers. Used by permission. All rights reserved.

Page design and typesetting by Lakeside Design Plus

Printed in the United States of America

Library of Congress Cataloging-in-Publication Data

Hart, D. G. (Darryl G.)
    Seeking a better country : 300 years of American Presbyterianism / D.G. Hart and John R. Muether.
        p. cm.
    Includes bibliographical references and index.
    ISBN 978-0-87552-574-7 (cloth)
    1. Presbyterian Church—United States—History. I. Muether, John R. II. Title.
BX8935.H37 2007
285'.109—dc22

                                                                2007014275

Contents

Preface

Now that American Presbyterians have had time to recover from the celebrations of their three-hundredth birthday, the time may be ripe for critical reflection on what they just celebrated. In point of fact, the festivities surrounding three hundred years of Presbyterian witness in America were subdued if not nonexistent in the denominations because of a widespread inability to appreciate the history of American Presbyterianism. Generally speaking, when American Presbyterians, whether liberal or conservative, turn to the past they read history selectively.

This is an obvious problem for such recent denominations as the Evangelical Presbyterian Church, the Presbyterian Church in America, and the Orthodox Presbyterian Church, where a sense of a new beginning and frustration with the mother church tempt Presbyterians to look to the past only as far as their denominations' founding. History before the beginning of the new church can yield only a depressing account of the difficulties that led to the break with the mainline church. But even in mainline Presbyterian circles, the temptation to confine one's interest in the past to the twentieth century is just as strong if not stronger. The reason is that for Presbyterians of a progressive mindset, the remote past is filled with the sorts of injustices and intolerance that only the recent church had the nerve to fix.

This book is written to cure the amnesia from which all Presbyterians suffer who trace their origins to the first presbytery founded in 1706 in Philadelphia. To be sure, the narrative that follows needs to be selective in its own right to fit within the confines of a volume accessible to lay people, pastors, and church historians. But we did write this book from the conviction and understanding that the church expressions of Presbyterianism in the Presbyterian Church (USA), EPC, PCA, and OPC have substantial and deep roots in the American Presbyterian experience begun when seven ministers assembled in Philadelphia for mutual edification and to ordain another man to the ministry of the Word and sacrament. As such our purpose is to help contemporary and future Presbyterians connect the dots between their own experiences in particular communions and the generations of Presbyterians who preceded them. Without those eighteenth-, nineteenth-, and twentieth-century saints, today's Presbyterians would be adrift.

This book is dedicated to a woman who has no such case of historical amnesia. In her work at the Presbyterian Historical Society, the archives of Westminster Theological Seminary and of the OPC, Grace Mullen has a wise understanding of the vicissitudes and riches of American Presbyterian history. And as a lifelong Orthodox Presbyterian, her historical awareness is tethered to a deep devotion nurtured by the Reformed faith. Both of us had the privilege of working with Grace when we served respectively as directors of Westminster's Montgomery Memorial Library—when, in fact, much of the direction came from our relying on Grace's own wise counsel as a librarian and archivist. As an acknowledgment of the debt we owe to her, and as a tribute to her insufficiently appreciated efforts to preserve Presbyterian history, we dedicate this book to Grace.

Introduction:
Of Sobriety and Legends

American Presbyterians are by most standards an impressive group. Of the fifty-six signers of the Declaration of Independence, Presbyterians accounted for eleven, and in the person of John Witherspoon boasted the only minister to have his name recorded on the nation's founding document. Presbyterians were less numerous in the production of the United States Constitution, but their six members of the fifty-five attending the Constitutional Convention in 1787 were nevertheless a striking showing.

Since the nation's beginning, eight presidents have been members of Presbyterian churches: Andrew Jackson, James Polk, James Buchanan, Grover Cleveland, Benjamin Harrison, Woodrow Wilson, Dwight Eisenhower, and Ronald Reagan. In cultural life, Presbyterians have been no less impressive. Writers with Presbyterian backgrounds include Mark Twain, Eudora Welty, and Frederick Buechner. Presbyterians have also produced a number of popular entertainers, from Jimmy Stewart, Shirley Temple, and Dick Van Dyke, to Frank Gifford, Fred (Mr.) Rogers, and David Letterman. In science, Presbyterians are common: C. Everett Koop, a leading pediatric surgeon, served as surgeon general of the United States, Edwin H. Armstrong invented the FM radio, and John Glenn and Sally Ride were astronauts who pioneered in space exploration.

Meanwhile, Presbyterians in business have made fortunes, from Andrew Carnegie to H. Ross Perot and Sam Walton. The success of American Presbyterians in these fields underscores the on adage about the social mobility of American Protestants: "Baptists are Methodists who can read, and Presbyterians are Baptists with shoes."

This book is only indirectly about these Presbyterians, however. A glance through the index at the end will reveal John Witherspoon and possibly one of the presidents mentioned above. The reason is that this brief history of American Presbyterianism is not about prominent Americans who happened to be Presbyterian. Instead, it is the history of the chief Presbyterian Church and its subsequent traditions. As such, this is a work of church history, not social history or collective biography. It provides an overview of the teachings and practices that set Presbyterians apart from other Christian communions in America.

This is not to say that the prominent Americans who worshiped in Presbyterian churches are insignificant for understanding the history of Presbyterianism in the United States. In fact, the pages that follow should be very instructive for understanding why a Protestant communion with doctrinal tenets (i.e., Calvinism) running directly contrary to American ideals of freedom and self-sufficiency became attractive to so many successful Americans. For at the beginning of American Presbyterianism's history, its status politically, socially, and culturally was much more like the adage about Presbyterians being Baptists with shoes than about those filling the lists of presidents, writers, and millionaires.

In sum, this book is about how a church with very humble origins became a communion known for belonging to that highly prized position of membership in the United States' Protestant establishment. The chapters that follow also raise questions, however, about whether being a religion of the affluent, successful, and powerful was supposed to be the point of being Presbyterian in America.

Presbyterian Primer

Anyone looking for an easy definition of Presbyterianism will likely be disappointed. For instance, none of the confessions or catechisms produced by the Reformed branches of the Protestant Reformation provides a summary statement on Presbyterianism. Dictionaries are not much help either. As a noun, *Presbyterian* refers to someone who is a member of a Presbyterian church. As an adjective, the word refers to a form of church government in which presbyters (i.e., elders) exercise rule. Since the Church of Jesus Christ of Latter-day Saints (Mormon) also involves the rule of elders, such definitions have serious limitations.

Presbyterianism, as the name suggests, is a form of church government different from either episcopal (more hierarchical) or congregational (more democratic) polities. But church government was only a part of what distinguished Presbyterians from other Christians, and possibly not even a major feature.

The Reformation of the sixteenth century produced three major branches of Protestantism that became part of the state-church order in Western Europe: the Anglican, Lutheran, and Reformed. Presbyterians were synonymous with Reformed, the latter being the term used on the Continent—Presbyterian designating similar beliefs and practices among the English-speaking Protestants in Great Britain and North America.

As the word *reformed* suggests, Presbyterians, like their Reformed siblings, were intent on reforming the church according to the Word of God. In theology, this meant an emphasis on human sinfulness, the complete sufficiency of Christ for salvation, a call to good works based not on merit but on love, and the elevation of Scripture over church tradition as the authority for determining ecclesiastical controversies.

In worship, Presbyterians and Reformed groups simplified services, eliminated practices that did not have direct warrant from Scripture (such as reducing the number of sacraments from seven to two), and devoted greater attention to the proclamation of the Word through preaching. In polity, Presbyterians and Reformed churches established the rule of elders through a series of graded courts, from the session at the local congregation, presbyteries and synods regionally, to the General Assembly as the body representing the whole church. (For Reformed groups, the different levels of church judicatories are consistories, classes, and synods.) These teachings and reforms took shape in the confessions and catechisms that Presbyterian and Reformed churches adopted during the sixteenth and seventeenth centuries, as well as in directories for public worship and church government.

Yet trying to define Presbyterianism as a body of ideas or a set of practices without reference to history is like trying to explain baseball to someone who has never seen a double play or sacrifice fly. Definitions of Presbyterianism only make sense in the light of historical experience. Even the creeds and confessions from which the most conservative of Presbyterians take inspiration and guidance are products of specific historical situations in which particular churches in unique circumstances determined what Presbyterianism meant. If this book has a lesson, this may be the most important: namely, that Presbyterianism understood apart from history is an abstraction bordering on fantasy.

This is not to say that Presbyterianism is relative. It is possible, we believe, to make judgments on better or worse forms of Presbyterianism, or when American Presbyterianism was in good or poor health. And the criteria for making these assessments are sometimes biblical or theological concepts that do transcend history. At the same time, however, it is important to see that even these ideas that appear to be the purest form of Presbyterianism are themselves the product of historical actors, often gifted with keen insight into Scripture and the history of Christian theology, who have emerged as authoritative guides to Presbyterianism and the Reformed faith. As this book makes abundantly clear, Presbyterianism did not fall from the sky with instructions on how to start a seminary, create committees, and serve communion. The elements and character of Presbyterianism have always been contested. This is especially true of the Presbyterian communion that emerged as the most numerous and influential in the United States.

Presbyterians and Calvinism

One reason for stressing the historical development of Presbyterianism, aside from the fact that this is a book of history, is that abstract notions of this Protestant branch can run into difficulty when the ideals don't line up exactly with historical realities. Take the example of Calvinism. One dictionary definition has it that a Presbyterian is a follower of Calvinism as taught in the Presbyterian Church. Historically, it is accurate to say that the founders of Presbyterianism in Scotland and later in America were stalwart defenders of Calvin's understanding of salvation. But to limit the identity of Presbyterianism to the five points of Calvinism is to foster confusion rather than clarity. For starters, other Protestants have been Calvinists but not Presbyterian, such as Particular or Calvinistic Baptists. To arrive at a doctrinal understanding of Presbyterianism that lacks the very feature highlighted in its name, that is, Presbyterian church government, is to commit an important historical mistake.

Just as significant here is the recognition that, whether for good or ill, not all Presbyterians have been Calvinistic. Cumberland Presbyterians, a group that left the American Presbyterian Church in the early nineteenth century because of objections to predestination and Calvinism's supposed disregard for human responsibility, were one of the first groups in the United States to divorce Presbyterianism and Calvinism. About a century later, liberal Presbyterians had moved well beyond objections to Calvinism to add other parts of historic Christianity to their list of doctrines in need of updating. And yet, in some sense, both of these groups were Presbyterian. They considered themselves part of the Presbyterian tradition not merely because they employed Presbyterian church government. They also traced their roots historically to the development of Presbyterianism in Great Britain and the United States. The following narrative attempts to account for this variety of Presbyterian expressions. To do so involves regarding Presbyterianism as more than the repristination of Calvinism, and instead looking at it as a religious or denominational tradition that has evolved to include a variety of perspectives on the nature of being Presbyterian.

Here the moral philosopher Alasdair MacIntyre's idea of tradition as an argument "extended through time in which certain fundamental agreements are defined and redefined . . ." is worthwhile for understanding the authors' approach to Presbyterianism. The history of Presbyterianism has in a sense been a lengthy debate about those features important to Presbyterian witness and identity. This book is about the American side of that argument. It has involved the way Americans appropriated their European past and developed their own expression of Presbyterianism. Some of the interlocutors in this argument about Presbyterianism have been better at seeing continuity and preserving the points at stake in earlier debates, while others have been more inclined to jettison those earlier speeches and venture out into newer lines of analysis. But to appreciate the full range of virtues and vices in American Presbyterianism, the authors have felt obligated to include the most important contributors to this argument even when some of those contributions were, in our estimation, unhealthy and detrimental.

Presbyterians and Puritans

Another possible source of confusion about American Presbyterianism that results from an overly abstract starting point is the relationship between Puritanism and Presbyterianism. Because both groups were in the Reformed wing of the Protestant Reformation and because both were Calvinistic, a common tendency is to lump them together as variations on the same theme. This is, however, a significant mistake since it distorts what has been a constant catalyst in the history of American Presbyterianism, namely, the disputes between immigrants to the United States with Presbyterian backgrounds and those with a Puritan heritage.

Presbyterians and Puritans were both Calvinistic and shared common ground in defending Reformed conceptions of sin and grace. But after this shared point the similarities quickly become harder to spot. The Puritans were Anglicans. That is, they were English and so members of the Church of England. They gained their reputation and name because they wanted to purify the Church of England, it in line with the goals of the Protestant Reformation. Some of those known as Puritans, a group increasingly hard to pin down, were Presbyterian and desired the abolition of bishops and priests in favor of a system of Presbyterian judicatories. But the interests of Puritans were different from those of the Presbyterians.

As the first chapter makes clear, Presbyterians were Scottish and Irish, and the Presbyterian Church was a body initially separate from the Church of England. The independence of Presbyterianism, however, became exceedingly difficult to maintain during the seventeenth century with its vexed political antagonism among the English monarchy, Parliament, and Scotland.

At certain points, Puritans and Presbyterians found themselves on the same side in these struggles. But at other times their interests differed, not simply because of variations in their religious outlook, but also because of practical realities in Scotland and England. The relationships between Presbyterians and Puritans in the North American British colonies and

6

then the United States were more cordial, thanks to the elimination of the threat of the Anglican establishment and to greater autonomy in the New World. Still, the Puritans in New England and the Scots and Scotch-Irish Presbyterians in the mid-Atlantic and Southern colonies and states did not always see things eye to eye. In fact, the major divisions in American Presbyterianism, the eighteenth-century Old Side-New Side struggle, the nineteenth-century Old School-New School division, and the twentieth-century modernist-fundamentalist controversy were outworkings of important differences between the heritages of English Puritanism and Scottish Presbyterianism.

Presbyterians and America

Yet another reason for stressing historical realities as opposed to religious ideals in trying to understand the history of American Presbyterianism is the uniqueness of the Presbyterian Church on the other side of the Atlantic Ocean from Scotland and Ireland. American Presbyterians are clearly indebted to developments in Scotland and Northern Ireland prior to the eighteenth century. Furthermore, the original membership of the Presbyterian churches in the United States was overwhelmingly Scottish and Scotch-Irish. Even so, the Presbyterianism that developed in America was significantly different from Scottish, Irish, or even Canadian Presbyterianism because of the unique set of circumstances that Presbyterians encountered in America. In fact, the subject of this book is the narrow one of Presbyterianism that was distinctly American as opposed to Americanized versions of Scottish or Irish Presbyterianism. This was also the first Presbyterianism to take formal shape in the New World with the creation in 1706 of the original American presbytery, the Presbytery of Philadelphia.

This book is about the denomination that grew from this first presbytery's roots, the Presbyterian Church (USA), as well as the denominations that at different times left this American denomination, such as the Cumberland Presbyterian Church, the Orthodox Presbyterian Church, the Presbyterian Church in America, and the Evangelical Presbyterian Church. All of these churches trace their roots to the founding of the Presbytery of Philadelphia in 1706.

Note - Presbytery of Philadelphia

As chapter one also makes clear, other Presbyterian churches came to America, for instance the Covenanters (Reformed Presbyterians) and the Seceders (Associate Reformed Presbyterians). But these were transplants from Scottish Presbyterianism. American Presbyterianism, however, was substantially an American original, being created without the oversight or support of Old World churches, figuring out what it meant to be a Presbyterian Church in America as circumstances allowed. Without historical awareness, the uniqueness of American Presbyterianism is either difficult to see or a source of confusion.

We have divided the history of this American Presbyterian Church into three main periods. The first runs from the founding of the Presbytery of Philadelphia in 1706 to the formation in 1789 of the first General Assembly of the Presbyterian Church in the U.S.A. American Presbyterianism during this era was characterized by basic questions of institutional identity. What sort of theological, educational, and spiritual criteria should be used to choose Presbyterian pastors? What are the functions of sessions, presbyteries, and synods? How should Presbyterians respond to America's religious diversity and freedom? These concerns were substantially responsible for giving an infant church of humble origins the institutional foundation on which future generations of Presbyterians would build. But American Presbyterianism during the colonial era was hardly set in stone, nor did it have many Old World models to emulate. The founders of the American church may not have been making it up as they went along, but the record shows that clarity of vision and purpose was not a trait of eighteenth-century American Presbyterianism. The formation of the American Presbyterian tradition was contested at practically every stage.

The second period covers the decades between the first General Assembly and the 1860s, when American Presbyterians decided to exist independently in regional churches that were divided by the politics of the Civil War. During this era American Presbyterianism matured and flourished, even though it took a division over the Second Great Awakening between Old School and New School Presbyterians to achieve such discernment. Substantial disagreements over the nature and function of the church animated Presbyterianism during this era—thanks to questions that arose over the church's involvement in the Christianization of the United States. But the Presbyterians who contributed to these debates, both among the Old School and New School, added intellectual heft to the institutional skeleton of Presbyterianism inherited from the colonial period. To the extent that American Presbyterians today have strong conceptions of Presbyterian identity, whether conservative, evangelical, or mainline, they owe a substantial debt to the concerted attention to Presbyterian faith and practice by nineteenth-century Presbyterians.

The third period extends from the 1869 reunion of the Old and New Schools in the North to the reunion in 1983 of northern and southern Presbyterianism. This stage of Presbyterian history is the most difficult to write because it involves covering both the northern and southern Presbyterian mainline denominations, plus keeping an eye on the sideline churches such as the Orthodox Presbyterian Church (OPC), Presbyterian Church in America (PCA), and Evangelical Presbyterian Church (EPC) that left those larger and more diverse communions.[1] This era was one marked by interdenominational cooperation and the pursuit of formal ecumenical ties among Protestants of all kinds, and later between Protestants and Roman Catholics.

As much as the reasons given for these ecumenical discussions appealed to Christ's prayer that his disciples be one, the politicization of American Presbyterianism during the Civil War was also crucial. Late nineteenth-century Protestants, often with Presbyterians leading the way, saw the divisions among Protestants as an impediment to the kind of cooperative good will and common action that the United States needed both to overcome domestic ills and to lead internationally in the cause of freedom and democracy. But despite the fraternal spirit of the times, the search for unity could not prevent smaller churches from leaving both the northern and southern churches over important disagreements about the limits of such denominational cooperation. Nor did the widespread support for ecumenism easily break down barriers between Presbyterians in the North and South who for over a century harbored suspicions of each other because of moral and political antagonisms. Our book concludes

---

1. This book differs from its predecessors, such as Lefferts A. Loetscher's *A Brief History of the Presbyterians* (1978) and James H. Smylie's *A Brief History of the Presbyterians* (1996), that, despite their titles, focused on the American mainline denominations and paid only passing reference to the denominations that formed as the result of controversies within mainline Presbyterianism in the United States.

with some reflection on the prospects for American Presbyterianism at the start of its fourth century of existence.

Anniversaries and Celebration

Anniversaries are generally times of celebration. Many readers of history read it for inspiration. Put those two impulses together, and you have a set of expectations that this book will likely not fulfill. The reason is not that the authors are, as Spiro T. Agnew put it, "nattering nabobs of negativism," though some have accused us of such. Instead, the lack of revelry here stems from our shared sense of all historical actors' clay feet. Even if history is not simply the story of human frailty and suffering, if it yields persons, events, and institutions with genuinely noble aspects, history is nonetheless not the place to go for assurance or vindication of one's deeply held convictions. For every Gilbert Tennent, Albert Barnes, and Harry Emerson Fosdick, there was also a John Thomson, Charles Hodge, and J. Gresham Machen laying claim to a legitimate position within the American Presbyterian Church.

Consequently, although this book uses the tercentenary of American Presbyterianism as the impetus for writing a new history of the Presbyterian experience in the United States, it is not a celebration of the church's past. As faithful and virtuous as many of our Presbyterian ancestors were, the thrill of recalling their accomplishments will not sustain the difficult work of contemporary Presbyterians seeking to be faithful and discerning.

Indeed, because the authors are interested in serving the church and assisting Presbyterians in their calling to be faithful disciples, we have decided to write a history that is more sober than enthusiastic, and more accurate than filled with legends. For what American Presbyterians need today, as they have throughout their past, is not a rosy or gloomy estimate of their prospects. Instead, they need a history that will yield discernment and wisdom about the strengths and weaknesses of their tradition, as well as the degree to which the circumstances of being American have affected their identities as Presbyterians. If the pages that follow avoid producing disillusionment and optimism but steer in the middle toward hopefulness that, in good Presbyterian fashion, is decent and well ordered, then this book should be worth reading.

PART 1

1706–1789

1706 - The first manifestation of Presbyterianism in America in Philadelphia.

1

Scotland to America

The older histories of American Presbyterianism often begin with brief narratives of the earliest congregations that emerged during the British colonial settlement of North America. You can read about Presbyterian outposts on Long Island as early as the 1640s, in New Jersey and Maryland during the 1680s, or Pennsylvania and Delaware during the 1690s. Some of these authors may even attempt to link the origins of American Presbyterianism to New England Puritanism, not only because of the cultural cachet that the Puritans possessed with their Ivy League colleges, idyllic town squares, and inspiring church steeples, but also because some Puritans favored Presbyterian church government over the Congregationalist scheme that prevailed in Massachusetts and Connecticut. But after all the scouring of congregational records has been finished, the fact remains that 1706 is the first manifestation of Presbyterianism in North America. The reason is simple: for Presbyterianism to exist it requires a presbytery, and the first presbytery in America began with the initial meeting of the Presbytery of Philadelphia. Without a presbytery, a minister or congregation that advocates Presbyterian church government is still only a congregation, and so abiding by congregationalist church polity.

No pageantry or ceremony of any means marked that first meeting of the Presbytery of Philadelphia. In fact, the records of this meeting have been lost. Nevertheless, it was the first gathering of ministers as presbyters to reflect the unity of their Presbyterian Church and to convene the agency that would settle disputes and regulate the life and teaching of their common church.

And the region over which this church court ruled was significant. Philadelphia was run by Quakers, who practiced religious toleration according to William Penn's convictions. This made the city, and the colony of which it was the commercial hub, a place teeming with various Protestant groups, from Moravians and Lutherans to Mennonites and Presbyterians. The city's ethnic diversity was indeed stunning for the time, and the Scotch-Irish who came to British North America through the port of Philadelphia bore all the marks of immigration's harsh circumstances. Philadelphia, then, was one of the few cities that could be a home for Presbyterianism. Boston conformed to the established Congregationalist churches; Williamsburg, Virginia, was firmly Episcopalian; and New York City was still sorting through the rival claims of the Church of England and the Dutch Reformed.

The reasons for stressing the "presbyterian" as opposed to "congregationalist" origins of American Presbyterianism and the place of the first presbytery have to do not only with theological and historical accuracy but also with underscoring the precarious, unpretentious, and humble roots of this Protestant church. *Presbyterianism* is a word that suggests a theological heritage rich in historical and cultural accomplishments, a church that was part of the momentous struggles of the sixteenth-century Protestant Reformation, influenced politics and church life in seventeenth-century Britain, and played a pivotal role in the founding of the United States of America—in sum, a church not on the margins but respectable, prestigious, even powerful. But Presbyterians on both sides of the Atlantic, in Scotland, Northern Ireland, Pennsylvania, and New Jersey, were not mighty or influential for much of their early history. In fact, for parts of their young existence, Presbyterians were as marginal and apparently crude as sixteenth-century Anabaptists, seventeenth-century Baptists, or eighteenth-century Methodists. To understand Presbyterianism's modest beginnings requires some awareness of the way a church that began in Scotland arrived in a land dominated by the English.

The Ordeal of Scottish Presbyterianism

The seventeenth century shines in Presbyterian history if only because it was the time when the doctrinal standards for Presbyterians around the world originated. In fact, it is not uncommon for Presbyterian tourists in London to practice a Protestant form of pilgrimage and pay their respects to the labors of the Westminster Divines who gathered between 1643 and 1649 at Westminster Abbey. This site that hosted the coronation of English kings was also where the ministers gathered who were responsible for writing the Westminster Confession of Faith, and the companion Shorter and Larger Catechisms. But one of the few rules of Presbyterian history is that looking to London for support and inspiration is a mistake, because that city, and England more generally, was Anglican, not Presbyterian.

Presbyterianism's roots, of course, were in Scotland. And during the decade that the Westminster Divines were writing the confessional standards that would eventually be normative for Presbyterian churches, England was in a fierce contest for control of the British Isles. As it turns out, the shining moment of the seventeenth century for Presbyterians was also the time of the English Civil War, a period when the prospects for a Presbyterian church in the English-speaking world looked bleakest.

The emergence of Presbyterianism in Scotland was part of the larger phenomenon of the Protestant Reformation. The earliest Protestant influences in Scotland were Lutheran. One particular pastor, Patrick Hamilton (1504?–28), who ministered in St. Andrews, had studied in Germany during the 1520s and came under Luther's influence. But his efforts to introduce Protestantism to Scotland met with swift resistance. Church authorities accused Hamilton of heresy and had him executed for his departure from Roman Catholicism.

John Knox (1514–72), generally regarded as the father of Scottish Presbyterianism, also began his life as a Protestant through reading the writings of Luther. Like Hamilton, Knox also ministered in the church at St. Andrews, but when he began to teach justification by faith alone

15

the new doctrine again met opposition. In this case though, the penalty for Knox was less drastic—he was condemned to work as a galley slave in France for nineteen months. During his indentured service Knox continued to study, and wrote a summary of the Christian faith based on Luther's commentary on Galatians.

In 1549, when set free, Knox went to live in England and actually served as a minister to Edward VI while contributing to revisions of the Book of Common Prayer. But in 1554 when Mary Tudor assumed the royal crown in England and tried to return the Church of England back to Rome's authority, Knox fled the country because of the queen's persecution of Protestants. He eventually found his way to Geneva where he preached to the English exiles in the city, and where he came under the Reformed Protestant influences of John Calvin. By 1559 Knox returned to Scotland and oversaw the reform of the Scottish kingdom's church.

The next year, 1560, witnessed the birth of Protestantism and Presbyterianism in Scotland. Parliament voted to abolish the authority of the pope in the realm, prohibited celebration of the Mass, and ratified the Scottish Confession of Faith, a creed that bears the decided influence of Knox. Four years later the Scottish church, again with the herculean efforts of Knox, produced the Book of Common Order (1564) to govern the liturgy. Having reformed its creed and worship, the Scottish church in 1578 composed the Second Book of Discipline to take care of church polity. Despite Knox's death in 1572, between 1560 and 1578 the building blocks were in place for Presbyterianism in Scotland.

But after a promising start, Presbyterians in Scotland ran up against the realities of British politics (though it should be acknowledged that Presbyterianism emerged in Scotland thanks as well to chinks in British politics). In fact, many of the setbacks the Scottish kirk endured during the seventeenth century stemmed from a Scottish monarch. James VI of Scotland, whose reign lasted from 1567 to 1625, was never a big supporter of Presbyterianism. In 1584 he tried to introduce an episcopal form of government, but Presbyterian opposition prevented his success.

But when James, a son of Mary Tudor, inherited the monarchy of England and became James I, ruling over both Scotland and England, he favored the Anglican church and began to impose Episcopalian government and Anglican liturgy on the church in Scotland. James took some of the pressure off the situation by approving the 1618 establishment of the Plantation of Ulster. It became the home for many Scottish Presbyterian immigrants to Northern Ireland as part of an effort to erode Roman Catholic rule among the Irish. Still, the English crown's hostility to Presbyterianism persisted. James I pushed through Parliament the Five Articles, which imposed further Anglican practices on the Scottish kirk. James's son, Charles I, who ruled from 1625 to 1649, flouted Presbyterian convictions and in 1638 attempted to force Presbyterians to use the Anglican Book of Common Prayer in worship.

The aggressive actions of the British monarchs toward Presbyterians in Scotland during the first third of the seventeenth century provided the backdrop both for the English Civil War (which historians now call "The Wars of the Three Kingdoms") and the Westminster Assembly. James I and his son Charles I were no less truculent regarding matters closer to home. Both of the Stuart monarchs believed in the divine right of kings, a theory that held that the monarch's power came directly from God and that he was similarly accountable only to God.

In 1639 this outlook precipitated a rupture between the crown and Parliament, with the latter going into permanent session and refusing to pass any new legislation or to raise revenue until the king backed down. The situation came to a head in 1642 with the beginning of the English Civil War, which pitted Charles I against Parliament. Because Puritans dominated Parliament, the war has also been called the Puritan Revolution. A year later Parliament gained a distinct advantage in this war when it formed an alliance with Presbyterian Scots by ratifying the Solemn League and Covenant.[1]

Obviously, the situation was now as complicated religiously as it was politically, with Presbyterians and Anglicans, Scots and English joining forces to battle a recalcitrant monarch. But this was precisely the setting in which the Westminster Assembly convened in 1643 to begin establishing a religious order that would both satisfy the Puritans in Parliament and prove workable for Presbyterians in Scotland. Some-

1. The Solemn League and Covenant was in effect an extension of the Scots King's Confession of 1581 and the National Covenant of 1638 to the political situation of England. The earlier statements expressed the mutual commitment of crown and Parliament to the true religion and political loyalty. When the English Parliament sought a political alliance with the Scots against the Stuart monarchy, it agreed to extend the terms of religious uniformity in Scotland to the United Kingdom (i.e., England and Scotland).

thing often forgotten about the Westminster Assembly is that, while its members were composing the Westminster Confession and the Larger and Shorter Catechisms, its patrons in Parliament were prosecuting a war against Charles I that resulted in the execution of a king. On January 30, 1649, after being tried by Parliament for treason, Charles I was beheaded. Not even the inspiring and precise prose of Westminster theology could escape the larger political realities that plagued seventeenth-century Presbyterianism.

For the next four decades after the death of Charles I, the ordeal confronting Scottish Presbyterians actually worsened. First, Oliver Cromwell invaded Scotland in 1650 because the Scots themselves had grown frustrated over their alliance with the English Parliament and crowned Charles II, the son of Charles I, as king of England, Scotland, and Ireland. Cromwell was successful in defeating the Scots and denying Charles II's rule for a decade. But, second, when Cromwell died in 1658 and the monarchy was finally restored in 1660 with Charles II on the throne, the prospects for Presbyterians in Scotland plummeted.

The English Parliament, in reaction against its Puritan predecessors, set out to establish Anglicanism throughout Great Britain, and the king could not prevent the enforcement of religious uniformity. As such, government officials threw out more than three hundred Presbyterian pastors from their congregations and replaced them with Anglican priests. In 1666, Parliament also passed laws requiring attendance at the state churches. Presbyterian ministers were conducting services and preaching in the open fields at this time.

The most zealous Presbyterians, who still affirmed the Solemn National Covenant of 1638, and so went by the name Covenanters, organized military resistance to this system of religious coercion. In turn, this Presbyterian defiance encountered even fiercer persecution by the English military. The worst of the escalating persecution of the Covenanters came at the end of Charles II's reign, from 1684 to 1685, the so-called "killing time." In that period, nearly one hundred and fifty Presbyterians were executed, many without even receiving a trial, for their religious practices and open rebellion against religious and state authorities.

Ironically, what ended the aggression against Presbyterianism in Scotland was the succession of James II, Charles's brother, to the throne.

A Roman Catholic, James met with immediate opposition from Parliament when he tried to throw the weight of his government behind Roman Catholicism. English Protestant statesmen in turn called James's son-in-law, William of Orange, from the Netherlands, to assume the crown. He landed in England in November 1688, and marched to London unopposed, thus accomplishing the so-called Glorious Revolution, under the reign of William and Mary.

In 1689 Parliament passed the Toleration Act, which granted religious liberty to non-Anglican Protestants in England. For the Scots the reign of William and Mary meant the establishment of Presbyterianism as the state church. In 1690, as part of the Glorious Revolution's settlement, the Presbyterian church became the Church of Scotland. This involved the abolition of the office of bishop in the Scottish church and the reinstatement of ejected ministers. It also brought restoration of late sixteenth-century acts that recognized Presbyterianism as the polity for the churches in Scotland—which included the authority of the General Assembly to oversee Scottish church life.

This ecclesiastical settlement was a compromise in several respects. It allowed Episcopalian priests serving in Scotland to remain as ministers as long as they could take an oath of loyalty to the General Assembly. Also, the settlement did not include an affirmation of the Solemn League and Covenant. This left the Covenanters no place in Scotland's official church, since they continued to insist that the king and Parliament recognize the 1638 promise between the British crown and the Scots. But despite these compromises, the settlement of 1690 did restore Presbyterianism in Scotland to the privileged position it had enjoyed in the late sixteenth century. Ironically, because of seventeenth-century British politics, the mainstream Presbyterian churches in Scotland would be only sixteen years older than their American counterparts, which started in 1706.

The other Presbyterian stronghold for the Scots was Northern Ireland, where the Plantation of Ulster had attracted Presbyterians during the first half of the seventeenth century. The Scotch-Irish Presbyterians of Ulster would become an important resource for American Presbyterianism, since more of the American church's founders came from Northern Ireland than from Scotland. In fact, some of the first Presbyterian congregations in Pennsylvania were the result of migrations to the New World by Scotch-Irish who were being persecuted by Charles II.

19

William of Orange secured a permanent place for Presbyterianism in Northern Ireland in 1689 during the Battle of Boyne, when he defeated Roman Catholic armies still loyal to his predecessor, James II. William's victory may have granted priority to Protestants over Roman Catholics in Northern Ireland. Yet it did not bring stability to Ulster Presbyters, who continued to be subject to difficulties, thanks to political struggles between England and Ireland throughout the eighteenth century. Even so, the resilience of Scotch-Irish Presbyterianism needs to be acknowledged in any account of American Presbyterianism.

Presbyterian Transplants

The ordeal of Presbyterianism in Scotland and Northern Ireland had important consequences for the emergence and development of Presbyterian churches in the United States. Arguably, the greatest was that American Presbyterianism rose and grew without the support and nurture of a mother church in Europe. Clearly, the situation in Scotland and Northern Ireland confronting Presbyterian bodies left them without resources to assist daughter churches in the New World. For this reason, American Presbyterianism would have to rely on its own wisdom and strength.

In fact, of the three major Presbyterian traditions to found denominations in the United States, the one with the least connection to Presbyterianism in the Old World emerged as the strongest or most numerous and influential, namely, the mainstream Presbyterian Church later known as the Presbyterian Church in the U.S.A. The other two, the Covenanters and the Associate Reformed Presbyterians, took shape with Scottish precedents in view even if not having formal ties to churches in the old country. Before turning the attention of this book to the mainstream Presbyterian body that started in 1706, some acquaintance with these other two Presbyterian traditions is useful, first, to underscore the difficult circumstances that Presbyterianism faced during its first two hundred years, and second, to recognize the uniqueness of mainstream American Presbyterianism in contrast with other Presbyterian communions.

Of the three Presbyterian branches in the United States, the Covenanters were the ones with the greatest stake in the struggles of seventeenth-century Scotland and for whom that history would provide

20

a major source of identity. They took their name from their support for the National Covenant of 1638, as well as the Solemn League and Covenant of 1643. During the period from 1638 to 1660 in Scotland, the Covenanters were synonymous with Scottish Presbyterianism, since they were the main opposition to the English monarchs' efforts to impose Anglicanism on the Church of Scotland. In fact, the chief impulse that has sustained the Covenanters throughout their history is the spiritual independence of the church from the state in order to protect and preserve the headship of Christ over the church. This was the principal rationale for their opposition first to Charles I and then to his son, Charles II.

Although they enjoyed significant influence on the English Parliament during the 1640s and 1650s as allies against the crown, after the restoration of the monarchy in 1660 and the subsequent subjection of the Scottish church to English norms, the Covenanters became a persecuted minority. From 1660 until 1690 the Covenanters were identified principally with those ministers who refused to submit to the new ecclesiastical norms and who suffered greatly for their resistance.

By 1690 when the Church of Scotland finally gained its standing as a Presbyterian body, the Covenanters, who since 1663 had been existing in the form of societies of believers without formal support or lawful ministers, remained separate from the kirk. Their reasons were elaborated in "The Reformed Presbyterian Testimony," which included four reasons for staying outside the established church, all of which concerned the unhealthy relationship between religion and politics throughout the seventeenth century and, in turn, compromised the original theological convictions of the Scottish Reformation. Finally in 1743, these informal dissenting groups of Presbyterians achieved a measure of stability by forming the Reformed Presbytery. As such, Covenanter is synonymous with Reformed Presbyterian.

The Covenanters' characteristics included not merely the affirmation of Christ as the sole and spiritual king of the church. The conviction of the church's spiritual independence from the state also committed Covenanters to holding that Christ is also head of the civil realm. The National Covenant and the Solemn League and Covenant were both explicit in pledging the support of the king and Parliament to the Reformed religion within the church and to Christ as "the King of kings" in civil society. For this reason, one of the characteristics of Covenanters in the United States, until as recently as 1980, was their refusal to participate in American electoral politics until the Constitution acknowledged the kingship of Christ.

The other noticeable difference between the Covenanters and mainstream American Presbyterians is worship. The Covenanters, like many conservative Scottish Presbyterians, insisted that metrical psalms were the only appropriate form of song for Christian worship. In addition, the Covenanters avoided most forms of worship that hinted of liturgy because of its negative associations with Anglicanism. Covenanter worship invariably avoided the praying of the Lord's Prayer, the recitation of the Apostles' Creed, or even the use of a bulletin or written form of worship. Congregational singing was also unaccompanied, although led by a precentor who in one period would sing a line for the congregation to repeat and later, when members knew the tunes, would set the initial pitch and keep the singing at the right tempo.

Although the Covenanters were a sizeable piece of seventeenth-century Presbyterianism, they took longer to take institutional form in the New World than the mainstream American Presbyterian communion. With other Scottish and Scotch-Irish immigrants to the British colonies in North America, the Covenanters often lacked ministers and worshiped when and where they could, sometimes attending mainstream Presbyterian congregations.

The first Covenanter society in America formed in 1743 in Middle Octarara (Lancaster County), Pennsylvania. What identified this congregation as Covenanter was its reaffirmation of the National Covenant of 1638. The Covenanters in America then petitioned the Reformed Presbytery of Scotland for supply preaching. In response to this request the Scottish Covenanters sent John Cuthbertson, who ministered almost single-handedly for twenty years in the New World among different groups of Covenanters. In 1774 he finally received help when the Reformed Presbytery of Scotland sent two additional ministers. At that point, with three pastors, the Covenanters in America formed their first presbytery in Paxton, Pennsylvania. By the close of the eighteenth century, 1798 to be precise, the Covenanters had grown sufficiently to become a separate denomination under the name the Reformed Presbytery of the United

States of North America (later to be called the Reformed Presbyterian Church of North America).

Not all of the original members of the Covenanters' presbytery joined this denomination, but some instead affiliated with the Associate Presbyterians, the second Presbyterian branch to emerge in the United States separate from the mainstream body. Also known as the Seceders, the Associate Presbyterians were another group of Scottish Presbyterians to emerge in the Old World and establish churches in North America. These Presbyterians had great sympathy for the Covenanters but, unlike them, decided in 1690 to join with the established Church of Scotland. But after that ecclesiastical settlement, a number of theological and political controversies emerged in the first three decades of the eighteenth century that revealed significant differences within the official kirk. The doctrinal conflicts centered on the nature of grace in salvation and the degree to which men and women can prepare for forgiveness of sins, along with the degree to which good works function as a form of assurance of grace. The political controversies concerned, yet again, the independence of the church from state oversight.

What specifically prompted a secession (hence Seceders) of ministers from the Church of Scotland and the formation of an Associate Presbytery in 1733 was the call of Ebenezer Erskine in 1731 by the parish of Kinross. The patron (or government official) of Kinross, however, disagreed with the congregation's wishes and installed the minister of his own choosing. This led to a conflict between the Presbytery of Dumferline and the Scottish General Assembly, with the former siding with the congregation, and the latter taking the patron's side. The upshot of these disputes among parish, presbytery, and General Assembly was the establishment of the Associate Presbyterian Church, with Ralph and Ebenezer Erskine providing leadership to these Seceders.

Because they shared a history with Covenanters in their opposition to the imposition of Anglicanism in Scotland and sympathies for the principles articulated in the National Covenant, Associate Presbyterians held convictions that looked similar. This overlap of sensibility helps to explain why in North America parts of each group have sometimes affiliated or joined the other's communion. But the Seceders, because of their entering the Scottish ecclesiastical establishment, took a different view of the relationship between church and state, looking for more

23

reciprocity than the Covenanters would allow. The doctrinal conflicts of the early eighteenth century in Scotland were also important factors in giving the Associate Presbyterians a separate identity. But on matters of worship and psalm-singing, and in jealously guarding the spiritual independence of the church, Associate Presbyterians were very close to the Covenanters.

The Associate Presbyterians were the most intentional of all American Presbyterian denominations in establishing a daughter church in the New World. They sent missionaries to the British colonies, and after several difficult tenures two of these ministers stayed long enough to form in 1753 the first Associate Presbyterian presbytery in southeastern Pennsylvania. By 1776 the Associate Presbyterians had two presbyteries, one in New York and one in Pennsylvania.

Because of their affinities with the Covenanters, in 1782 the Associate Presbyterians merged with some of the Reformed Presbyterians to become the Associate Reformed Presbyterian Church. This would be the largest of the predominantly Scottish Presbyterian communions in the United States, eventually yielding two denominations, the United Presbyterian Church of North America, a denomination made up of two of the Associate Reformed Presbyterian Church's synods (the North and West), as well as the Associate Reformed Presbyterian Church in the South (the ARP's southern synod), which continues in the twenty-first century, to perpetuate this distinct version of Scottish Presbyterianism transplanted in America.

American Orphan

Unlike the Associate Presbyterians or Covenanters, the mainstream American Presbyterian tradition that began in 1706 emerged not as the daughter church to Old World sponsors but as a Presbyterian expression without deliberate missionary strategy or oversight. Its history is unlike that of other Reformed denominations in the North American British colonies which are bound up with the story of their European mother churches. The Dutch and German Reformed each were under the oversight of synods in Continental Europe and did not gain independence from their religious supporters until the United States itself gained political independence from England. The same is true for the

Associate Presbyterians. But the mainstream American Presbyterian Church was different, even novel, in the history of Reformed Christianity in the United States. It began virtually at the initiative of New World ministers who were without substantial accountability either to ecclesiastical or political bodies in the Old World.

Although some of the Puritans who migrated to the New World were Presbyterian by conviction (that is, holding to a Presbyterian form of church government as opposed to Congregationalism), the growth of an American Presbyterian church would depend on the migration of people inclined to form Presbyterian congregations. This helps to explain why some of the first congregations that historians count as Presbyterian could be identified as such. These emerged in the 1640s on Long Island, pastored by ministers from New England who, as Charles Briggs described them, adhered to "the Puritan type of Presbyterianism." John Young in Southold Abraham Pierson in Southampton, and Francis Doughty in Mespat, were Puritan types who took calls on Long Island outside the jurisdiction of New England's Congregationalist establishment.

But Presbyterianism would need more than ministers. It would need church members, and such people did not begin to make their religious needs known until after 1680, when for a variety of circumstances a trickle of Scottish emigration to the New World began to collect as a noticeable Presbyterian presence.

The Scots were, in fact, responsible for two colonies in the lands that would become the United States. In the decade prior to the Glorious Revolution of 1688, the Covenanters attempted to establish a colony in the Carolinas that they formed specifically to escape religious deprivation under the reign of Charles II. But this colony never attracted many settlers. Once the persecution of Covenanters ended, thus removing the rationale for migration, the colony became an easy target for Spanish attack, which occurred in 1686 and finished off the effort. The other Scottish colony of note, also starting in the 1680s, was the one in East Jersey, an endeavor conceived and executed by Scottish Quakers. Because of the Scottish ties, this colony and region would eventually attract Scots of Presbyterian faith. But this would not happen for another four decades. In the meantime, Scottish culture in East Jersey would be more Quaker than Presbyterian.

More typical of the earliest Presbyterian experience in the British colonies than either the case of Long Island or Carolina was a haphazard movement of families from Scotland and Northern Ireland, looking for means of physical and spiritual sustenance. Two cases in particular help to illustrate the fragile condition of American Presbyterianism at its beginning. The first is that of Francis Makemie, the so-called father of American Presbyterianism, who ministered to these recent migrants scattered throughout the lands surrounding the Chesapeake Bay. The second is that of Jedediah Andrews, the first settled Presbyterian pastor in the city of Philadelphia.

Born in Donegal County, Ireland, in 1658, Makemie studied for the ministry at the University of Glasgow and was subsequently ordained in 1681 by the Presbytery of Laggan. His reasons for moving are unclear (since most of the records have not survived), but he left his homeland initially to minister on the Caribbean island of Barbados. By 1684 Makemie had helped to organize a Presbyterian congregation in Snow Hill, Maryland. He recorded that the population in this small peninsula between the ocean and the bay was sparse and the society was devoid of towns. The subsistence existence of these settlers prevented them from taking on any real form of social organization, let alone religious affiliation. According to Makemie:

> Towns and cohabitation would highly advance religion, which flourishes most in cohabitations; for in remote and scattered settlements we can never enjoy so fully, frequently, and certainly, those privileges and opportunities as are to be had in all Christian towns and cities; for by reason of bad weather, or other accidents, ministers are prevented, and people are hindered to attend, and so disappoint one another: But in towns, congregations are never wanting, and children and servants never are without opportunity of hearing, who cannot travel many miles to hear, and be catechized.

For these reasons, Makemie's efforts involved as much finding those who would hear his sermons and receive his instruction as the actual preparation of what he proclaimed and taught. In fact, the Snow Hill congregation would not be Makemie's only charge. For most of his work as a Presbyterian pastor, he functioned as an itinerant missionary, primarily on the Chesapeake Bay's eastern shore, but also in Virginia, with occasional trips to preach to groups of believers in the Carolinas.

The condition of these churches, combined with his own limited resources to minister to them, prompted Makemie to take the initiative in seeking assistance both in New England and the old country for a Presbyterian witness. He corresponded with ministers in Boston and London, asking them to send ministers who might be willing to shepherd in these hardscrabble conditions. Makemie even traveled to London to visit with pastors there and communicate the need for Presbyterian ministers in the New World. On another trip he visited Cotton Mather in New England to see whether the churches there might spare young men seeking to minister the Word. On one of these expeditions, Makemie recruited a minister for the work in Maryland. But this effort practically came to naught, thanks to the spread of the Church of England in the late seventeenth and early eighteenth centuries as the established religion in numerous colonies such as Maryland and New York. In fact, the change of religious establishments led to one of the most dramatic affairs of Makemie's known life, and through it he emerged as the obvious leader of the young Presbyterian Church.

The incident that would call on Makemie's courage and wisdom did not occur until 1707, a year or so after the founding of the Presbytery of Philadelphia. It also was another aspect of the difficulties that Presbyterianism faced in gaining a foothold on North American soil, in this case legal and political, rather than merely human and financial. During one of his many travels, Makemie headed north toward New England with John Hampton, one of the Irish Presbyterians, to assist in the work of planting Presbyterian churches. While passing through New York, Makemie tried to preach in the pulpit of a Dutch Reformed congregation, but the authorities forbade Makemie from preaching. So he led services in a private home in the city. Meanwhile, Hampton also preached in the public meetinghouse in Newtown, Long Island. Three days later, with Makemie having joined up with Hampton in Newtown, the local sheriff arrested the two Presbyterian ministers for preaching in the colony of New York without a license from the royal governor, Lord Cornbury.

The legal proceedings against Makemie would last for the better part of five months, all of which he spent in jail (Hampton had been released because his offense was less grave, having preached in a public setting). In his first exchange with Lord Cornbury, Makemie answered the charge that he was spreading "pernicious doctrines" contrary to the Church of England, first by citing King William's Act of Toleration of 1689 and the protections it guaranteed for Protestant dissenters under English rule. Makemie also argued that none of his preaching was contrary to the Thirty-Nine Articles, except for those parts that the law specified as legitimately contested by dissenters.

Another part of the charge against Makemie was that he had been preaching in a private setting, a sure indication of objectionable teaching and a breach of the public decorum that official religion helped to maintain. Makemie's response included pointing out that once he was refused a license for preaching in public he had tried to minister the word in as public a manner as possible "with open doors." Ultimately, however, Makemie admitted that he had no plausible defense against the colony's laws or the governor's arbitrary rulings if he was prevented from preaching the gospel. He told Lord Cornbury that even though he tried "to live always so as to keep a conscience void of offence towards God and man," he neither could nor would refuse to preach if asked "by any people" no matter what the law or the government.

After considerable time in prison, and negotiations with the legal authorities and petitioning Lord Cornbury, Makemie finally received a trial by jury. Here the Presbyterian minister showed himself knowledgeable of English law and reasonable in his objections to what appeared to be the arbitrary decisions of the royal governor. The jury acquitted Makemie of all charges, except for the legal fees associated with the trial, which he was still compelled to pay. During the late eighteenth century this incident would become a staple in the case for Presbyterianism's support for freedom of religion. Just as pertinent, however, was not simply the intolerance of ecclesiastical establishments. Makemie's submission to the penalty of law, no matter how seemingly unfair, was a wound that Presbyterians during the American Revolution often recalled to oppose English plans to install an Anglican bishop in North America. And yet, thanks to this Irish Presbyterian's indefatigable efforts, both on behalf of small, impoverished congregations and as a public spokesman on behalf of a larger Presbyterian body, American Presbyterianism did establish a secure, even if modest, foundation during the late seventeenth and early eighteenth centuries.

A second example of the conditions that colonial Presbyterians faced was that involving the ministry of Jedediah Andrews, a man of Presbyterian conviction sent by New England authorities to Philadelphia, likely at one of Makemie's pleas for assistance. Andrews was born in 1674 in Hingham, Massachusetts. He was graduated from Harvard College in 1695, and three years later had taken up residence in the port city of Philadelphia. Because of incidents like those faced by Makemie in New York, and because of the Church of England's control of religious life in most southern colonies, the mid-Atlantic settlements in Pennsylvania, New Jersey, and Delaware would be especially fruitful for Presbyterian congregations, with Philadelphia providing the most resources in those colonies, thus making it the informal capital of American Presbyterianism.

When Andrews arrived in Philadelphia, his congregation was a motley assortment of English-speaking Protestants. Records indicate that as many as nine Baptists were in the congregation, as well as émigrés from Scotland, Wales, New England, and even Sweden. According to one Episcopalian observer who reported on Andrews's 1701 installation in Philadelphia, "The Presbyterians have come a great way to lay hands on one another, but, after all, I think they had as good a stay at home, for all the good they do . . . In Philadelphia one pretends to be a Presbyterian, and has a congregation to which he preaches." Two years later another Philadelphian remarked that Presbyterians did have a meeting place in the city and a minister but "they are not likely to increase here." In point of fact, Presbyterians did persist and grow in William Penn's city, thanks to the religious freedom Quakers afforded to all sorts of dissenting religious groups (including swarms of German-speaking Protestants).

But Presbyterianism increased in Philadelphia and elsewhere thanks to devoted ministers such as Andrews who were able to take a diverse array of congregants and instill in them a measure of Presbyterian identity. In 1704 and 1705 Andrews baptized a handful of new adult members each year. And in 1705 his congregation had become sufficiently stable to begin the construction of a meeting place for their worship services, thus vindicating Makemie's wisdom about the congeniality of towns for congregational life. According to a seemingly jealous Episcopalian, the new meetinghouse, "I am afraid will draw away a great part of the Church, if there be not the greatest care taken of it." That Philadelphia meetinghouse would a year after its completion be the site in 1706 for the first gathering of the first presbytery in North America, the Presbytery of Philadelphia.

Undoubtedly, Andrews's labors within the bustling young city, soon to attract a wave of immigrants from Scotland and Northern Ireland, were responsible for Presbyterian success in southeastern Pennsylvania. But the stability of a meetinghouse and town life did not prevent Andrews from itinerancy comparable to Makemie's. In addition to his duties in town, Andrews also preached in nearby Bucks County and farther north into the region of East Jersey where he performed supply preaching for local groups of believers who lacked pastors. According to Charles Hodge, a native of Philadelphia Presbyterianism himself, Andrews was "one of the most laborious and useful members" of the original presbytery. Although Makemie would die only two years after the presbytery's founding, Andrews lived on to the relatively ripe age of seventy-two. During those years between the presbytery's founding and his death in 1747, Andrews did not miss a meeting of presbytery and served as its treasurer and clerk for many of those years.

The labors of Andrews and Makemie, then, were crucial to the formation of an American Presbyterian church. Their efforts illustrated the hardships and difficult conditions under which Presbyterian ministers worked. They also showed how much the creation of an American church was the product of ministers who impressed upon their congregations a Presbyterian stamp through preaching and teaching Reformed Christianity. Andrews and Makemie also recognized the need for a Presbyterian form of government and the unity and order it provided. As such, their leadership and support in calling and hosting the first meeting of the Presbytery of Philadelphia in 1706 was largely responsible for the small but influential effort to give shape and identity to the chaotic, and at times desperate, life of those people in the New World who worshiped together as Presbyterians.

So difficult, in fact, were the conditions of early American Presbyterianism that the records of the first meeting of the Presbytery of Philadelphia have not survived. The first official acts that have been preserved related to the 1707 ordination of John Boyd for the congregation in

East Jersey at Freehold. From that record we know that the Presbytery of Philadelphia originally consisted of seven ministers. In addition to Makemie, the first moderator, and Andrews, were John Hampton, George Macnish, John Wilson, Samuel Davis, and Nathaniel Taylor.

The lack of preserved records for the first meeting prevents any historical effort to reconstruct a dramatic scene at which Presbyterians announced to the New World their inauguration and purpose. American Presbyterians, for that reason, lack a "city-on-a-hill" speech to rival the coming of Puritanism to North America. But the lack of fanfare is fitting. The original Presbyterians in America were not ambitious, nor did their resources promise an auspicious church to emerge from their disorganized beginnings. American Presbyterians were much closer in condition to their Anabaptist neighbors in Germantown, Pennsylvania, than they were either to the Puritans in the North or Anglicans in the South. Presbyterianism's roots theologically may have been in the magisterial Reformation of the sixteenth century. But their historical origins in America were significantly lacking in majesty.

Even after the formation of the Presbytery of Philadelphia, the identity and existence of an American Presbyterian church were very much up for grabs. The reason has much to do with the obstacles that Presbyterianism faced from its initial expression in sixteenth-century Scotland. To say that the Presbyterian church in the British Isles was a mere pawn in the contest between the British monarchy and the English Parliament may be an overstatement. But the assertion contains enough truth to indicate that the Protestant church John Knox nurtured into existence never had a chance to blossom until at least some of the political struggles in British politics achieved resolution. Along the way, even the most devout of Scottish Presbyterians drew motivation for their faith sometimes as much from political resentments as from theological conviction. Furthermore, even by the time of an officially recognized and sanctioned Presbyterian Kirk (1690), the Presbyterian faith was still captive to political pressure.

Ironically, then, at the beginning of the eighteenth century America may have offered the best prospects for a Presbyterian witness. It was also a place that appeared to be the least conducive for establishing a Presbyterian church. It offered small groups of people scattered across the frontier. Colonial America featured religious establishments that were hostile to the Presbyterian ministry, thus making Quakerism an odd cobelligerent of the earliest American Presbyterians. The New World also provided an inhospitable environment for Presbyterian ministers hoping to use their talents and calling to further the Presbyterian faith.

All of these factors made the original American Presbyterian Church remarkable, the efforts of its ministers heroic, but its presence in the New World ultimately unpromising. The formation of American Presbyterianism lacked strategic thinking, aristocratic patronage, political heroics, and even stunning theological wisdom. It was the product of obscure and diligent labors by men who lacked any significant model for starting a Presbyterian church. But although the efforts of pastors such as Makemie and Andrews and the formation of a presbytery were without precedent, these became the basis for a Presbyterian church that would rival the witness of any branch of European Reformed Christianity. As inauspicious as its beginning, it proved to be an unusually resilient start for a theological tradition in desperate need of freedom and stability to develop its own identity and character.

2

In Search of Presbyterian Identity

In 1730 one of the oldest Presbyterian congregations in North America, this one in Freehold, New Jersey, gathered to consider the best location for the construction of its meetinghouse. According to legend, while the men debated the advantages of one site over another, a feisty woman of Scottish descent rose from her seat, picked up the cornerstone, carried it up a small hill to the church's eventual foundation, and complained, "Wha ever heard o' ganging doon to the House o' the Lord, an no o' gangin oop to the House o' the Lord?"

Janet Rhea was the woman's name and her biblical knowledge, as well as her decisive action, have long provided evidence of the steely devotion of those first Presbyterian saints who endured innumerable hardships to settle in America and practice the faith of their parents. (At the least it indicated the resolute conviction of the female saints who in this case forced the men to abandon the favorite Presbyterian pastime of committee deliberation and take action.) But, Rhea's bravado was part of a wider constellation of factors that suggest a different perspective on the piety of the earliest Presbyterian settlers in North America.

The congregation in Freehold was not nearly as Presbyterian as this strong woman's accent implies. Rhea herself came to North America in 1680 or thereabouts, not as a Presbyterian but as a member of the Society of Friends. Other participants in the debate about where to construct the meetinghouse in Freehold also indicated the breadth of personal and religious backgrounds that informed the American Presbyterian church.

The pastor of the Freehold congregation in 1730 was John Tennent, one of the sons of the famous Tennent clan that by the middle decades of the eighteenth century became a catalyst for controversy and renewal within the American church. Tennent had come to British North America in 1718 with his father, William Sr., from Northern Ireland and as a member of the Anglican church, which by then, thanks to English policy, had become the established church in Ulster Province.

Another prominent figure in the Freehold discussions was Walter Ker, a Covenanter who had been banished from Scotland during the era of intense opposition to conservative Presbyterians by the English monarchy. Rhea, Tennent, and Ker all possessed Scottish ancestry, but that common ethnicity in no way signified a common faith. One reason is that Scotland was hardly uniform in its religious practices, with Highland and Lowland Scots themselves owning characteristically different forms of piety. The lesson, then, at least if the experience of this Freehold congregation is any indication, is that, as Ned Landsman has observed, "one should beware of taking too much for granted about either the nature of the significance or the ethnic heritages of America's colonial ancestors."

The lesson for American Presbyterian history may be even more pointed than Landsman's general caution about colonial history. Charles Hodge, who wrote a two-volume account of American Presbyterian origins and whose roots were among the Scotch-Irish who settled in Philadelphia, could not restrain his ethnic pride when describing the character of the original American Presbyterian Church. He wrote that it was "but a sectional vanity little less than insane" to assert, as many Presbyterian historians have, that New England Puritanism "was the basis for presbyterianism in this country, and that the presbyterian church never would have had an existence, except in name, had not the congregationalists come among us from New England."

Compared with the twenty thousand or so English immigrants to New England in the early seventeenth century, Hodge explained, the Presbyterian immigrants to America during the eighteenth century were far greater, numbering "between one and two hundred thousand." Far more accurate, in Hodge's estimate, was an assertion that posed Presbyterianism as the basis for several other American denominations rather than Puritanism as the foundation for American Presbyterianism. The Princeton professor's arithmetic makes some sense, as well as the point he made with it, namely, that if Presbyterians had kept their own folk in the fold, the Presbyterian Church would have been huge. But the difficulty in Hodge's logic was the very situation at the Freehold congregation. He assumed that all immigrants from Scotland and Northern Ireland were Presbyterian, when in fact those settlers were as diverse as Great Britain was itself.

Over the course of the first four decades of the eighteenth century, American Presbyterianism would grow because of an influx of immigrants from Great Britain. It would also attract new members of English and Dutch backgrounds from New England and New York. Meanwhile, the need for ministers would only increase as newly arrived Presbyterians sought pastors who could preach and administer the sacraments. The collection of these diverse groups threw into question the identity of the American Presbyterian Church. Without the overt guidance and support of a parent denomination, American Presbyterians would be on their own to figure out the character of their church's ministry and witness. None of the people contributing to these debates doubted they were Presbyterian. But determining what Presbyterianism involved—that was the real question.

Presbyterian Melting Pot

The primary semblance of order that the American Presbyterian Church possessed between 1706, when the Presbytery of Philadelphia was formed, and 1729, when the church first adopted a constitution, was the presbytery. Unlike later in American Presbyterian history—when ministers and elders gathered regularly to conduct joint affairs of the local congregations under their jurisdiction—the first presbyteries in the colonial church were mainly ministerial associations. According to Francis Makemie, in one of his letters, the aim of the presbytery was:

> . . . to meet yearly, and oftener if necessary, to consult the most proper measures for advancing religion and propagating Christianity in our various stations, and to maintain such a correspondence as may conduce to the improvement of our ministerial abilities, by prescribing texts to be preached on by two of our number at every meeting, which performance is subject to the censure of our brethren.

Obviously, the initial plans for presbytery could not be ambitious, since the churches that these ministers served were barely surviving. But the presbytery was more than simply a conference for ministers seeking encouragement and camaraderie. The initial American presbyteries did undertake the business of ordaining or receiving ministers into membership. And as Makemie's letter indicates, the design was also to oversee the quality of ministerial service being offered by members of presbytery. Still, beyond these basic functions the original presbyters were unprepared to go. For instance, presbytery did not require sessions in the local congregations to maintain records until 1714, and ruling elders did not begin to attend presbytery meetings until 1716.

The initial growth of the American Presbyterian Church depended on the reception of ministers into the Presbytery of Philadelphia. The colonies of Pennsylvania, New Jersey, Maryland, and New York might have had numerous groups of people who met for religious instruction and worship. But their path to becoming part of the Presbyterian Church lay in the ordination or reception of a minister whom the presbytery recognized as being called to a particular congregation (or in the case of many ministers, multiple congregations). This growth of Presbyterian ministers also resulted in the growth of presbyteries. By 1717 the American Presbyterian Church had attracted a sufficient number of ministers to comprise three presbyteries. This was also the year that American Presbyterians formed a higher judicatory to which all the presbyteries were accountable, the Synod of Philadelphia.

The composition of the first three presbyteries is fairly revealing of the diverse currents flowing within the mainstream of American

Presbyterianism. It also gives some indication of migration patterns in colonial America among Reformed believers. By 1717 the Presbytery of Philadelphia included six ministers, spread out over eight to nine congregations. Of these, two were from England, one was from Wales, one from Scotland, one from Northern Ireland, and one from New England (Jedediah Andrews). The Presbytery of New Castle (Delaware), which at the time of the formation of Synod had absorbed the Presbytery of Snow Hill, included eight ministers, four with Scotch-Irish backgrounds, three from Scotland, and one with a Welsh heritage.

The youngest presbytery, the Long Island Presbytery, formed at the same time as the Synod in 1717, had only two members, one from New England and one from Northern Ireland. But the youngest presbytery would soon become the most numerous and the most hospitable to ministers from New England. Of the twenty-seven ministers to be ordained between 1717 and 1729, eleven came from New England, and they found calls relatively evenly sprinkled among congregations in Long Island, New Jersey, and New Castle. But most of these Presbyterians with Puritan backgrounds were in the vicinity of New York City, either on Long Island or in northern New Jersey (which was still under the jurisdiction of the Presbytery of Philadelphia).

Of course, geography and ethnicity could not by themselves determine a minister's understanding of Presbyterianism. Among the newcomers to the Presbyterian Church, three stood out in the denomination's early history. Two of these came from Northern Ireland and the other from New England, but they became representatives of three different strands of Presbyterian witness that were also responsible for significant division within the young church.

The first of these three new arrivals of note was William Tennent Sr. (1673–1746). He may have been born in Scotland, and his training at the University of Edinburgh is one reason why this may be likely. But he eventually moved to Northern Ireland, where he became a minister in the Church of Ireland, which was part of the Anglican establishment in Great Britain. Tennent's decision to minister in an Anglican church was not entirely unusual, since policies restricting the Presbyterian churches in Northern Ireland were more severe even than in England. He and his family migrated to the American colonies in 1718, at which point Tennent renounced Anglicanism as unscriptural. He first arrived in

Connecticut, but soon moved to New York where he gained admittance to the Presbyterian Church and pastored a congregation in Bedford. In 1727 Tennent moved to Bucks County, Pennsylvania, just north of Philadelphia, where he established what became known as the Log College, a school named for the simple log building in which students met and received training for pastoral work.

Tennent's influence on colonial American Presbyterianism was enormous, thanks to his training of Presbyterian ministers both formally at Log College and informally in his home. An obvious concern of the young Presbyterian Church was the training of pastors. Because of the assumed need for university training before being called to the ministry, the American church had only two live options. One was to continue to recruit men who had been trained at Scottish universities, the graduates of Glasgow and Edinburgh being the most familiar to the presbyteries in the colonies. The second was to look to the colleges of New England, Harvard and Yale, for adequate learning. The founding of the Log College raised directly the question of what constituted a proper training for Presbyterian pastors, either that of established European or American schools, or that of a college without a solid reputation in either the liberal arts or divinity.

Even more important than the education Tennent provided through the Log College may have been the training he imparted to his sons, all of whom would become ministers in the American church. Of his four boys, Gilbert Tennent (1703–64) was the most important and the most controversial. He was born in Northern Ireland, and once his father moved the family to the colonies Tennent received his education in America, taking his college degree at Yale. After graduation he pastored briefly at the congregation in New Castle (Delaware) before receiving a call to the church in New Brunswick (New Jersey). There he came under the influence of Theodore Frelinghuysen, a rambunctious Dutch Calvinist minister, who had discovered that preaching the "terrors of the law" was an effective means of awaken sleepy church members from their spiritual doldrums and driving unbelievers to faith in Christ. This kind of preaching, which Gilbert adopted, became one of the chief catalysts for the revivals that began to transform American Presbyterianism in the 1720s and 1730s. It also became a great source of controversy among American Presbyterian ministers. Although Gilbert learned to preach a certain way from Frelinghuysen, the type of intense Christian experience at which such sermons aimed was close to the experiential piety that Gilbert had learned while growing up under the supervision and care of his father, William. In fact, William Sr. and his sons reflected a strain of Presbyterian devotion, infused from Northern Ireland, that was more informal and subjective, owing to the particular difficulties presented to Northern Irish Presbyterianism at the hands of the Anglican establishment.

Another newcomer to the American Church from Northern Ireland was John Thomson (1690–1753), a man who reflected another strain of Presbyterianism among the Scotch-Irish. He was born in Northern Ireland, and like many Presbyterians there went to Scotland for university training, receiving his degree from the University of Glasgow. Thomson migrated to the colonies in 1715 and took his first call to the congregation in Lewes (Delaware). For many years he served as the moderator of the Presbytery of New Castle, the jurisdiction where Scottish and Scotch-Irish congregations were most prevalent.

John Thomson

Thomson's strain of Presbyterianism was more formal and doctrinally precise than the one promoted by the Tennents. It became a significant force within the American church when in the early 1720s Thomson began to advocate subscribing to the Westminster Standards as a requirement for all licentiates and ministers in the Presbyterian Church. He emerged as an important critic of the revivalist-inspired piety that during the awakenings of the 1730s and 1740s began to stamp American Presbyterianism with an indelible imprint. Thomson's most important work, *The Government of the Church of Christ* (1741), was indicative of a strain of Presbyterianism that was less individualistic and more ecclesial.

Formal and doctrinally precise

The third newcomer of note to the colonial Presbyterian Church, unlike Thomson or the Tennents, was not an immigrant from overseas. Jonathan Dickinson (1688–1747) was part of the third generation of New England Puritans. Born in Massachusetts and educated at Yale College in Connecticut, Dickinson's familial and cultural ties were to the English Protestants whose "errand into the wilderness" was part of the larger Puritan hope for reform of the church in the Old World.

Jonathan Dickinson

In 1709, at the young age of twenty-one, Dickinson accepted a call from a congregation in Elizabethtown, New Jersey. Eight years later, at the time of the creation of the Synod of Philadelphia, he became a member of the Presbytery of Philadelphia. Dickinson emerged as a leader within American Presbyterianism thanks to his learning and devotion. In such works as *The Reasonableness of Christianity* (1732) and *Five Points: The True Scripture-Doctrine Concerning Some Important Points of Christian Faith* (1741), he established a reputation for defending not simply the Christian religion but also the Calvinist understanding of salvation.

In addition to his theological writing, Dickinson also defended the revivals that broke out in the 1730s and 1740s, though he was also critical of their excesses. For this reason, some have regarded Dickinson as colonial Presbyterianism's Jonathan Edwards. Whether or not a fair comparison, Dickinson was one of those influential ministers to join the American church between 1706 and 1717 whose Presbyterianism reflected a strand of Reformed faith and practice that was distinct from the views of other Presbyterian ministers. Reconciling these differences would become the major occupation of the infant Presbyterian church.

The Search for Order

Accounting for the variety of understandings of Presbyterianism within the American church is not hard to do. Especially with some awareness of the obstacles that Presbyterians faced throughout the seventeenth century in Scotland and Northern Ireland, combined with the meagerness of resources that any immigrant communion would naturally face, the diversity of expressions in the American church makes good sense.

By 1720 American Presbyterianism contained four types of Reformed Christianity: one with some affinity to Scottish Presbyterianism, though likely the smallest in number; two with different conceptions of Presbyterianism from Northern Ireland exemplified in the ministries of the Tennents (i.e., experiential) and Thomson (i.e., creedal and formal); and one that tapped the outlook and inclinations of New England Puritanism. These tendencies within the American church could sometimes form different alliances. But during the 1720s two distinct parties within the American church began to emerge. One of these looked more conservative in the sense that it stressed order, uniformity, and the importance

40

of doctrine. The other, in contrast, appeared to be more tolerant and emphasized freedom and the primacy of experience.

Two different issues emerged during the 1720s that exposed the formation of these two Presbyterian parties. The first concerned the authority of Synod in overseeing the conduct and life of the church. Two minor disputes—one involving the confessed sin of a minister and a subsequent relatively light penalty to which some ministers objected, the other concerning the call of a minister in New York despite the protests of members of Long Island Presbytery—directly raised the question of synodical power and control. In both cases, Synod became the court of appeal for dissenting ministers.

But five ministers, led by Dickinson, objected to the increasing power of Synod in the affairs of congregations and presbyteries, and to a 1721 resolution passed at Synod that determined this was a legitimate use of the body's collective authority. The exact language now appears mild: "for the better carrying on in the matter of our government and discipline" a minister "may bring [an overture] against next Synod." But the resolution passed the following year, in response to the objections of Dickinson and other ministers, indicated a deep reluctance to grant any sort of regulatory power to Synod.

The Synod of Philadelphia affirmed it and similar that bodies had executive power and even the powers of the keys of the kingdom. Synods, likewise, could make recommendations to presbyteries and congregations concerning the government and better ordering of the church. But granting such power to synods was acceptable only as long as presbyteries, congregations, or individual ministers could "conscientiously dissent from them." This resolution and its peculiar language gained the assent of a majority of Synod, which included particularly those ministers from New England whose experience of church power had been congregational rather than presbyterian. But to the more conservative element in the church, which included ministers from Scottish and Scotch-Irish backgrounds, this understanding of church authority was defective.

The second issue to reveal the differences between the strict and tolerant parties in the American church was creedal subscription. Again, it is important to stress that in the matter of adopting the Westminster Confession of Faith and Larger and Shorter Catechisms, American Presbyterians were on uncharted sea. The kirk in Scotland had at its

41

reinstitution in 1690 required subscribing to the Westminster Standards for ordination. But that practice had been in effect for only thirty years by the time Americans began to debate it. Meanwhile, the practice of subscription in Northern Ireland differed, with only some presbyteries requiring it. As such, American Presbyterians lacked a clear precedent for what some ministers were proposing. Meanwhile, with the inclusion of ministers who grew up in New England, where Puritans had different doctrinal standards (slightly modified versions of Westminster in the Cambridge Platform [1648] and the Saybrook Platform [1708]) and did not require subscription for ordination, the American church reflected at least two minds on the propriety and necessity of ministers giving their assent to a common creed.

The Presbytery of New Castle, the home of the stricter Presbyterian party, took the lead by requiring candidates for licensure to subscribe to the Westminster Confession of Faith. The language of the vow read as follows: "I do own the Westminster Confession as the Confession of my faith." The controversial Presbyterian biblical scholar at Union Seminary, Charles Briggs, in his history of American Presbyterianism, denounced this requirement as a "usurpation of Presbyterial power," acting "in defiance of Presbyterian law and precedent." But in the light of Synod's resolution in 1721 that significantly diminished synodical authority in favor of the independence of presbyteries, sessions, and individuals, Briggs's objection is hard to understand. The effort to pacify both sides in the American church had left the affairs of presbyteries to each presbytery. New Castle appeared to be acting in accord with that agreement, even if its own understanding of Presbyterian identity was stricter than other presbyteries.

New Castle continued to pressure the church to design some form of creedal subscription. John Thomson, a member of that presbytery, submitted an overture to Synod in 1727 that called on the church to adopt "publicly and authoritatively . . . the Westminster Confession of Faith, Catechisms, &c., for the public confession of our faith, as we are a particular organized church." The overture was comprehensive in requiring subscription for those seeking licensure, ordination, or transfer into the American church. It even included the hope that Synod would recommend the Westminster Standards to church members, "to entertain the truth in love, to be zealous and fruitful, and to be earnest with God by

prayer to preserve their vine from being spoiled by those deluding forces
. . . with the damnable errors of our times." Synod did not take action
on Thomson's measure in 1727, but the following year he brought the
same overture again before his peers. This time, Synod saw the matter
of subscription to be "a very important affair" and unanimously decided
to put the question on the docket for the 1729 meeting.

Thomson's concerns were the impurity of the young Presbyterian
Church and the dilution of its witness, but his opponents saw that
matter differently. With ties to Northern Ireland, Thomson was likely
troubled by an emerging liberal element in the Presbyterian Church in
Ireland that also opposed creedal subscription—not simply because of
concerns over church power, but also because of explicit departures from
the teachings of the Westminster Standards.

But to ministers such as Jonathan Dickinson, the issue before the
American Church was not its theological fuzziness but the danger of
an authoritative church. In a letter he wrote prior to the 1729 meeting of Synod, Dickinson argued that the history of Christianity was
littered with the harmful consequences of subscription. Prior to the
Council of Nicea the church had other means to "detect heresies, resist
gainsayers, to propagate the truth; and to keep the church not only a
garden enclosed, but a garden of peace." He admitted that the Council
of Nicea had imposed subscription but the effect was "horrible schism,
convulsions and confusions, until the church was crumbled into parts
and parties, each uncharitably anathematizing one another." Dickinson
believed that even down to contemporary times, subscription was more
a curse than blessing. Here he referred to the situation in Northern
Ireland where subscription had "consumed their glory; and this engine
of division broke them in pieces." The best means for protecting the
church was not subscription but "strict" examination of candidates,
"strict" discipline of scandalous ministers, and the "diligent, faithful,
and painful" discharge of ministerial duties. As Charles Hodge put it,
Dickinson "belonged to that small class of persons who are opposed to
all creeds of human composition."

At the 1729 meeting of Synod, then, the question of subscription was
firmly before the American church, with two parties holding markedly
different notions about the value of creeds for maintaining a faithful
ministerial witness. According Charles Briggs, who provided a scorecard

on the composition of the 1729 Synod, the strict subscriptionist party was led by Thomson and James Anderson, one of Thomson's colleagues from the New Castle Presbytery. The anti-subscription party enjoyed the leadership of Dickinson and John Pierson, a minister in Woodbridge, New Jersey. The total number of ministers present for the meeting of Synod was twenty. The trick was to find some ground that would keep the entire body together.

On the surface, the views of Thomson and Dickinson do not appear to be capable of harmony. For that reason, when Synod proposed and accepted the Adopting Act of 1729 it appeared to signal a real defeat for the anti-subscription party, since the formula adopted did endorse and require subscription. To write as Briggs does that the Synod of 1729 was a vindication of Dickinson is truly a strange reading of this pivotal episode in American Presbyterian history. But the Adopting Act was not exactly what Thomson and the strict subscriptionists had in mind either. It represented something of a compromise, the nature of which requires closer scrutiny.

Subscription American Style

The ministers who debated subscription at the Synod of Philadelphia in 1729 ratified a series of paragraphs that when cobbled together are generally referred to as the Adopting Act. But in C. W. Baird's *Digest of the Acts and Deliverances of the Assembly* only one of those paragraphs possesses the heading, "Adopting Act." It reads as follows:

All the Ministers of this Synod now present, except one, that declared himself not prepared, viz., Masters Jedediah Andrews, Thomas Craighead, John Thomson, James Anderson, John Pierson, Samuel Gelston, Joseph Houston, Gilbert Tennent, Adam Boyd, Jonathan Dickinson, John Bradner, Alexander Hutchinson, Thomas Evans, Hugh Stevenson, William Tennent, Hugh Conn, George Gillespie, and John Willson, after proposing all the scruples that any of them had to make against any articles and expressions in the Confession of Faith and Larger and Shorter Catechisms of the Assembly of Divines at Westminster, have unanimously agreed in the solution of those scruples, and in declaring the said Confession and Catechisms to be the confession of their faith, excepting only some clauses in the twen-

44

tieth and twenty-third chapters, concerning which clauses the Synod do unanimously declare, that they do not receive those articles in any such sense as to suppose the civil magistrate hath a controlling power over Synods with respect to the exercise of their ministerial authority; or power to persecute any for their religion, or in any sense contrary to the Protestant succession to the throne of Great Britain.

The Synod observing that unanimity, peace, and unity, which appeared in all their consultations and determinations relating to the affair of the Confession, did unanimously agree in giving thanks to God in solemn prayer and praises.

What this resolution reveals is that, despite the variety of backgrounds represented in colonial Presbyterians, all the ministers—the Scottish, the Irish, Welsh, and New England Puritan—were agreed in their understanding of the Reformed faith and comfortable employing the language of the Westminster Standards to express that agreement. These ministers also affirmed, we should note, that they were comfortable using the words of the Westminster Assembly to summarize their own personal convictions. Their only reservation concerned the Westminster Confession's teaching about the magistrate, a matter of theology that would eventually force American Presbyterians to revise the revered Westminster Standards (see chapter four below). But the Adopting Act per se did not really address subscription. In effect, those present at Synod subscribed to the Westminster Standards—that is what the Adopting Act proper indicated. Only in the preliminary paragraphs did Synod address the matter of how the American church should employ the Westminster Standards as a form for subscription.

In the very first paragraph of its 1729 decision, Synod chose words that certainly modified its members' own act of subscription and that reflected the anti-subscriptionist views of Dickinson. Synod's declaration begins:

Although the synod do not claim or pretend to any authority of imposing our faith upon other men's consciences, but do profess our just dissatisfaction with and abhorrence of such impositions, and do utterly disclaim all legislative power and authority of such impositions, and do utterly disclaim all legislative power and authority in the Church, being willing to receive one another, as Christ has received us to the

45

glory of God, and admit to fellowship in sacred ordinances all such as we have grounds to believe Christ will at last admit to the kingdom of heaven; yet we are undoubtedly obliged to take care that the faith once delivered to the saints be kept pure and uncorrupt among us, and so hand down to our posterity.

This statement was a clear affirmation of the Protestant doctrine of liberty of conscience, itself a notion straightforwardly taught in chapter twenty of the Westminster Confession, which declares: "God alone is Lord of the conscience, and hath left it free from the doctrines and commandments of men . . ." (20.2). Less clear, however, was that the fathers of the American church were aware that in announcing their loyalty to the Westminster Standards they were also affirming a notion of church power that the preamble to the Adopting Act apparently denied. For instance, in the chapter on Liberty of Conscience in the Westminster Confession, the divines stated that Christian liberty was not "intended by God to destroy, but . . . to uphold and preserve" both civil and ecclesiastical power (20.4). Later in the confession, the divines also described the very activity in which the 1729 Synod was engaged as ordinances "to be received with reverence and submission; not only for their agreement with the Word, but also for the power whereby they are made, as being an ordinance of God appointed thereunto in his Word" (31.2).

At some level, then, the preamble to the Adopting Act was in tension, if not at odds, with the view of church power contained in the creed to which members of Synod subscribed.

In the next two preliminary paragraphs before the Adopting Act proper, Synod employed language that has bedeviled American Presbyterians ever since. They introduced the phrase "essential and necessary articles" twice to modify the nature of the subscription they would require. On the one hand, members of the Synod of Philadelphia would be expected to adopt the Westminster Standards: "all the Ministers of this Synod, or that shall hereafter be admitted into this Synod, shall declare their agreement in and approbation of the Confession of Faith with the Larger and Shorter Catechisms of the assembly of Divines at Westminster, as being in all the *essential and necessary articles*, good forms of sound words and systems of Christian doctrine; and do also adopt the said Confession and Catechisms as the confession of our faith" (italics added).

On the other hand, Synod also asserted that presbyteries would be expected to use the same creedal standard in their examination of candidates, an assertion that clearly spread the practice of creedal subscription from the Presbytery of New Castle to those of Philadelphia and Long Island as well. In Synod's exact words:

> all the Presbyteries within our bounds shall always take care not to admit any candidate of the ministry into the exercise of the sacred function, but what declares his agreement in opinion with all the *essential and necessary articles* of said Confession, either by subscribing the said Confession of Faith and Catechisms, or by a verbal declaration of their assent thereto, as such Minister or candidate for the Ministry shall think best. And in case any Minister of this Synod, or any candidate for the ministry, shall have any scruple with respect to any article or articles of said Confession or Catechisms, he shall at the time of his making said declaration declare his sentiments to the Presbytery or Synod, who shall, notwithstanding, admit him to the exercise of the ministry within our bounds and to ministerial communion if the Synod or Presbytery shall judge his scruple or mistake to be only about articles not *essential and necessary* in doctrine, worship or government. But if the Synod or Presbytery shall judge such Ministers or candidates erroneous in *essential and necessary* articles of faith, the Synod or Presbytery shall declare them incapable of Communion with them (italics added).

To underscore that Synod was adopting the Westminster Standards in a less-than-strict manner, the last paragraph before the Adopting Act proper included a declaration of intent to treat all the members of Synod, even if not in complete theological agreement, with Christian charity. According to the preamble, Synod agreed that "none of us will traduce or use any opprobrious terms of those that differ from us in these *extra-essential and not necessary* points of doctrine, but treat them with the same friendship, kindness and brotherly love as if they had not differed from us in such Sentiments" (italics added).

Historians of American Presbyterianism have long debated what the phrase *essential and necessary* meant. For some, it was everything except those articles about the magistrate that the Adopting Act proper had in view. In other words, the form of subscription approved in 1729 was strict except for those passages about the magistrate's rule that were clearly out of synch with realities among dissenting Protestants. Charles Hodge, in his history, for instance, argues that Synod affirmed a strict view, with those minor exceptions regarding the magistrate, because that is the fair meaning of the words and because Thomson and Andrews were satisfied with the declaration.

Charles Briggs, for different reasons, regarded the Adopting Act as a mechanism for flexibility in examining candidates for the ministry. Specifically, for Briggs it was an adaptation of Irish and Scottish methods of subscription to the new environment of America, and so more liberal in its provisions than any form yet tried in the Old World. This argument does not mention Dickinson's agreement with the decision, but Briggs could just as easily have used Hodge's logic that because the leader of the anti-subscription party did not oppose the Adopting Act, it must have been compatible with Dickinson's views.

Synod itself recognized the ambiguity of the Adopting Act. A year later at its regular meeting it received an overture asking for clarification. In turn, the 1730 Synod declared "that they understand these clauses, that respect the admission of itinerants or candidates, in such a sense as to oblige them to receive and adopt the Confession and Catechisms at their admission, in the same manner, and as fully as the members of Synod did, that were then present." This would seem to imply that with the exception of those clauses regarding the civil magistrate, future ministers of the Presbyterian Church were expected to adopt the Westminster Standards in a fairly strict manner.

To add to this clarification, Synod also called for a report on all ministers admitted between 1729 and 1730 to see whether they had affirmed the Westminster Standards in the right way. Then again six years later, as the differences between the various Presbyterianisms consolidated in the American church became more apparent, the Synod of 1736 explained the nature of subscription called for in the Adopting Act of 1729. It announced that Synod had "adopted, and still do adhere to the Westminster Confession, Catechisms, and Directory, without the least variation or alteration, and without any regard to said distinctions." In addition, the 1736 Synod averred its "hope and desire, that this our

48

Synodical declaration and explication may satisfy all our people, as to our firm attachment to our good old received doctrines contained in said Confession, without the least variation or alteration. . ."

The practice of creedal subscription is another question altogether. Because the records of practically all of the original presbyteries do not survive, determining whether the execution of Synod's intention was as thorough as the Adopting Act or its later explanations is impossible. Chances are that the practice varied from presbytery to presbytery, hence the number of calls to Synod to explain its actions. The state of affairs, then, at the local level may have been more like Briggs's understanding of loose subscription, while at the synodical level the strict subscriptionists may have had a sufficient majority to employ their own understanding of creedal definition.

American Presbyterianism Organized

Even so, the Adopting Act of 1729 was a major step in the consolidation of an American Presbyterian Church. At the same meeting of Synod, members also voted to adopt the Directory for Worship, Discipline, and Government, with again some allowance for differences between England in the 1640s and Philadelphia in the 1720s. In addition to a confessional standard, the young American church now also possessed the foundation for uniformity of worship and church polity. By 1730, then, this mainstream American Presbyterian communion, organized by the Synod of Philadelphia, was still the only Presbyterian denomination in British North America. And in only twenty-five years the original presbytery of seven ministers had grown to three presbyteries covering most of the Middle Colonies, with a synod overseeing the work of the church at large.

In other words, the American church was still unclear about the nature, limits, and meaning of its newly achieved organized life. But considering its original perilous conditions and grim prospects, the founding generation of ministers had taken a huge step toward establishing Presbyterianism with its own identity, mission, and structure as a solid, even if small, part of church life in colonial America.

49

3

Enthusiasm and Order

During the year prior to the pivotal meeting of the Synod of Philadelphia held in 1729, a series of strange occurrences took place at the Presbyterian congregation in New Brunswick, New Jersey, that portended the future of American Presbyterianism.

Gilbert Tennent was the pastor of the church, having been called there in 1726. Two years later his brothers, John and William Jr., joined him in effect as pastoral interns. Although learning from and being supervised in the basic work of congregational ministry by a sibling may have been unusual, these internships were not nearly as bizarre as what transpired in 1728 within the New Brunswick church.

Shortly after their arrival, both of Gilbert's brothers fell ill. Whether the cause of the physical discomfort was natural or spiritual is a matter of debate, because the immediate remedies recommended were largely spiritual. First, Gilbert's mentor, Jacob Frelinghuysen, confronted John Tennent, who seemed to be like "a man going to be put upon a rack, or gibbet," with the depravity of his past. John battled the torments of guilt and sin for several days and nights until Gilbert thought the encouragement of forgiveness found in the gospel might be a better pastoral strategy. The calming effects of Gilbert's counsel were not immediate, but within a day or so John had found relief and was in a stable state of mind.

The resolution was not so easy, however, for William Jr. He lost consciousness and descended into a coma that caused those around to think he was dead. Gilbert went ahead with plans for his brother's burial. But a physician looking in on the patient detected the slightest pulse and called off the funeral. Nevertheless, William persisted in the state of a coma for several days. Growing impatient, Gilbert insisted that plans for burial go forward. When he entered William's room, to his alarm Gilbert discovered the physician dropping small amounts of oil on William's tongue in the hope of sustaining him with some nourishment. As the story goes, at this moment, with Gilbert in the room, William "gave a dreadful groan and sank again into apparent death." Instead of being a fatal reaction, this stress actually confirmed the physician's diagnosis. And over the next several months, Gilbert and his sister nursed their brother back to health. Once he had recovered, William recalled having been received during his illness into a place where he witnessed "an innumerable host of happy beings surrounding the inexpressible glory" and participating in "acts of adoration and joyous worship."

Some historians have speculated that this extraordinary combination of physical and spiritual distress was characteristic of certain strains of Scottish Presbyterianism. This was particularly the case in those regions farther from urban centers and without the oversight of clergy, either because of remoteness or government surveillance. Whatever the origin, this type of piety would cause distress not only for individual members of the Tennent family but also for the Presbyterian Church at large. In his preaching, Gilbert Tennent used the story of his brother John's joyous discovery of spiritual relief (he may have chosen to ignore William's example because of his own conduct in urging burial) to ignite a series of small revivals in New Jersey in his own congregation and during pulpit supply to churches on Long Island.

These revivals in 1729 and 1730 were the seeds of a transcolonial spiritual awakening that would blossom a decade later with the arrival of the great evangelist, George Whitefield. But these revivals, both Tennent's less-publicized and Whitefield's famous ones, would turn out, just as in the case of John and William Tennent, to be a mixed blessing. The zeal and excitement that the revivals nurtured did heighten an interest among the laity in spiritual realities and truths. But the methods and consequences of revival also increased antagonisms within the still young and frail American church to the breaking point.

Presbyterian Predicament

During the 1730s the American church grew at unprecedented rates that seriously tested the settlement of 1729 in the Adopting Act. Could the young church cope with an expansion of membership, congregations, and new pastors on the basis of Synod's decision regarding creedal subscription and church polity? Although a noticeable influx of immigrants from Scotland had commenced as early as 1717, the growth during the 1730s was especially significant. Newspapers in Philadelphia regularly recorded the arrival of large parties of Irish. In September 1736 alone, one thousand families came from Belfast owing to financial hardships in the old country.

The effect of this influx of Presbyterian émigrés on individual congregations was soon evident. In New York City, for instance, the congregation had languished for almost two decades, meeting in a dreary home with boarded-over windows that let in enough light for only a dozen or so worshipers. But by the middle of the 1730s the congregation's pews were full, and the giving from members was sufficient to convert the boards into windows that flooded the church with light. In Philadelphia, the growth in Presbyterians prompted the congregation there to call an associate pastor to assist longtime minister Jedediah Andrews.

The structures of the American church also reflected the addition of new members. Between 1733 and 1738 the Presbytery of New Castle generated two new presbyteries, Donegal (in Lancaster County, Pennsylvania) in 1734, and Lewistown (Delaware) in 1738. Likewise, the Presbytery of Philadelphia was reorganized in 1733 to give way to the Presbytery of East Jersey. By 1738 sufficient congregations existed also to form presbyteries in New Brunswick (New Jersey) and New York.

With growth, however, came uncertainty about how to maintain uniformity of witness and practice. Responses came primarily in two forms, one a desire for greater doctrinal integrity, the other a call for increased spiritual zeal or holiness among ministers and members. The occasion for the former was the first heresy trial in the history of American Presbyterianism.

The minister called to assist Andrews in Philadelphia was a recent immigrant from Northern Ireland, Samuel Hemphill, a man educated at the University of Glasgow and ordained by the Presbytery of Strabane, Ireland, specifically for pastoral work in America. Soon after his arrival in 1734, Andrews and other members of presbytery began to object to Hemphill's preaching. Not only had the influence of Enlightenment philosophy led him to express notions that were clearly Arian and Socinian, but ministers also discovered that Hemphill was plagiarizing his sermons.

The Synod of Philadelphia appointed a commission to investigate the matter, consisting of nine ministers, which included John Thomson and Jonathan Dickinson. Andrews, Hemphill's senior colleague at the Philadelphia congregation, led the charge by bringing six objections against the assistant pastor, which included denials of conversion, the merits of Christ, faith as a work of the Holy Spirit, and justification by faith. For all intents and purposes, Hemphill had been preaching Christianity as the culmination of the religion of nature, something accessible to all people with the exception of the sacraments and Christ's work. The case generated publicity when Benjamin Franklin decided to defend Hemphill through a number of pamphlets and stories in the press. (Franklin had heard Hemphill preach on a number of occasions and thought the preacher's rational Christianity was the sort of religion most compatible with the advance of science and morality.) But Hemphill found no support from fellow Presbyterians. Synod convicted and ejected him without debate.

Despite unanimity on Hemphill's errors, the case did raise questions about the effectiveness of creedal subscription as a means of maintaining the purity of the church. After all, the wayward pastor had subscribed to the Westminster Standards when ordained in Northern Ireland. Then when admitted to the Synod of Philadelphia he reassured his future pastoral colleagues that he had no reservations about the Westminster Confession and Catechisms.

The case of Hemphill was the chief factor in the 1736 Synod's declaration that it had "adopted & still do adhere to the Westminster

Confession, Catechisms, and Directory, without the least variation or alteration, and without regard to said distinctions," with the exception of the articles regarding the civil magistrate. Significantly absent from the 1736 Synod was Dickinson, who was still not convinced about the necessity or desirability of strict subscription. What is more, no matter how strongly Synod might declare its intentions in the Adopting Act, the case of Hemphill proved that tight subscription was not foolproof. Even the affirmation of the Westminster Standards required honesty on the part of candidates for the ministry as well as discernment by the ministerial examiners. In the end, the Hemphill case showed the limits of Presbyterian conservatives' plan to enforce doctrinal orthodoxy as the way to maintain the health of the church.

Attempts to improve the subscriptionist strategy soon gave way to the second method for bolstering the faith and practice of the American church, namely, through the pursuit of greater personal holiness. In 1734, Gilbert Tennent presented a memorial to Synod calling for greater spiritual rigor among American Presbyterians, both ordained and church members. The document advised that "due care [be] taken in examining into the evidences of the grace of God" in candidates for the ministry and for the Lord's Supper as well as "other necessary qualifications . . . as it is recommended in the Directory for worship and government." Tennent's motion went on to call Synod to "take special care not to admit into the sacred office, loose, careless, and irreligious persons, but that they particularly inquire into the conversations, conduct, and behaviour of such as offer themselves to the ministry" including an examination of all candidates for the ministry of "their experiences of a work of sanctifying grace in their hearts."

Although the memorial to Synod concluded with another reference to the "due care" that ministers should give to anyone seeking to partake of the Lord's Supper, Tennent's chief concern was declining standards of ministry. Since this resolution, which gained the assent of Synod, preceded the Hemphill trial, Tennent likely did not have the Philadelphia situation in view. But, like the strict subscriptionists, he feared for the health of the church because of lax ministers. For Tennent, however, the key to ministerial integrity was religious experience, not theological precision.

Head versus heart has become a cliché in distinguishing diverse Christian temperaments. But it is also tiredly familiar because since the 1730s American Presbyterians have divided over these two efforts to isolate the essence of genuine Christianity. By 1736 the American church was clearly of two outlooks concerning the best way to build and maintain a Presbyterian witness. If debates over the Adopting Act had left any doubt about the nature of disagreement in the church, the Hemphill trial and Tennent memorial underscored the fundamental tension in colonial Presbyterianism, namely, whether to test the church's ministry by the objective measure of conformity to received teaching or by the subjective gauge of spiritual zeal.

This basic division would continue to bedevil the American church during the last years of the 1730s, which was arguably the pivotal decade of the colonial era of American Presbyterianism. The specific issue that 1730's initially crystallized the split was not a new one, but the ongoing dilemma of standards for ministerial ordination. The question that particularly proved divisive after the Hemphill trial was theological education. To which schools should the American church send its candidates for ministry?

Because of their own European training and undoubtedly because of a perceived inferiority of colonial education, some ministers clearly preferred that candidates pursue their studies at one of Scotland's universities. But this was obviously a short-term and expensive solution. Other ministers who had trained at Harvard or Yale desired Presbyterian candidates to study at one of New England's established institutions.

If these had been the only options, either Scotland or New England, theological education would likely not have been as divisive as it became, even though Presbyterians would have eventually had to consider their own school or college, a topic that could easily have generated strong opinions. But a new school had been created that forced Presbyterians to reckon with educational requirements for the ministry. It was the Log College, established in 1727 by William Tennent Sr. This school had the advantage of being centrally located, about fifteen miles north of Philadelphia, and so accessible to the presbyteries in Delaware and New York. The Log College was supervised by an American Presbyterian. But the school was also the creation of the Tennent family and nurtured an introspective and enthusiastic piety among its students that could lead to the excesses of religious experience that afflicted the Tennent sons mentioned above. From the perspective of strict subscriptionists, Log College was also clearly on the wrong side of the debates about ministerial qualifications.

For its first several years, the consequences of a Log College education went largely unnoticed by Presbyterian authorities, though the Tennents themselves were not lacking in notoriety. But with the redrawing of presbytery lines over the course of the 1730s, the influence of William Tennent Sr.'s school and the network of ministers it fostered became more evident. Once the Presbytery of New Brunswick emerged in 1738 as a separate authority, Log College had a region in which to consolidate its aim of training ministers who were not afflicted with what they regarded as dead orthodoxy but exhibited and encouraged genuine Christian devotion. With a presbytery in place that could ordain the graduates of Log College, the debate over Presbyterian theological education quickly became bound up with the ongoing contest over subscription and the appropriate requirements for ordination.

Ministers from other presbyteries had for several years expressed reservations about Log College's training and tactics. The Presbytery of Lewes (Delaware), another of the presbyteries to emerge from restructuring and growth, made these concerns explicit with a motion to the Synod of 1738 that was designed to curtail the appeal of Tennent's school. It called for a synodical committee to examine every candidate for the ministry who had not been trained either in New England or Europe. The task of this body was to test how well each candidate knew "the several branches of philosophy, and divinity, and the languages." Since Log College was basically a form of internship with one minister and so lacked the resources of several faculty and an appropriate library, the requirement for a liberal arts education left little doubt that this resolution was written to impede the influence of the Tennents' school.

But theological education was not the only item of business in the proposal from Lewes. It also called on all ministerial members of Synod to refrain from preaching "in any congregation belonging to another Presbytery whereof he is not a member" if advised that such preaching outside his own presbytery will produce "divisions and disorders." Here the Lewes proposal took aim at the habit of Log College graduates, and especially Gilbert Tennent, of itinerant preaching without invitation from the local Presbyterian authorities.

To be sure, itinerancy had been a fact of life for colonial Presbyterianism. But the reference to splits in churches indicated that the experiential preaching for which the Tennents were known was contested. This was especially the case on those occasions when such preaching not only recommended godliness but also raised suspicions about ministers who did not exhibit the same kind of zeal. In effect, the design of this motion was to quarantine the Log College education by confining it to the Presbytery of New Brunswick and by forcing its graduates to gain the approval of Synod.

As might be expected, the members of the Presbytery of New Brunswick objected to these measures, which gained approval of Synod by a large majority. The Synod of 1739 in turn received responses from the Tennents and other presbyters that led to some slight modifications in the terms of the 1738 action. But the effect was still to create the impression that a Log College education was inferior and that its graduates had a tendency to be divisive in the prosecution of their callings. The restraints imposed by Synod, consequently, were not welcome to the Log College party and in 1739 they displayed their displeasure with an act of defiance. At its regular meeting, the Presbytery of New Brunswick disregarded the act of Synod and its new procedures for ordination by licensing a Log College student, John Rowland. Synod objected and refused to recognize Rowland as duly licensed. In 1739 it also rebuked the Presbytery of New Brunswick and established a committee to "prosecute the design of erecting a school or seminary of learning," which would serve the entire synod, not one presbytery.

With the controversy over Log College and the qualifications of its graduates for ministry, the older debates over subscription had acquired new and greater significance. The debate over subscription had always concerned standards for ministry, with affirmation of the Westminster Standards indicating a man's understanding of Christianity and his intention to teach and preach Reformed doctrine. The Tennents expanded the debate by adding two questions about adequate ministerial qualifications. The first and most obvious was education. In effect, which schools did the American church approve as providing a fitting training for Presbyterian ministry? The second was religious experience. Did a man need to give an account of his own conversion in order to show his fitness for ministry? The Log College was clearly implicated in these two issues, but also its advocates and supporters were the Presbyterians with the greatest reservations about the necessity or effectiveness of subscription.

But just as the subscription controversy had included an argument about the power of church authorities, so the debate over Log College and ministerial qualifications also revolved around the authority of Synod to make such determinations. The Log College group, led by Gilbert Tennent, complained in its 1739 defense of the licensure of Rowland that Synod's actions rested on a "false hypothesis," namely, that synods or church judicatories have the power "committed to them from Christ, to make new rules, acts, or canons about religious matters . . . which shall be binding upon those who conscientiously dissent therefrom . . ."

Here were echoes of the older objections by Dickinson to Synod's decision to make creedal subscription the basis for ministerial membership. In a conciliatory gesture, at its 1740 meeting Synod unanimously agreed that, as a regional judicatory, it was not the best body for examining the qualifications of ministers. This was a matter appropriately left to the local authorities in presbyteries. But Synod also determined that it had legitimate authority to determine the qualifications for its own membership. And by licensing or ordaining men contrary to the qualifications established by Synod, a presbytery could, as New Brunswick had, "impose" its own standards on Synod. Over time, these members could multiply and "cast the Standards out of doors."

By 1740, then, the American church was apparently at an impasse. The most glaring dispute was between the Presbytery of New Brunswick and the rest of the church, though supporters of the Tennents clearly could be found in other presbyteries. American Presbyterianism's growing pains were not merely the result of adding new immigrants to the church. They also involved the capacity of the church to produce and train its own ministers. Unable to rely on educational institutions in the Old World, the American church needed its own school, but the one that had sprouted up on its own soil, the Log College, had substantial liabilities. As it turned out, the synodical committee appointed to study the establishment of a Presbyterian school of theology was never able to complete its business. A war between England and Spain had prevented its members from traveling to London to solicit financial support. A different kind of war also erupted in America that kept the dispute between Synod and the Presbytery of New Brunswick from reaching a congenial compromise. To understand that conflict requires some familiarity with George Whitefield and the First Great Awakening.

Awakening and Division - Whitefield·

The timing of George Whitefield's arrival in British North America in 1739, the second of seven preaching tours in the colonies over the course of his life, was a mixed blessing. From the perspective of Presbyterians such as the Tennents who sought greater zeal and holiness for their church, Whitefield, a Church of England priest and colleague of John and Charles Wesley who possessed amazing speaking talents and entrepreneurial instincts, was an unalloyed good.

Between 1739 and 1741 Whitefield's itinerant preaching and marketing genius turned the local revivals that towns such as Northampton, Massachusetts (thanks to Jonathan Edwards), and New Brunswick, New Jersey (thanks to Tennent), had experienced into a transcolonial and trans-Atlantic affair—prompting many onlookers to designate it a Great Awakening.

During those two years of itinerancy up and down the Eastern seaboard, the evangelist preached with the good wishes and cooperation of most of the Presbyterian ministers in the presbyteries of New York and New Brunswick. To read his itinerary in New York, Pennsylvania, New Jersey, and Delaware is to see a list of the Presbyterian congregations in the American church. Here was a minister doing on a large scale what some could accomplish only on the local level, and then without the same sensational results. Whitefield was so appealing that even skeptics such as Ben Franklin became fans of his ministry, though apparently never embracing the evangelist's call for faith and repentance.

For ministers already suspicious of the Log College and its graduates, Whitefield was hardly a welcome addition. In fact, he only aggravated the antagonisms within the church. On the one hand, Whitefield further utilized the practice of itinerant preaching that many believed threatened the bonds between a congregation and its minister. The zeal to preach the gospel and holy living to people wherever they might be found ran up against the formal relationships and constraints of Presbyterian church government, which delegated spiritual oversight to pastors and sessions at the local level, and to presbyteries and synods regionally.

In effect, Whitefield threatened Presbyterian propriety. His methods also contravened Presbyterian decorum and order. Whitefield's preaching could be highly emotional and theatrical. To some it looked manipulative. As did the Tennents, he preached in a threatening manner, sometimes referred to as "the terrors of the law," as a way to arouse nominal Christians and the spiritually nonchalant. He also expressed himself in vernacular language that could sound like a trivialization of Christianity's weighty claims. For such reasons the same ministers in the presbyteries in Philadelphia and Delaware were critical of Whitefield in ways similar to their objections to the Tennents and the Log College. The popularity and fanfare of the Great Awakening, consequently, shifted the ongoing debate within the American church over ministerial qualifications from subscription and formal education to religious experience.

The controversy over Whitefield was not confined to American Presbyterians. He also encountered opposition in New England from those who regarded his message and manner as a threat to the established churches there. But the controversy over the awakening among Presbyterians was pivotal for upsetting an already fragile harmony. Indicative of the increasing antagonism was Gilbert Tennent's abusive sermon, "The Danger of an Unconverted Ministry," preached on March 8, 1740, close to the peak of Whitefield's popularity in the middle colonies and the nadir of intransigence within the Synod of Philadelphia. Tennent's performance at Nottingham, Pennsylvania, well outside the boundaries of his own Presbytery of New Brunswick, was calculated as retaliatory fire to the shots aimed at Whitefield and at Log College graduates by the presbyters in Pennsylvania and Delaware. It came only two months before the next meeting of Synod and was largely responsible for the eventual division in the church between the Old Side and New Side Presbyterians.

In this sermon Tennent argued sensibly that unregenerate ministers should not be tolerated. Less plausible, however, was his identification of the revivals' opponents as unregenerate ministers. In fact, Tennent followed the highly partisan tactic of conceiving of his own position as the only legitimate expression of Presbyterian faith and practice. That position included a new conception of conversion as a deep and abiding experience that transformed believers, a requirement that ministers demonstrate having experienced such a conversion, and a suspicion of ecclesiastical rules and policies that might become a barrier to the spiritual influences rippling out of the awakening. The rhetorical flourish of Tennent's concluding comments was a testimony to his own skills as a preacher and to the highly pejorative nature of his argument:

> I beseech you, my dear Brethren, to consider, That there is no Probability of your getting Good, by the Ministry of Pharisees .... They are as good as non, nay, worse than non, upon some Accounts .... They strive to keep better out of Places where they live; nay, when the Life of Piety comes near their Quarters, they rise up in Arms against it, consult, contrive and combine in their Conclaves against it, as a common Enemy, that discovers and condemns their Craft and Hypocrisie. And with what Art, Rhetoric, and Appearances of Piety, will they varnish their Opposition of Christ's Kingdom? As the Magicians imitated the Works of *Moses*, so do false Apostles, and deceitful Workers, the Apostles of Christ.

With some understatement, Charles Hodge commented on the "unhappy violence" of this sermon as "one of the principal causes of that entire alienation of feeling, which soon resulted in an open rupture."

But Tennent would not let up and carried such vituperation with him to Synod in May of 1740. The initial business of that body called for an effort to hammer out an agreement on the divisive issue of the role of Synod in licensure and ordination. Despite Tennent's inflammatory sermon, the opponents of revival, who had a clear majority, sought a compromise to which both sides might agree. Tennent and his party refused such a conciliatory effort because he argued that compromise was impossible. Members of Synod then offered two other olive branches. The first called for two members of Synod to be present at the examination of candidates by presbyteries, and for these synodical delegates to report back to the main body if they suspected any foul play. The second proposed that presbyteries prepare reports for Synod on the licensure and ordination of their candidates when presented for installation as members of Synod.

But in each case Tennent was adamant that each presbytery retain its own sovereignty in the examination and ordination of its members. As Richard Webster depicted Tennent's stubbornness, the New Brunswick minister's idea was to give each presbytery the power of a "private mint to put the guinea-stamp on pieces of such weight and such alloy as it chose, and to circulate them through the dominions of the synod currency, as of equal value with the standard coin." Webster added that this understanding of the power of presbytery "disrobed" Synod of "all its dignity" and left each presbytery free "to disregard and annul" synodical decisions.

Tennent and one of his like-minded colleagues, Samuel Blair, followed their refusal to work toward compromise with papers that discredited the critics of revivals, many of whom were the audience for their remarks, in terms similar to Tennent's Nottingham sermon. When asked whether they had conferred with those opponents of revivals they had in mind, Tennent and Blair admitted that they had not. Even so, Synod demonstrated remarkable patience with the advocates of revival by passing a resolution that called on its members to contemplate the seriousness of Tennent's and Blair's charges "as they will answer it at the great day of Christ" and for presbyteries to make sure their members were acting appropriately with regard to the awakening. Webster observed that "it is difficult to conceive" why Tennent and Blair "were not rebuked or suspended for their representations" since the ministers against whom the revivalists inveighed were not only present but "respectable for their number, age, long-tried fidelity, and admitted ability." And yet, despite all of the ingredients necessary for a split in the American church, the 1740 Synod managed to adjourn without one.

The uneasy peace of the 1740 meeting, however, did not characterize the intervening year. Instead, from 1740 to 1741, the controversy over revivalism became transcolonial, with preaching tours by the famous Whitefield and lesser-known such as Tennent in New England functioning as the proverbial gasoline on the fire. In the meantime, charges went back and forth between the two sides, both with great publicity in the press, but also in less public settings such as pulpits and meetings of presbyteries. By the time of the 1741 meeting of Synod, a division between the pro- and anti-revival parties was inevitable. Contributing to the timing of the split between the New and Old Sides in 1741 was the complete absence of the members of the Presbytery of New York at the annual synodical gathering. With the nascent Old Side Presbyterians comprising almost the entire attendance at Synod, the protest that Robert Cross presented and that had signatures of half of the synodical delegation found a receptive and cordial audience. This so-called "Protestation of 1741" was the formal declaration of an intention to divide the American church into its Old Side and New Side branches.

This document, which ran on for several pages, summarized the frustrations of those who had been most zealous for creedal subscription and for ecclesiastical order. The hope behind the Protestation was "to preserve this swooning church from a total expiration." The method for doing so was to remove the influence of the Tennent group and "their unwearied, unscriptural, antipresbyterial, uncharitable, divisive practices."

Positively, the Protestation advocated a return to The Westminster Standards and Directories as the basis for membership in Synod, and the refusal of anyone who would not submit to this basis. But the document went on to list objections to the pro-revival group, which included their "anarchical principles" of church government, their habit of preaching without invitation by local ministers and presbyteries, their uncharitable and unfounded charges against fellow ministers, their manner of preaching (i.e., the "terrors of the law"), and their teaching that so divided good works from the assurance of faith as to encourage licentiousness. *[margin note: substance of the objections]*

More basic than these lists of principles or grievances was a recognition that the unity of the Presbyterian Church was a sham. "How monstrously absurd," the authors wrote, that men who openly condemned particular members of Synod "without judicial process, or proving them guilty of heresy or immorality," refrained from "Christian communion" with their opponents, "to join with us, or we with them as a judicatory, made up of authoritative officers of Jesus Christ." As such, the protest called for Synod to unseat the ministers from the Presbytery of New Brunswick. *[margin note: — unseat the ministers]*

The Protestation was a controversial move, and not only because of its explicit renunciation of the revivalist party in New Brunswick. The measure included signatures of twelve ministers, mainly from Philadelphia and Delaware, and nine ruling elders. Yet because the Presbytery of New York's ministers were all absent, the Protestation carried a slim majority two votes. Even some of the more conservative ministers, such as Jedediah Andrews and George Gillespie, did not approve of the Protestation. Also unusual was Synod taking action against fellow ministers without the due process of charges and a trial. Still, even those who did not vote for the measure were in sympathy with it.

Soon after Synod, Andrews, who was moderator of Synod, wrote a letter of explanation to one of the absent New York ministers. The New Brunswick men "have called themselves members with us, but have been continually acting against us, and endeavoring to make all that don't follow them to be looked on as carnal, graceless, unconverted hypocrites, to destroy our usefulness and bring as many as possible over to them. . ." But this was not all. Andrews added that "both town and country are full of Antinomian notions, which if we say anything against, in pulpit or out, 'tis almost as much as our lives are worth, and we feel ourselves bound in conscience to give people warning and endeavor to preserve them from destruction."

The judicial aspect of the Protestation of 1741 and the subsequent division between the Old and New Sides takes on a different light when seen in the context of subsequent developments. For four years, moderates within the Synod of Philadelphia, led by the likes of Andrews, Gillespie, and Jonathan Dickinson, continued to seek a compromise that would allow the members of the Presbytery of New Brunswick to regain their membership in Synod. The decision to bar New Brunswick's members, then, was in effect on more a procedural move to restore harmony than it was a judicial decision to remove men from the ministry.

Once the efforts to find a resolution failed, the procedural character of 1741 became even clearer. In 1745 the Presbytery of New York joined with the Presbytery of New Brunswick to form the Synod of New York, which was the New Side Synod. The Old Side remained as the Synod of Philadelphia. These synods continued to work independently by each having different members and somewhat different terms for admission. But they also continued to communicate with each other for the purpose of restoring unity in the American church. The Old and New Sides, then, were two variants of the American Presbyterian Church, not two different Presbyterian denominations.

Each synod stood for a different emphasis within American Presbyterianism, with revivalism holding the key to understanding their disagreements. The New Side, represented best by Gilbert Tennent and Jonathan Dickinson, sought a Presbyterian Church that would be characterized by its zeal and genuine Christian devotion. This godly piety took precedence over such formal restrictions as creedal subscription, presbytery boundaries, ministerial prerogatives, or appropriate levels of theological education for ministers. In Tennent's case, the stress on Christian earnestness could take an uncompromising and radical form, but it was leavened by Dickinson's moderation, especially in the formation of the Synod of New York. In 1745 when that Synod was established, the terms for membership were substantially similar to those of the Old Side in Philadelphia, except that these rules placed no explicit prohibition on itinerant preaching (requiring instead only an avoidance of divisiveness) and so were generally favorable to the prosecution of revivals. Still, what defined the New Side first was religious experience, which then should as much as possible be embodied in a Presbyterian form of church life and doctrinal expression.

The Old Side, in contrast, gave priority to the outward forms of Presbyterianism while still seeking to encourage godliness among clergy and laity. John Thomson and George Gillespie were the best exponents of Old Side convictions. For them, the zeal of revivals should not ordinarily conflict with the good order of the church, whether in the training of ministerial candidates, the authority of sessions or presbyteries, or its doctrinal witness. In fact, if the spiritual energy of revivals disrupted church life, they reasoned, then generally speaking it was not a legitimate expression of Christian faith. Instead of testing the genuineness of faith on the basis of individual experience, whether the convert seeking admission to a local congregation or a candidate being examined for licensure or ordination, the Old Side looked at the corporate or collective expression of Christian faith in the form of the Presbyterian Church's witness as a whole. A church's creedal witness, its church government, and its learned ministers were as much indications of true Presbyterianism as what an individual Christian might experience.

During the disruption between the Old and New Sides, the latter flourished at least numerically, while the former languished by comparison. As near as spotty records will allow, the New Side received close to fifty new ministerial members between 1745 and 1758, while the Old Side received only nine. In addition, none of the Old Side's new members were as noteworthy as the New Side's David Brainerd, a missionary to the Native Americans in Pennsylvania and author of a spiritual diary that remains in print, or Samuel Davies, an itinerant preacher in Virginia and president of the College of New Jersey.

The temptation has been to attribute these different outcomes to the superior zeal and understanding of the faith that the New Side exhibited over the Old Side. But equally important to consider for the Old Side's limited growth are several institutional factors. Because of its proximity and ties to New England, the New Side was able to recruit the ministers from the orbit of New England Congregationalism, while the flow of ministers from Scotland and Northern Ireland to Old Side churches virtually dried up. In addition, the New Side in 1746 was able to secure from New Jersey a charter for its own college, the aforementioned College of New Jersey, which inherited most of the networks and support of William Tennent's old Log College. The Old Side attempted in 1743 to start its own academy in Delaware for the training of ministers but the school lacked adequate funding and students.

Another important factor was the New Side's favorable attitude toward itinerant preaching, an outlook that gave it an advantage in sending out ministers to immigrants from Scotland and Ireland who were surging down the Shenandoah River Valley into parts of Virginia and the Carolinas. For instance, the Synod of New York had members who were ministering in the South, even though the Old Side's Synod of Philadelphia was geographically closer. A combination of religious and institutional factors, then, contributed to the growth of the New Side and the stagnation of the Old Side during these years of disruption.

Even so, during the years from 1745 to 1758, the Synods of New York and Philadelphia continued to correspond for the purpose of reuniting as one body. Many of the Old Side's objections had already been removed with the formation in 1745 of the Synod of New York and its affirmation of creedal subscription and insistence that members submit to synodal decisions.

Also conducive to warmer relations was Gilbert Tennent's 1749 sermon, "*Irenicum Ecclesiasticum*," in which he argued strongly for union of the two synods and recanted from his vitriolic remarks in "The Danger of an Unconverted Ministry." When he said that "it is cruel and censorious Judging, to condemn the States of those we know not; and to condemn positively and openly the spiritual *States* of such as are sound in *fundamental Doctrines*, and *regular in Life*," Tennent took a major stride in backing away from an attitude that had directly prompted the Protestation of 1741.

Matters that still divided the two Synods concerned the power of Synod (as opposed to presbyteries) to determine the doctrinal norms for ordination, and whether Old Side and New Side presbyteries in the same region should be merged in a proposed reunion. In 1754 both sides agreed in principle to a form of reunion that would simply merge both Synods and their respective presbyteries, thus putting off any sort of redrawing of presbytery boundaries. Still, it took four years before each party could muster the willpower to sign an agreement, which they did on May 15, 1758, when the Synod of New York held its annual meeting in Philadelphia while the Synod of Philadelphia was already in session.

reunion of 1758

Presbyterians Revived and Reunited

The reunion of 1758 merged the two separate Synods of Philadelphia and New York as one: The Synod of New York and Philadelphia. The fact that New York preceded Philadelphia in the name was indicative of the majority that the New Side enjoyed in 1758. Of the united Synods' ninety-four ministerial members, seventy had come from the former Synod of New York. The terms of reunion were also appropriately favorable to the New Side. This is not to suggest that the Reunion of 1758 was a complete rout of the Old Side. The composition of each group had changed, moderate heads on both sides had prevailed, and the terms of reunion were agreeable to both parties. Still, the Plan of Union was a vindication of the New Side, thus resulting in a settlement of colonial Presbyterian tensions on grounds that predisposed the American church to revivalism and the piety it nurtured.

terms of reunion

Of the major issues that had triggered the division, the terms of reunion did uphold Old Side concerns. For instance, though the language was not exactly the same as the Adopting Act of 1729, the first article of the Plan reaffirmed the Presbyterian Church's loyalty to the Westminster Standards and Directories for government and worship. Also, on the question of candidates for licensure and ordination, article six stated that a man needed to show adequate learning and accept the Westminster Standards as "the confession of his faith." Less agreeable to the Old Side would have been that same article's assertion that candidates also demonstrate "experimental acquaintance with religion," a phrase that catered to the New Side's demand that candidates recount a conversion experience.

The article did not mention which schools might be acceptable, a silence indicative of the College of New Jersey's legitimacy as a training ground as good as Yale or Harvard for Presbyterian ministers. Furthermore, articles two through five addressed the Old Side's concern for good order in the church by forbidding dissension and false accusations against other ministers, requiring submission to the vote of the majority, and outlining procedures for appropriate protests of synodical decisions. In these various ways, the Plan of Union did address the convictions that had led the Old Side to take action against the New Brunswick Presbyterians.

But the Plan was ultimately a victory for the New Side because its eighth article, and by far the longest (almost half the entire document), was about the awakenings that had divided the church. It declared that the former Synod of New York continued to hold that the recent revivals of religion were "a blessed work of God's Holy Spirit," a phrasing that may have exempted the Old Side from taking the same view. It also delineated in careful detail the signs of spiritual renewal that were to characterize the experience of conversion, a level of specificity that would have troubled Old Side leaders. To be sure, this description of the work of the Spirit on the life of a sinner was contrasted with visions, hearing voices, and extraordinary manifestations that were deemed clearly delusional. As such, this was a moderate affirmation of revival piety and the introspection it so often encouraged.

But however balanced the eighth article was, and no matter how much it bore the imprint of Dickinson's moderate understanding of the work of the Spirit, the Plan of Union stamped the Presbyterian Church as a communion that would encourage and benefit from revivals. Although that form of piety could lead as it did to new members and greater godliness among its ministers and members, it was also a form of devotion that was in tension with the covenantal faith of the Reformed tradition that stressed children growing up and inheriting the faith of parents rather than having to undergo a religious experience as a Christian rite of passage.

Indeed, as the form of religious experience outlined in the Plan of Union became more and more the norm for American Presbyterian piety, the American church's reliance on the older forms of Protestant church life—catechesis, family visitation, the faithful work of the settled ministry—dwindled. The effects of the colonial church's settlement of the question of Presbyterian piety would not become evident until the nineteenth century, when another series of revivals again divided the Presbyterian Church.

4

From a Colonial to a National Church

John Witherspoon is one of the heroes of American Presbyterianism, and for good reason. He provided leadership to the American church at a crucial time in its history. He presided over the College of New Jersey for the longest period of any of its early presidents, thus giving the institution stability and turning it into a school that would provide steady service to the church. As the sole minister to sign the Declaration of Independence, he was also one of American Presbyterianism's most eloquent and fabled patriots at the time of the American founding.

And yet, Witherspoon was an import from Scotland, not a product of the colonial Presbyterian Church. When he arrived in America with his wife and five surviving children in the summer of 1768, the reception he witnessed was almost prophetic of his future greatness. In Philadelphia, the Witherspoons received a cordial welcome from city dignitaries, complete with the publication of a special edition of one of Witherspoon's most popular books, *Ecclesiastical Characteristics*. From Philadelphia the family headed north toward Trenton, New Jersey, and along the way the trip turned into a victory tour with local officials and families coming out to greet and escort the newly arrived Presbyterians. A mile from the village of Princeton itself, town leaders, faculty, and students were on hand to greet the new president and accompany him and his family during the last leg of the trip.

What had Witherspoon done to merit this remarkable outpouring of support? In point of fact, this display of good will was more indicative of difficulties within American Presbyterianism than of Witherspoon's own accomplishments, which were many. Born in 1723, the son of a minister in the Church of Scotland, Witherspoon followed in his father's footsteps and also went into the Presbyterian ministry. He served in two Scottish parishes before accepting the invitation to preside over the College of New Jersey. During those pastorates, Witherspoon emerged as one of the leaders of the evangelical wing of the kirk, through books such as *Ecclesiastical Characteristics*, originally published in 1753 as a parody of the moderate or liberal leadership of the Church of Scotland. His defense of orthodox theology, careful exegetical preaching, and regular appeal to Scripture were partly responsible for the interest Witherspoon generated among American Presbyterians. Gilbert Tennent and Samuel Davies had first met the Scot during a trip in 1754 to secure financial support for the college. By 1766, when the trustees first voted to invite Witherspoon, he had solidified his reputation as an orthodox minister and a man of learning whom the Americans needed.

Witherspoon was also the choice of Presbyterian leaders who were still suffering the effects of the division between the Old and New Sides. As much as the reunion of 1758 had restored harmony at the synodical level, local skirmishes continued to disrupt the church. Although the College of New Jersey had been and remained a New Side stronghold, that wing of the church lacked an obvious leader who could ensure the institution's reputation. In addition, trustees, always in need of financial support, recognized the advantage of enlisting the Old Side in the college's affairs. The choice of Witherspoon for president was, then, something of a compromise. His evangelical views were agreeable to the New Side, while his Scottish pedigree pleased the Old Side.

American Presbyterians on both sides also got more in Witherspoon than they had bargained. One of the great attractions of his presidency was the need for a professor at the college who could teach theology and help train ministers that the American church desperately needed. As early as 1760, Synod had begun to explore possible sources of funding for a professorship of divinity at the Princeton college. Witherspoon filled that need, even if he could not devote his complete attention to classroom instruction. As a college president he would leave an indelible intellectual stamp on American Presbyterian theology by introducing Scottish philosophy at the College of New Jersey. In addition, as a churchman he would help to consolidate the colonial Presbyterian Church and establish structures for its ministry in the new political landscape of American independence. And as a political activist, Witherspoon would emerge as a spokesman for colonial Calvinists suspicious of the Anglican establishment and its head, the British monarch. In sum, Witherspoon signaled a new era in American Presbyterianism, one in which the old tensions of the church's infancy would make way for a more ambitious agenda.

Lingering Divisions

In some ways, the antagonisms that determined perceptions of the new president of the College of New Jersey were virtually irrelevant by the time Witherspoon settled in Princeton. Thanks to another wave of migration of Scottish and Scotch-Irish immigrants, from 1760 on the Presbyterian Church received a plethora of new members and congregations. These new churches and members were largely ignorant of the arguments that distinguished the Old and New Sides. Plus, they resided and worshiped in places far removed from the sites of greatest dispute.

In fact, patterns of migration shifted the demographic heft of the Presbyterian Church from the corridor between New York City and Philadelphia, with Princeton in the middle, to territories south and west. Scotch-Irish settlers flooded into western Pennsylvania during the years after reunion and became a political thorn in the side of colonial authorities, owing to ambiguities in policies governing Native Americans and to rivalries between the French and English empires in the New World. Another wave of these immigrants continued to travel south through the Shenandoah River Valley into Virginia and North Carolina. But they did not stop there. They kept going into the new territories of Kentucky and Tennessee. (Andrew Jackson, the seventh president of the United

States, was a descendent of these Scotch-Irish migrants who settled in Tennessee.) When looking for pulpit supply or a settled pastor, the last item on the list of these frontier Presbyterians was a minister's Old Side or New Side credential.

Another consequence of this influx of new members was the dilution of the New England presence in the American church. For the time being, during the decades prior to the War for Independence, the Scottish and Scotch-Irish identity of American Presbyterians was arguably the strongest it has ever been. Even so, formerly New Side presbyteries grew the fastest as places that attracted and ordained new ministers. Between 1758 and 1776 the presbyteries of the American church received new ministers in the following numbers: New Brunswick, twenty-four; New Castle, thirteen; New York, eleven; Donegal, nine; First of Philadelphia, eight; Hanover, six; Suffolk, six; Lewes, four; Second of Philadelphia, three; Dutchess County, two; Orange, two; and Lancaster, one.

Although the division of 1741 faded in significance at the level of congregational membership, the statistics for the admission of new ministers suggests that the issues dividing the church would not go away entirely after 1758. This was partly the result of the Plan of Reunion's terms of settlement. The Plan had not addressed the manner of incorporating presbyteries in the same region that were divided along Old Side/New Side lines. New churches, but even older ones, could choose to identify with the Old or New Side presbytery in their vicinity depending on theological affinity. The fact that Philadelphia had two presbyteries was one indication of this problem. But also in parts of southeastern Pennsylvania and Delaware the competition between both parties was still fierce.

The basis for this friction continued to be different notions of ministerial qualifications, with New Siders still insisting on a conversion experience for candidates for the ministry, and Old Siders being content with affirmation of the church's creedal statements and directories. But because the Plan of Union delegated the power of ordination solely to presbyteries, without the possibility of synodal review or veto, different standards continued to divide those bodies where Old and New Side sentiments remained. The reunion of 1758 may have healed the division of 1741 but it did not resolve the original points of disagreement.

73

For instance, in 1765 the Presbytery of Donegal petitioned the Synod of New York and Philadelphia to be divided into two presbyteries, along the lines that would have separated the former Old and New Side ministers in its midst. Donegal had been an Old Side presbytery, but in redrawing of presbytery boundaries following reunion, it had become a fairly acrimonious region, in part because it had been reconfigured with an Old Side minority. In the intervening six years following the redistricting, the Old Side pastors, some of whom had been transferred to Donegal from Delaware because of similar presbytery rearrangements in New Castle, had objected to their minority status.

To keep the peace, the 1765 Synod reassigned some of Donegal's pastors to New Castle, where the original Delaware Old Side pastors were transferred, and some farther west to the newly formed Presbytery of Carlisle. But this also proved disagreeable since the Old Side now constituted a minority in the Presbytery of New Castle. The Old Side pastors who had been forced to switch jurisdictions twice gave up and decided to constitute themselves as an independent body. They appealed to the 1768 Synod to be acknowledged and received, but Synod would only take back individual pastors who would then be assigned, depending on their location, to the presbyteries of Donegal, New Castle, or Second of Philadelphia. Four of the pastors chose this option and were received by the Second Presbytery of Philadelphia. The others affiliated with their former presbyteries.

A similar set of difficulties became a nuisance for the Second Presbytery of Philadelphia, the body created in 1762 precisely to maintain the witness and affiliations of previously Old Side ministers in that area. Because the former Old Side ministers in Philadelphia felt marginalized by the Presbytery of Philadelphia after reunion in 1758, Synod had allowed for the creation of a presbytery based on theological affinity. The result was two presbyteries in Philadelphia, First (formerly New Side ministers) and Second (previously Old Side pastors). The reception of four ministers from Donegal into Second Presbytery obviously increased their resolve. The issue that had been responsible for the division in 1762 was the ongoing question of whether candidates for licensure or ordination were required to give evidence, as one Presbyterian Church historian felicitously put it, of "their experimental acquaintance with religion."

74

In 1762 Synod tried and failed to unite the two Philadelphia presbyteries, despite the objections of synodical members that the perpetuation of the Second Presbytery tolerated an unhealthy "temper of schismatical tendency." Perhaps in retaliation, Synod in 1772 required the Second Presbytery to receive as a member George Duffield, who would become famous for serving as chaplain of the Continental Congress. He was objectionable to the Old Side pastors because of his associations with New Side members in Donegal Presbytery, even though the formerly Old Side congregation at Pine Street Church had called him.

Duffield's installation in Philadelphia showed how lingering suspicions in the church played out after 1758. Those tensions mattered more to pastors, many of whom had roots in the church prior to reunion, than to the laity, many of whom were new to colonial America. Even so, Second Philadelphia was one of the rare presbyteries from the former Old Side to withstand what one historian has called "a case study in ecclesiastical manipulation" by the New Side. After reunion, to quell the Old Side element, Elizabeth Nybakken continues, Synod created "presbyteries with a New Side majority," consulting "neither ministers nor congregations as it created, abolished, and reshuffled presbyteries by mandate amid howls of protest from the Old Side." This may explain why men of Old Side backgrounds training for the ministry began with increasing frequency to seek ordination in the Episcopal Church, or why a small number of Old Side ministers simply gave up on the American church and joined other Presbyterian communions such as the Reformed Presbyterians.

Ironically, the Synod of New York and Philadelphia was softer on other Reformed churches in colonial America than on the Old Side. In 1768 Synod initiated correspondence with Reformed bodies in Europe, including the Netherlands, Switzerland, Scotland, England, and Ireland. Undoubtedly, the chief aim of this interest in fraternal relations was to secure new ministers for congregations in America. As one letter indicated, a great number of the colonial churches "could support ministers singly, than could procure them, and the rest by joining two or three together."

But beyond the need for pastors, Synod also indicated through such correspondence its sense of being part of a larger Reformed witness that extended from centers of Old World Protestantism to frontier outposts in the New World. This awareness accounts in part for Synod's appointment in 1769 of a committee to study the possibility of establishing a union with Associate Presbyterians (Seceders) in Pennsylvania. Nothing ever came of this interest formally. The Associate Presbyterians still had strong formal ties to their Synod back in Scotland, which was jealous of its membership and associations, and which expressed displeasure with the possible union with the American Presbyterians. In 1774 the clerk of the Pennsylvania Associate Presbyterians sent the Synod of New York and Philadelphia a letter saying that his body was not "disposed" to carry forward any attempt at union. Even so, the effort did show that American Presbyterians had an interest in cultivating formal ties to other Reformed communions.

The Sacred Cause of Liberty

Other Protestants with whom Synod began to establish closer relations during the final decades of the eighteenth century were the Congregationalist churches of Connecticut. Regular correspondence between Presbyterians and Congregationalists began in 1766. Its aim was an annual convention of ministers from both churches to study their "united cause and interest," to "collect accounts relating thereto; to unite their endeavors and counsels for spreading the gospel and preserving the religious LIBERTIES of the churches; to diffuse harmony, and to keep up a correspondence throughout this united body, and with friends abroad." This convention was to meet alternately at Congregationalist and Presbyterian sites. The first in 1766 took place in Elizabethtown, New Jersey, and it continued to meet for the next ten years until the Revolutionary War prohibited ministers from attending. Its first order of business was to draw up a plan of union between the Congregationalist churches in Connecticut and the American Presbyterian Church, a foreshadowing of the Plan of Union that went into effect in 1801.

In the meantime, this convention of Presbyterians and Congregationalists became a chief outlet for nurturing among American Calvinists a sense of wariness about the changing political environment in the colonies. Here the mention of religious liberties as part of the rationale for this convention was significant. During the decade before the Declaration of Independence, the Church of England, already the established church in New York and Virginia, had stepped up its presence within the colonies and had begun to explore the possibility of establishing an American bishop.

For dissenting British Protestants, the thought of an American bishop did prompt fears of turning the status of the American churches into that of non-conformists, thus being forced to yield many of the rights and privileges they enjoyed as communions with their own authority. Francis Makemie's own experience in the early eighteenth century when he was imprisoned for not having a license to preach in New York was one example that came readily to mind for American Presbyterians. But the actual situation of Presbyterians in Virginia, who provided important support and arguments for the principles informing state laws on religious toleration, was another case in point. There the Anglican authorities posed a variety of obstacles, formal and informal, that prevented Presbyterian ministers from executing their duties.

A pastoral letter from Synod in 1775 was indicative of American Presbyterians' initially cautious support for political independence. It recommended not only allegiance to King George III "as the first magistrate of the empire," but also "esteem and reverence" for a sovereign who had "merited well of his subjects on many accounts, and who has probably been misled into the late and present measures by those about him." The letter added, "It gives us the greatest pleasure to say . . . that the present opposition to the measures of the administration does not in the least arise from disaffection to the king, or a desire of separation from the parent state." Consequently, Synod advised Presbyterians "to continue in the same disposition" and to desire only "the preservation and security of those rights which belong to you as freemen and Britons . . ."

The same letter also recommended the union of the colonies and respect for the work of the Continental Congress: "Let your prayers be offered up to God for his direction in their proceedings" and "adhere firmly to their resolutions." This pastoral advice from Synod concluded with a brief affirmation of the principles of liberty, warning that "there is no example in history in which civil liberty was destroyed, and the rights of conscience preserved entire."

A small minority of colonial Presbyterians identified more closely with Synod's recommendations about loyalty and respect for the king, but the majority threw their support behind the Continental Congress and the logic of the letter tying religious liberty to the preservation of civil liberties. John Witherspoon's fast-day sermon of May 17, 1776, "The Dominion of Providence Over the Passions of Men," was arguably the most important the Princeton president ever gave. It was based on Psalm 76:10 ("Surely the wrath of men shall praise thee; the remainder of Wrath shalt thou restrain") and delivered on a day set aside by the Continental Congress for prayer.

At the time, Witherspoon was a member of the Continental Congress. Because of his high visibility in colonial affairs no doubt, his sermon was published and distributed widely throughout America. In the sermon, which warned of divine judgment against nations that failed to honor God, Witherspoon also expressed confidence in the patriots' purpose. "[T]he cause in which America is now in arms," he declared, "is the cause of justice, of liberty, and of human nature." Witherspoon observed that the colonists had not been motivated by "pride, resentment, or sedition" but instead by "a deep and general conviction" that religious and civil liberty, as well as "the temporal and eternal happiness of us and our society," depend on political autonomy. Here Witherspoon was not simply regarding religious liberty as a subset of a broader group of civil liberties. Rather, he had a more precise relationship between civil and religious liberty. "The knowledge of God and his truths have from the beginning of the world been chiefly, if not entirely, confined to those parts of the earth, where some degree of liberty and political justice were to be seen . . ."

In effect, Witherspoon was articulating the logic of most American Presbyterians in which they assumed that true religion flourished only where civil magistrates protected civil liberties. "There is not a single instance in history," the Princetonian warned, "in which civil liberty was lost, and religious liberty preserved entire." For this reason, if the colonists were to "yield up our temporal property" to Parliament through unfair taxes, they would also be delivering their consciences "into bondage."

Other Presbyterian ministers were not as well known as Witherspoon but no less assertive in offering fulsome support for independence. John King of Mercersburg, Pennsylvania, preached a number of sermons on behalf of American interests and served as a chaplain during the Revolutionary War. One of his sermons provided an example of other

78

arguments American Presbyterians used to declare and fight for their independence from England. Like the pastoral letter from Synod, King expressed toleration for the king but objected vigorously to Parliament's increasing usurpation of the colonists' rights. "They call themselves . . . the mother-country," King asserted, but "is it fatherly or motherly to strip us of every thing, to rob us of every right and privilege, and then to whip and dragoon us with fleets and armies till we are pleased?" The answer was obvious. "When the king uses the executive branch of government which is in his hand, to enable one part of his subjects to lord it over and oppress another, it is a sufficient ground of our applying to the laws of nature for our defence."

The combination of arguments such as those of Witherspoon and King made American Presbyterians notable in the revolution. According to one Hessian captain fighting for the British, "call this war . . . by whatever name you may, only call it not an American rebellion, it is nothing more or less than an Irish-Scotch Presbyterian Rebellion." As objectionable as an Anglican establishment would have been, and as onerous as Parliament's policies of taxation were, Presbyterian leaders did not show the greatest theological insight in their support for independence. After all, a strong strain of biblical teaching, such as Paul's instruction in Romans 13, counseled not a Christian duty to defend political rights but to be subject to the political authorities that God had established.

Equally germane was the Presbyterians' own confession of faith. In its chapter on Christian liberty, the Westminster Confession clearly states that the freedom believers enjoy because of Christ's having liberated them from the tyranny of sin and death is no basis for resisting the lawful authority of both state and church. To be sure, political theorists in Reformed countries had long debated the legitimacy of political resistance to obvious tyrants. But American Presbyterians often assumed the conclusion to those arguments rather than identifying carefully the nature of Christian obligations in a time of political upheaval.

Nevertheless, Presbyterians' overwhelming support for political independence was by no means a position of ease or sloth. In fact, Presbyterians individually and corporately paid dearly for their political convictions. Because Presbyterian clergy were outspokenly in favor of the war, and because some served in official capacities in colonial politics, while many others accompanied troops as chaplains, British soldiers often singled them out as "ringleaders of rebellion." This meant that services were often disrupted because of rumors of Hessian soldiers nearby who were intent on capturing the local Presbyterian minister. Other ministers were imprisoned, and stories even circulated of Presbyterian pastors who decided to surrender to enemy troops but were shot and killed despite their pacifistic intentions.

Churches were also a casualty of war, with British soldiers either mistreating a meetinghouse in the course of their setting up camp, or in a punitive fashion destroying whatever they could find within a Presbyterian church, in one case stripping the pews and using them for firewood. Estimates run as high as fifty Presbyterian congregations' church buildings having been destroyed during the war.

The razing of church edifices also extended to the experience of several Presbyterian ministers who served either as chaplains or in the local political associations. The Hessians sometimes identified their homes and raided them, destroying personal possessions and libraries in the process, or worse. So cautious and alarmed were Presbyterian pastors and congregations during the war that some ministers conducted services in their home churches with rifles close at hand behind the pulpit. Nor was it unusual for Presbyterians serving as chaplains to be conducting a service for the Americans, only for their singing to alert enemy soldiers of the company's position and send the worshipers scattering with gunfire aimed at more than simply ending the religious activities. Under such circumstances congregations were in no condition to pay their pastors the salary on which many ministers depended.

Obviously, the conditions of war were infelicitous for local congregations whose pastors either had left to serve as chaplains or soldiers, or whose meetings were conducted with fear of British reprisal. But the war also took a terrific toll on meetings of presbyteries and Synod. During the years of violence, for instance, Synod averaged only sixteen ministers in attendance at a time when its total ministerial membership was slightly more than one hundred. The highest number (twenty) found their way to Synod in 1779. The previous year was the lowest attendance, when the British militia had occupied Philadelphia and only eleven ministers could make the trip to Bedminster, Pennsylvania, where Synod was forced to conduct its business. The agenda for these meetings during the war was hardly ambitious. Churches often sent applications for assistance, both financial and spiritual, but Synod was in no position to respond. The most Synod could muster was a continual call to Presbyterians for days dedicated to fasting, humiliation, and prayer.

Somewhat surprisingly, when peace returned the level of participation in Synod did not resume its former pre-revolution level of involvement. Attendance figures often doubled or tripled what they had been during the war. Still, the lack of ministers at Synod became a matter of some concern for Presbyterian leaders. Clearly, several factors were at work. The effects of the war continued to be felt and proved to be pressing matters needing ministers' immediate attention. The size of the American church was also a problem; it had outgrown its mid-century organization of Synod and presbyteries.

But the war had also proved to be a distraction from the Presbyterian Church's original and primary calling as a witness to the gospel, thus causing the frenzy of war and euphoria of political independence to sap Presbyterian zeal for religious, as opposed to political, matters. One indication of this change of perspective was the decline in numbers of the College of New Jersey's graduates going into the ministry. President Witherspoon's involvement in the life of the new nation inspired more of the college's graduates to pursue political rather than ministerial callings.

Another indication of the war's effect on the Presbyterian Church's sense of mission was the pastoral letter that the 1783 Synod sent to its presbyteries and congregations. Its tone and content were less measured than in the comparable letter of 1775, just prior to the war, and suggest a different set of loyalties for the American church. Synod wrote first of Presbyterians' commitment to the political principles of freedom without the qualifications that had previously colored their perspective on the conflict with Great Britain:

> We cannot help congratulating you on the general and almost universal attachment of the Presbyterian body to the cause of liberty and the rights of mankind. This has been visible in their conduct, and has been confessed by the complaints and resentment of the common enemy. Such a circumstance ought not only to afford us satisfaction on the

review, as bringing credit to the body in general, but to increase our gratitude to God, for the happy issue of the war.

Finally, Synod recommended gratitude to God, despite real hardship, for the outcome of the war:

> Had [the war] been unsuccessful, we must have drunk deeply of the cup of suffering. Our burnt and wasted churches, and our plundered dwellings, in such places as fell under the power of our adversaries, are but an earnest of what we must have suffered, had they finally prevailed. The Synod, therefore, request you to render thanks to Almighty God, for all his mercies, spiritual and temporal, and in a particular manner for establishing the Independence of the United States of America.

These were plausible sentiments given the consequential events of the prior decade. But they also indicated an unhealthy identification with and disproportionate allegiance to the United States that would haunt the Presbyterian Church, especially during the Civil War.

The First General Assembly

At the same time that the Continental Congress was deliberating the best way to organize the new North American nation, Synod was also meeting to find a better form of government for the Presbyterian Church's ministry to the United States. This coincidence has tempted some to read the principles of Presbyterian government into the efforts of America's founding fathers. According to Charles Briggs, for instance, "the ecclesiastical polity of the Presbyterian churches influenced the government of the State, and the government of the American Presbyterian Churches was in no slight degree assimilated to the civil government of the country." Briggs even asserted that the choice of a republican form of government in the United States followed the model of Presbyterianism, which "is an organized representative and constitutional government." Undoubtedly, the pattern of Presbyterian government bears clear resemblance to the polity that the Continental Congress and the states embraced and that Presbyterians, such as Witherspoon, who participated in those deliberations, likely drew from their own church polity. But the reorganization of the Presbyterian Church during the 1780s had less to do with national than with ecclesiastical realities.

As mentioned earlier, attendance at Synod between 1775 and 1785 fell off sharply, with an average of only sixteen ministers and six ruling elders being present for these annual gatherings. Not even the presbyteries of New York and Philadelphia had particularly good records of attendance. Even though roads to Philadelphia, where Synod usually met, were good, the Presbytery of New York on average sent only 40 percent of its ministers to the meetings. The Presbyteries of Philadelphia may have managed to send more than New York, but their average of 50 percent attendance was by no means exemplary, given their proximity to the proceedings.

In addition to the distraction of war and nation-building, another reason for the poor showing of Presbyterian officers was the increasing size of the Presbyterian Church. The premise behind the synodical structure of the colonial church had been to regard Synod as a "presbytery of the whole" or super-presbytery. It was a meeting of all the presbyteries, and its task was to conduct business that each presbytery and session could not perform on its own. As such, Synod expected all ministers to attend, and each congregation was supposed to send one ruling elder. But with considerably less than half the ministers attending, Presbyterian leaders recognized a problem in need of attention. In 1785 a pastoral letter from Synod to the four southernmost presbyteries summed up the growing concern. The missive feared that "a habit of neglect" would contribute to the "weakening of each other's hands, the discouraging the comparatively few that attend, and the great injury, if not entirely moldering away of the body."

At the same meeting in 1785 came the first steps to remedy the declining importance and vigor of Synod. One motion called for a committee to consider the "constitution of the church of Scotland, and other Protestant churches, and agreeably to the general principles of Presbyterian government, compile a system of general rules for the government of the Synod. . ." Another motion to the 1785 Synod expanded the interest in a constitution for the church by prescribing the establishment of a general assembly, with the reorganization of the existing presbyteries into three regional and subordinate synods. It aimed to create a representative body for the entire church whose members would be delegated from their presbyteries and synods. The function of synods would remain the same, but their work would now be overseen and coordinated by a general assembly. The proposal was delayed until the 1786 Synod, when the members reached a consensus on reorganizing the church's sixteen presbyteries into four subordinate synods. But Presbyterians were still not ready to erect a general assembly.

The reason for hesitation about a general assembly was a debate within the committee assigned the task of writing a constitution. These officers were divided between two models for the proposed assembly. One was that of the Church of Scotland, which gave the assembly relatively broad powers over synods and presbyteries. The other was the inspiration of ministers of New England Puritan background whose congregationalist instincts made them suspicious of church power beyond the local session. What finally prevailed in committee was a plan closer to the Scottish model, but that allowed greater autonomy for presbyteries (e.g., the authority to license and ordain ministers belonged to presbyteries).

The Synod of 1787 considered the plan, performed some minor revisions, and ratified a motion that established a committee to include these changes in the proposed form of government and to have it printed and distributed to the presbyteries for their consideration. Synod also assigned to this committee the task of including in the constitution revised editions of the Confession and Catechisms, as well as the Directory for Public Worship. The reasons for revision of these parts of the constitution owed to teaching in the Westminster Standards about the civil magistrate that were now obviously out of place in the American situation of religious disestablishment, and to the debates at several recent synods about the church's commitment to psalm singing in worship.

Two of the three parts of the American church's constitution were generally unexceptional. In fact, the founding documents for the national Presbyterian body, complete with General Assembly, consolidated the order that had emerged during the eighteenth century. The Plan of Government, for instance, reflected the American church's fear of centralization and hierarchy. It stated directly that General Assembly's role would not supplant the authority either of congregations or presbyteries. Sessions were free to determine their own rules for the admission of members, and congregations had the liberty to apply the rules of presbyterian government according to their own situation. Meanwhile, presbyteries retained all the powers of licensure and ordination. The plan did recommend that prospective ministers be college educated and know Greek, Hebrew, and Latin. It also elaborated the questions to be put to a candidate for the ministry, which included his reception and adoption of the Westminster Standards. Presbyterian rules extended to assertions about the need for godliness in ministers, a further indication of the New Side victory in the reunion of 1758.

But if any feared a top-down structure in American Presbyterianism thanks to the inauguration of the General Assembly, their worries were easily cast aside. The American model of Presbyterian government, in clear distinction from the Scottish pattern, was to vest great power in local sessions and presbyteries—with General Assembly providing a way for the churches to organize and conduct their larger affairs, and to hear and decide complaints sent to it from those local authorities. This reflected the history of Presbyterianism in the New World.

It was unlike that in Scotland, where the Parliament first created the General Assembly, which then set the tone and order for subsequent developments in the kirk. In America the presbytery came first, and then the Synod, with the General Assembly being created to coordinate national efforts and function as a final court of appeal. Consequently, when the first General Assembly convened in 1789 and took the name, the Presbyterian Church in the U.S.A., it did not possess a grand mandate for positioning and extending American Presbyterianism. The presby- 1789 teries and synods had been around longer and knew that the newly delegated assembly would not infringe on their longstanding and, in some cases, hard-won powers.

The Directory for Worship also more reflected the decentralized character of the American church than did it establish uniformity of practice. In fact, worship had not been a source of controversy throughout the colonial era the way that subscription or qualifications for ministry had. Of course, the debates over revivalism were also in effect a disagreement about worship, since the question of religious experience would be decisive for future Presbyterian tussles over the exact content and atmosphere of public worship. Still, the closest the colonial Presbyterian Church came to a disagreement regarding worship was in the efforts of some of the former Old Side ministers to restrict congregational song to psalmody. Committees did meet during the mid-1780s for constructing an American psalter. But their work was no longer necessary once Synod in 1787 sanctioned a version of Isaac Watts' hymns for public worship. Not for another forty years would the American church address the question of psalms and hymns again. In the meantime, the Directory for Public Worship offered guidelines less specific than those provided by the Westminster Assembly. It included suggestions about the administration of the sacraments, the officiation of funerals and weddings, and even the conduct of worship in the home. But since its contents were essentially advisory, it was hardly a stumbling block to the constitution's ratification.

Arguably the item of greatest significance in the first constitution of the Presbyterian Church in the U.S.A., aside from the erection of a General Assembly, was the revision of the Westminster Standards. But as unprecedented as the task of changing the hallowed words of the Westminster Divines might appear, the revisions provided by American Presbyterians were substantially those planted by the Adopting Act of 1729, and so passed with little fanfare.

In its infancy Synod had declared that certain phrases in the original Westminster Confession on the authority of the magistrate were objectionable to all of its members. Those sections included the end of chapter 20, which read that persons who abused Christian liberty to disobey the state or the church "may be proceeded against by the censures of the Church, *and by the power of the civil magistrate*" (italics added). The Adopting Act also specified that chapter 23, section 3 of the original was objectionable since it granted the civil magistrate the authority to protect the peace and purity of the church by calling synods, being present at them, and providing "that whatsoever is transacted in them be according to the mind of God." This ecclesiastical role of civil government did not make sense for colonial Presbyterians where they had no Presbyterian magistrate to whom to turn, and it made even less sense after the United States established itself as a new nation committed to a sometimes confused sense of religious liberty.

In addition to revising these two passages that clearly spoke of a civil rule that contradicted the American Presbyterian situation, the American revision of 1788 eliminated a similar section in chapter 31 and also a passage in the Larger Catechism which, in its explanation of the second commandment, implied national religious uniformity. Although some might regard these revisions as evidence of the Americanization of the Presbyterian Church, in this particular case, as nineteenth-century theologians would demonstrate, the changes were important for regaining the independence of the church from the state and for protecting the prerogatives of the church to be the church.

The Voluntary Church

In 1788 the Synod of New York, and Philadelphia received the proposed constitution, which included the Plan of Government, the Directory for Public Worship, and the Westminster Standards. Still functioning as the "presbytery of the whole," Synod adopted the constitution without the subsequent normal procedure of sending the document out for the presbyteries to ratify. With that decision, the Synod of New York and Philadelphia, the creation of the Reunion of 1758, went out of business, both as the highest court in the Presbyterian Church and as a clerical body overseeing the upper mid-Atlantic presbyteries.

With the creation of the First General Assembly also came a reorganization of the denomination. In 1789 the Presbyterian Church in the U.S.A. consisted of four synods: New York and New Jersey, which included four presbyteries; Philadelphia with five presbyteries; Virginia with four presbyteries; and the Carolinas with three presbyteries. The Assembly's statistics showed that the church had a total of 177 ministers, 111 licentiates, 215 congregations with ministers, and 205 without regular ministry. The shortage of clergy was very much an issue, but one with which the colonial church had constantly struggled.

As it turned out, the creation of the General Assembly and its first meeting changed very little in American Presbyterianism. The new constitution reflected most of the tensions that had caused controversy and division, and the church at large still could not supply enough ministers to those Presbyterians who sought a settled ministry. Between 1706 and 1789 the American church had made significant strides and overcome numerous obstacles. Nevertheless, the church of the constitution and General Assembly was essentially the same as the body that had struggled to find a measure of coherence for common Presbyterian endeavor throughout the colonial era.

From its inception, the American church attempted something unusual within the history of Reformed Christianity. Its leaders had set up a church that was independent of the state, either for financial or legal support. American Presbyterianism was a voluntary faith. It depended both on the assent of ministers who agreed to submit to each others' rule in presbytery and synod, and also on the choices of church members who formed local congregations and looked for Presbyterian ministers to be their pastor. Most of the other Reformed churches in Britain and on the Continent had depended on the support and sanction of the state.

The defect of the American pattern was a church with more variety than some conservatives wanted, and more order than less-strict Presbyterians desired. It was a church without commanding authority or binding address because by its very nature, ministers and members could leave its fellowship and structures without penalty from the state or other institutional authorities. The virtue of the voluntary character of American Presbyterianism was a church that would not have to conform its witness or practices to the whims of the state. It would not be an unwilling pawn in the game of building nation or empire.

In the end, this is the predicament of American Presbyterianism, a church too broad for some and too narrow for others. If the American political experiment with constitutional republicanism was a novelty in the late eighteenth century, the formation of the Presbyterian Church in the U.S.A. was no less a test to see whether Presbyterianism could grow and flourish without the aid on which the churches had depended for almost fifteen hundred years since Constantine made the Christian religion the established faith of the empire. The subsequent history of American Presbyterianism would show that Presbyterians in the United States could not escape the anomalies inherent in a voluntary church.

PART 2

1789–1869

5

Presbyterianism's Ferment

The disestablishment of Christianity that defined the American founding may have represented a decisive turn in the history of the West but it constituted business as usual for American Presbyterians. Beginning in the fourth century, Christians had sometimes enjoyed and at other times suffered from lack of the crown or empire's support. Now, in the late–eighteenth-century, revolutions in America and France seriously upset the church's settled status as part of the political establishment. Still, the United States Constitution's silence about religion and its rejection of church membership as a basis for holding public office did not significantly change American Presbyterianism.

Since the founding of the Presbytery of Philadelphia in 1706, Presbyterianism in colonial America had been an unofficial religion, that is, a church lacking the financial and legal backing of the state. To be sure, federal disestablishment did not prevent the states in the Union from having established churches. In fact, of the original thirteen colonies to ratify the Constitution, nine supported an official church even after ratification, and some such as Massachusetts would continue to do so until the fourth decade of the nineteenth century (New Jersey,

Delaware, Pennsylvania, and Rhode Island were the colonies without a religious establishment). Yet, since Presbyterians in the colonies had never depended on state support, the new political order did not pose new obstacles.

Continuity between pre- and post-revolutionary arrangements did not mean, however, that Presbyterians were indifferent to a series of conditions that seemed to threaten the vitality of religion in the new nation. The founding fathers, many of them deists, agreed with more conventional Protestant leaders that the well-being of the United States depended on virtuous citizens and that healthy churches were essential to a responsible and free republic. For that reason, when signs of religious infidelity became more noticeable to the nation's elites in the decades after the revolution, Presbyterians and other Protestants quickly denounced the new ideas and defended Christian orthodoxy as the surest basis for a free society.

Free thinkers including Thomas Jefferson, who successfully ran for president in 1800, gave one indication of the questionable ideas circulating among the new nation's citizens. Tom Paine's *Age of Reason*, published in the 1790s, with its attack on the supernatural aspects of Christianity, was another source of anxiety. Liberal theological trends were even evident in sectors of New England Congregationalism where an overly rational approach to Christian teaching caused some, who would eventually become Unitarians, to express reservations about the deity of Christ. Finally the bloody and despotic turn of the French Revolution in the early 1790s confirmed in many Protestant leaders the conviction that social chaos and immorality were the sure consequence of unbelief.

The new situation in the United States, consequently, posed a number of dangers to which Presbyterian pastors and theologians felt obligated to respond. One such rejoinder came from Ashbel Green, a Princeton minister who would eventually preside over the College of New Jersey, in a fast-day sermon preached on May 9, 1798. From the text, "the LORD is with you, while ye be with him" (2 Chron. 15:2), Green appealed to the religious calculus that had prompted so many American Calvinists to support the American Revolution. "The nation that adheres to the laws of God shall be protected and prospered by him," Green declared, "but the nation that forsakes and disregards those laws he will destroy." He firmly believed that Christianity was the basis for "those civil institutions and those excellent social dispositions and habits which have rendered our country the envy of the world." But he feared that unbelief was rapidly submerging America in "this guilty age—this age of *infidel reason.*"

Green's worries were not isolated. That same year the General Assembly sent a letter to Presbyterian congregations and presbyteries that spoke of a "deep concern and awful dread" that "the eternal God has a controversy with our nation and is about to visit us in his sore displeasure." The evidence of irreligion was easy to spot: "a great departure from the faith and simple purity of manners for which our fathers were remarkable," "a visible and prevailing impiety and contempt for the laws and institutions of religion," and "an abounding infidelity which in many instances tends to atheism itself." In response, the 1798 Assembly called for a church-wide day of fasting and prayer.

Beyond this one day of religious observance, American Presbyterians would take other steps to shore up genuine piety and faith in their new environment. In some cases, the ordinary work of establishing and maintaining congregations was just that—ordinary. In other cases, though, Presbyterians would attempt other means, some acceptable and others unusual, to promote their witness in the new nation. In either case, the Presbyterian Church in the U.S.A. had ventured into a period of uncertainty, both for the nation and for American Presbyterianism itself.

— uncertainty

Presbyterians on the Frontier

Although American Presbyterianism now had a national body, the General Assembly, and a national identity, the Presbyterian Church in the U.S.A., life for most Presbyterians continued to be largely a local affair. And even here, the character of church life varied according the age of a given presbytery and the region it served. Two examples, one from the Synods in Pennsylvania, the other from the Synod of the Carolinas, help to illustrate the different strands of American Presbyterian experience at the beginning of the nineteenth century.

Pennsylvania had a reasonable claim to being the most settled of territories among American Presbyterians, but the life of the church there was hardly routine. At the beginning of the nineteenth century, the Synod of Philadelphia consisted of six presbyteries—Philadelphia (the Old Side or Second having been removed from the rolls in 1786 and its members distributed among other presbyteries in Pennsylvania and Delaware), Carlisle, Huntingdon, Redstone, Erie, and Ohio. Even though Philadelphia had the longest history, it had the fewest congregations, twenty, an indication that American Presbyterianism was growing through migration to the West. In fact, the Presbyterian Church in Pennsylvania grew between 1800 and 1820 in almost the same proportion as the state's population, about 33 percent. The other presbyteries averaged roughly thirty congregations each, though the numbers of ministers serving those churches was insufficient. The total number of Presbyterian ministers in Pennsylvania at the beginning of the century was eighty-two, and the total number of congregations was 180. Two decades later those figures had jumped to 158 ministers and 333 congregations. Most of the growth, however, had been in the western part of the state, where in 1820 there were ninety-four ministers and 216 congregations. Meanwhile, to give oversight to Presbyterianism in western Pennsylvania, in 1802 the church established the Synod of Pittsburgh and over the next several decades redrew presbytery boundaries to create four new presbyteries.

The congregations in Philadelphia, because the oldest, were the most stable but also had the least amount of growth. By the third decade of the century the city had twelve congregations within Philadelphia's borders, each creatively named for the order in which it had been founded—First through Twelfth. One of the numbered congregations that was an exception was First African Church, a ministry founded in 1807 with the support of Third Presbyterian Church and the Evangelical Society of Philadelphia. The pastor of the African-American congregation, though never ordained or installed by the Presbytery of Philadelphia, was John Gloucester, a former slave from Tennessee, who had attracted the interest of his master because of his piety and natural gifts. Gloucester's labors began with preaching in private homes among free blacks, but this soon became inadequate and his congregation found a school in which they could meet, though in good weather he often preached outside. On these occasions, Gloucester, who possessed a "strong and musical voice," would stand at the corner of Seventh and Shippen streets and, while singing a hymn, wait for listeners to gather. His labors were greatly appreciated by the presbytery, and before his death in 1822 he had secured the liberty of his family. In 1811 First African Church completed a building for worship, located at the place where Gloucester sometimes preached.

Another somewhat unusual congregation started around the same time in the Northern Liberties section of the city, a neighborhood known for its poverty, lack of education, and vice. The founding pastor of First Church, Northern Liberties, was James Patterson, who came to Philadelphia by way of Brook, New Jersey. When he started in 1813 the church had fifty-three members. But following the lead of a congregation in New Brunswick, Patterson started a Sabbath-School Association that provided instruction in reading and writing for the local children. He attracted more than one hundred pupils. Patterson also began to hold prayer meetings during the week among young and old alike. These were small gatherings, in some instances only two or three, which included prayer and brief instruction. Sometimes Patterson conducted as many as forty-four such meetings during one week. Through such endeavors the congregation in Northern Liberties grew faster than the established churches in the city.

The condition of Presbyterianism in Pittsburgh, though more active than Philadelphia, was much less settled. As E. H. Gillett put it, "There was not in the whole region a church-spire to greet the traveler's eye." Presbyterians in Pittsburgh, which in the early nineteenth century was a frontier town, met mainly in structures made of logs, sometimes in the shape of a parallelogram, others in that of a cruciform, "but the twelve sides and the twelve corners were not accounted symbolic." Pastors there invariably had several congregations under their charge. George Hill, a pastor in Ligonier, was known to cross rivers on horseback during high water, preach in his wet clothes at a congregation five miles from his home, and return the same day.

The work of many pastors was basically that of home missionaries, though in Pennsylvania the work in the West also involved mission work among the Native Americans. In 1806 the Synod of Pittsburgh initiated a plan to send a minister to the Wyandotte tribe in the Western Reserve for the purpose of religious instruction and initiation into the arts of civilized life, which included a farm to serve as a model for Native American agriculture. The mission to the Wyandottes lasted only until the War of 1812 when its buildings were destroyed and its work, which had always been precarious, was impossible to sustain.

The situation in North and South Carolina was not entirely different from that in western Pennsylvania, though not nearly as packed with Presbyterian congregations. At the start of the nineteenth century, the Synod of the Carolinas consisted of six presbyteries, with Orange, South Carolina, Concord, and Hopewell supplying the most vigor to southern Presbyterianism. By 1813 the growth of the southern churches had become too large for the one Synod of the Carolinas. In that year, the Synod was divided into two synods, those of North Carolina and South Carolina. But the latter extended well beyond that state to include presbyteries in Georgia and Alabama.

During the first two decades of the nineteenth century the growth of North Carolina Presbyterianism generally kept pace with the size of the state's population. But the pool of ministers did not increase at a similar rate. In 1800 North Carolina had twenty-nine Presbyterian ministers and seventy-three congregations; by 1820 the ministers numbered only thirty-eight while the congregations had escalated to 112. In South Carolina the growth was not as rapid. There the number of pastors in 1800 was eighteen, a figure that grew in 1820 to thirty-four, while the congregations increased only by ten during these same years, going from fifty in 1800 to sixty in 1820. Once again, the experience for many average Presbyterians was that of having no regular minister but depending on the sometimes infrequent visits from pastors performing pulpit supply.

The ministers in the southern Presbyterian churches often were natives to the South, though some from Northern Ireland and Scotland still found their way directly to pulpits in the region. For example, in the Presbytery of Orange, Malcolm McNair and Ezekiel B. Currie, both ordained in 1802, had been born and reared in North Carolina and served in a variety of congregations in Robeson County. John McIntyre, another minister near McNair and Currie, was a Scot who in 1791 immigrated to North Carolina after working as a shoemaker in Glasgow. At the ripe age of fifty-three he began to study Latin, and eventually in 1807 was ordained and pastored four small congregations for the next three decades (McIntyre lived to be 103). Another notable minister in the South was James Hall of Concord Presbytery. Born in Carlisle, Pennsylvania, Hall moved with his family at a young age to North Carolina where he lived and worked for the remainder of his life. His initial pastoral charge was in Bethany, but Hall distinguished himself among his peers for indefatigable missionary labors. His itinerant work extended from North Carolina to Georgia and Mississippi. According to one of his contemporaries, "in the power and majesty of pulpit eloquence he had no superior."

The demand for ministers was so great that as a general rule the presbyteries sent out licentiates to perform the difficult work of ministering to small congregations scattered far and wide. E. H. Gillett's history of American Presbyterianism from the colonial era to the Civil War, one of the fullest accounts of the church, renders a fairly vivid portrait of the hardships endured by these southern Presbyterian missionaries:

> A meagre salary was given them; for the churches from which the necessary funds were raised were few and feeble. But it sufficed to furnish them with "scrip and staff;" and, thus, equipped, they were commissioned to take practical lessons in preaching, by itinerating in the wilderness, looking after the scattered sheep, supplying the vacant congregations, and addressing such assemblies as they could draw together. It was a rough experience. It required men of energy and vigor, mental and physical, as well as no small measure of self-denying love for souls, to meet it. But the training in such a school was worth the price of tuition; and it brought into the field some of the most efficient and successful ministers of the day.

Presbyterianism in the Wild

Presbyterians on frontier experienced a different kind of worship.

One of the reasons for the popularity of such ministers as James Hall in North Carolina, aside from remarkable gifts and maximum effort, was the ability to elicit enthusiastic responses from his listeners. According to one of Hall's contemporaries, "his solemn and fervid manner generally awakened the bodily exercises incident to that day." Hall's congregations would often "cry out in distress and plead aloud for mercy, or give thanks to God for their feelings of joy and offer audible supplication for their families and friends." Although Presbyterians would become known for their reserve and formality in worship, these remarks demonstrate that Presbyterians on the frontier experienced a different kind of worship. Indeed, Hall's own itinerant ministry drew him into the sort of camp meeting revivalism that has long been associated with the rural South and which gained its greatest notoriety during the revivals of the Cane

Ridge area of Kentucky. What is seldom remembered is that these revivals drew directly on Presbyterian ministers such as Hall and practices such as the communion season. In addition, these revivals were not only part of southern life but also broke out in Presbyterian strongholds including western Pennsylvania.

The characteristic feature of a camp meeting revival was its outdoor setting, usually held in the summer in a place that could accommodate several thousand people. These people not only listened to sermons, but also needed space to camp, since these meetings went on for several days. Here the ties to older Presbyterian practices of communion seasons are striking. During the seventeenth century, Scottish Presbyterians developed the tradition of celebrating the Lord's Supper outdoors once a year. Church members from the region would come for several days of preaching and instruction in preparation for the Lord's Supper, with a service of thanksgiving on the Monday following to close the festivities. These five-day gatherings were likely the original basis for the revivals in the camp meeting tradition.

The one in Cane Ridge, which took place in 1801, became legendary because of the number of people present and because of the intensity of emotion. The site was chosen in part because of the Presbyterian church nearby, pastored by Barton Stone (1771–1844), who began his ministry there in 1796. Stone conducted communion seasons according to Scottish Presbyterian custom, but soon began to include ministers from other denominations, among them Baptists and Methodists who had their own traditions for itinerant outdoor preaching and revivals.

Although reared a Presbyterian and born in Maryland, Stone had always maintained doubts about Calvinist theology, even raising questions about the teaching of the Westminster Standards at the time of his ordination. The camp meeting he organized in 1801 at Cane Ridge exceeded anything he had put together before. Some estimate that it attracted upward of twenty thousand people, though more realistic estimates place it between two thousand and five thousand. Just as amazing were the physical and emotional reactions among those gathered. One spectator wrote, "I saw at least five hundred swept down in a moment, as if a battery of a thousand guns had been opened upon them; and then immediately followed by shrieks and shouts that rent

98

the very heavens." "My hair rose upon my head," he continued, "my whole frame trembled, the blood ran cold in my veins, and I fled for the woods."

The Presbyterian origins of camp meeting revivalism are even stronger when considered in relation to the North Carolina minister, James McGready (c.1758–1817). Born in Pennsylvania of Scotch-Irish parents, McGready moved with them to North Carolina while still a child. His training for the ministry came mainly through an apprenticeship with a minister back in Pennsylvania. The Presbytery that ordained him in 1788 was Redstone, part of the Synod of Pittsburgh. Like revivalists before him, McGready was known for preaching the terrors of the law, which he did once he returned to North Carolina shortly after ordination. His preaching in the western part of that southern state, and also into Kentucky, regularly prompted revivals characterized by many of the emotional excesses common in the First Great Awakening some four decades earlier.

One of McGready's converts during this time was Barton Stone. McGready also influenced Stone by fashioning the original structure for the camp meeting that eventually generated so much attention in Cane Ridge. In 1800 he decided to publicize an upcoming communion service to be held at the Gasper River congregation in Kentucky. Because of the popularity of revivals throughout the South in the late 1790s, McGready's announcement brought great response. Large numbers of farmers and pioneers came from as far as one hundred miles away, hoping to witness an extraordinary work of the Spirit. But it was not as big as Cane Ridge, which became the epicenter of southern revivalism at the turn of the nineteenth century.

These kinds of revivals were not confined to the South, however. They also transpired in places such as western Pennsylvania. Here McGready's ties to Redstone Presbytery were likely an important link. Still, the practice of communion seasons was undoubtedly more important. In 1802, Elisha Macurdy led a communion season at Three Springs in the Presbytery of Ohio that bore features characteristic of the southern camp meetings. "Numbers sank down in their distress, and gave evidence of great concern and anguish of spirit," Gillett wrote. This marked the beginning of a series of revivals in the region led by Macurdy and other Presbyterian pastors. One difference between these and the ones in Kentucky is that the northern revivals did not appear to include ministers from other denominations and were still tied to the sequence of services in the typical communion season, from Thursday through Monday. Also, the northern revivals did not generate the throngs who came to McGready's and Stone's. Still, the "evidences" of the Spirit were remarkably similar, with groaning, wailing, fainting, sobs, and shouts of joy punctuating the services.

Because the revivals in western Pennsylvania remained under Presbyterian auspices, they did not become as controversial as the ones in Kentucky. At the time of the Cane Ridge revival, Kentucky had three presbyteries, Transylvania, West Lexington, and Washington, each of which was still overseen by the Synod of Virginia. By 1802 the churches of these presbyteries had become sufficiently active and numerous to warrant the formation of the Synod of Kentucky. In the same year Kentucky added a new presbytery, that of Cumberland. This new presbytery became the site of an intense controversy over the revivals that were increasingly dominating the Synod. Cumberland had two distinct groups, equally divided at the outset, with McGready the most prominent among the pro-revival party, and Thomas Craighead emerging as the spokesman of those opposed to camp meetings and the enthusiasm associated with them. Soon, however, the anti-revivalists were in the minority, thanks to the licensure and ordination of several men whose views were at odds with the Westminster Confession. In 1804 Craighead petitioned to Synod about the irregularities of his presbytery, and the following year Synod appointed a committee to investigate what appeared to be significant violations of Presbyterian practice. During the investigation members of the synodical committee also learned that several of the licentiates were not only lacking in formal education but also dissented explicitly from the Calvinism taught by the Confession. The result was a replay of colonial contests between presbyteries and synods over the prerogative of licensure and ordination. But Synod would not relent and dissolved Cumberland and annexed its ministers to the Presbytery of Transylvania.

Still, the pro-revival members of the old Cumberland Presbytery dug in and in 1807 the case went before the General Assembly. The advice to Kentucky from the Assembly was that, although grateful for its zeal, Synod should show moderation in dealing with Cumberland

Cumberland

Presbytery. In response, Synod allowed for the reconstitution of Cumberland. By 1810 the reestablished presbytery, now firmly in the hands of the pro-revivalists, began to ordain the same sort of ministers who had launched the controversy. But without the anti-revivalists around, the Cumberland Presbyterians went forward unabated. By 1813 they had grown to encompass sixty congregations, at which point they formed their own Synod.

1813

In 1814 their autonomy became even more apparent when they revised the Westminster Confession to eliminate objectionable language *for new* that seemed to teach fatalism, or the idea that persons were doomed to *own* damnation because of original sin and the eternal decree. Specifically, *Synod* they objected to the doctrine of predestination. For instance, in their version of the Shorter Catechism on the Decrees of God, the Cumberland Presbyterians revised the answer to read, "The decrees of God are his purpose according to the counsel of his *own* will, whereby he hath foreordained *to bring* to pass what *shall be* for his own glory: *sin not being for God's glory, therefore he hath not decreed it*" (italics theirs). Although the Cumberland Presbyterians never formally broke their ties to the Presbyterian Church U.S.A., by 1825 the latter's General Assembly ruled that the Cumberland Synod had no authority from or within the Presbyterian Church U.S.A. and that its status was that of *1825* "other denominations, not connected with our body."

This was the first significant departure from the Presbyterian Church since 1789, and it was one that would hurt the denomination in those regions where Cumberland Presbyterians flourished. In 1906 a significant block of the Cumberland Presbyterian Church would reunite with the Presbyterian Church U.S.A. But in the early nineteenth century, the controversy over camp-meeting styled revivalism was a reminder of Presbyterianism's unruly and sensational past in the seventeenth century, which at the beginning of the nineteenth century did not seem too distant.

Presbyterians as Congregationalists

At roughly the same time that Kentucky Presbyterians were experiencing the contortions of revival, Presbyterians in the more settled parts of the Northeast entered into a formal relationship with New England

Congregationalists. The Plan of Union of 1801 was originally the strategy of two ministers, John Blair Smith (Presbyterian) and Eliphalet Nott (Congregationalist), both of whom served at different times as president of Union College in Schenectady, New York. (The college took its name from the cooperative efforts of Presbyterians and Dutch Reformed in that part of New York State, which through the Plan of Union soon involved Congregationalists.)

The discussion between Smith and Nott took place in 1795, when Smith was at Union and Nott was pastoring in nearby Albany. Still, their idea that Presbyterians and Congregationalists were basically the same except for church polity built on decades of informal coopera- tion and good will between the two denominations. Some of that had originated because of mutual concerns about the establishment of an Anglican bishop before the War for Independence, and common political convictions during the Revolution. Between 1795 and 1801 both sides appointed committees to study the matter, and by the meeting of the 1801 General Assembly a plan agreeable to both sides had emerged. Jonathan Edwards Jr., the president of Union College between the ten- ures of Smith and Nott, presented the Plan to the Presbyterian Assembly of 1801.

Although the denominations involved in this union effort represented some of the oldest Reformed witnesses in North America, the Plan was devised with the experience of the American frontier almost exclusively in mind. Soon after the founding of the new nation, the American population spread out from the Eastern seaboard dramatically. In New England this meant that inhabitants of its states, looking for land and autonomy, sought opportunities in western New York State and the Northwest Territory (Ohio, Indiana, Michigan, Illinois, Wisconsin). Many of these migrants passed directly through the area around Union College on their way west. Congregationalists had an obvious interest in the new communities being planted in the West, many of which bore the marks of New England patterns of settlement. But Presbyterians in New York had also begun to establish mission works in the western part of their state similar to those somewhat haphazard efforts of Presbyteri- ans in western Pennsylvania and in western North Carolina, Kentucky, and Tennessee.

The Plan of Union was essentially a formal means of cooperation between the two denominations to supply adequate visitation and preaching for the congregations emerging in the upper Midwest. It also was designed to prevent the sort of denominational rivalry and competition that might naturally result from a church-planting situation. Its explicit purpose was "to promote union and harmony in those new settlements" -4 in which Presbyterians and Congregationalists lived. It did so through ~~Guidelines~~ four general guidelines.

First, the Plan "strictly enjoined" all pastors to new churches "to endeavor, by all proper means, to promote mutual forbearance, and a spirit of accommodation, between those inhabitants of the new settlements who hold the Presbyterian, and those who hold the Congregational, form of Church government." The second and third guidelines outlined what to do in the case of a congregation that called a pastor from the other denomination; if difficulties arose between congregation and pastor, the church would appeal either to the presbytery or the Congregational association of which he was a member. The fourth provision outlined what congregations that were a mix of Presbyterian and Congregationalist members should do in cases of discipline: for Presbyterian members it would involve going through the appropriate presbytery and synod; for Congregationalists discipline would come through the Congregationalist members of the local congregation.

The Plan clearly had any number of chinks through which serious problems might bubble up. But it was an indication of the warm relations between Presbyterians and Congregationalists that they regarded their differences as so slight that only technicalities of church polity would be noticeable. In 1807 the relations between Presbyterians and Congregationalists in New York became so strong that the Synod of New York invited the Middle Association of Congregationalist Churches to become a constituent branch of synod, an invitation approved in 1808 by the General Assembly.

E. H. Gillett commented on the cooperation with Congregationalists as a reason for celebration because "at this crisis in the religious progress of our country such liberal and Christian views prevailed." He added that the great "struggle" of the century, namely, "to shape the future destiny of a growing nation," had begun, and it called for "the hearty cooperation, on broad principles, of all who loved the common cause."

But another way of looking at the Plan of Union, along with similar missions endeavors in the South, was to wonder about the identity of the Presbyterian Church. Presbyterianism in one part of the country could wind up with a form of Christianity that questioned some of the central tenets of Reformed theology. And in New York the same Protestant communion could agree to a form of cooperation that seriously undermined the chief arguments for Presbyterian church government. In other words, the Plan of Union was an early iteration of a phrase that would gain great urgency later in the nineteenth century, "doctrine divides, ministry unites." Yet, if Presbyterianism were so malleable as the conditions of the church indicated during the first two decades of the nineteenth century, what made the Presbyterian Church U.S.A. Presbyterian?

The Advent of Presbyterian Identity

One of the reasons for the seemingly incoherent diversity of the Presbyterian Church was the disparity of standards for ministerial education. This is not to suggest that the identity of a church depends solely on the outlook of its clergy, or that theological education is the only source of denominational identity. Worship and church government may play equally important roles in shaping the character of a church. Likewise, the influence of the laity in forming the ethos of a local congregation, and especially in calling ministers appropriate to it, is a crucial aspect of church life (so important that one could plausibly argue that the quality of a denomination's pastors is simply a reflection of its church members).

The point here is simply that at the beginning of the nineteenth century the Presbyterian Church U.S.A. had no formal agencies or structures beyond the regular meeting of its presbyteries, synods, General Assembly, or committees thereof. The usual pattern of institution formation for most new churches is to start with schools for the training of its ministers. So to say that the Presbyterian Church's diversity stemmed from the different kinds of training its clergy received is only to suggest that once the denomination began to formalize and regularize its theological education its diversity would begin to diminish. For with the establishment of schools for theological education normally come requirements for aspiring ministers to attend the institutions sponsored by the denomination.

Of course, the College of New Jersey was one such agency of Presbyterian education. It had originally been founded to train pastors for the Presbyterian Church, especially those inclined to the experiential piety of the colonial revivals. But during John Witherspoon's administration and the era of the American Revolution, the college's educational reputation shifted from one of schooling pastors to one of preparation for careers in law and public life. Part of the reason for this owed to important and valuable changes that Witherspoon made to the curriculum at the college that proved to be as useful for a career in politics as for the church. From 1776 to 1783, 21 percent of the college's eighty-two graduates went into the ministry, and from 1784 to 1794, the last decade of Witherspoon's tenure, the figure declined to only 13 percent of the school's 222 alumni. It was for good reason that one historian of the college called it during this era, "the school for statesmen," since so many of its graduates were going on to careers in public service.

To be fair, however, the problem was not entirely Witherspoon's or the College of New Jersey's. Since the founding of their first college, Presbyterians had established other institutions of learning that might conceivably take up the slack. For instance, by 1800 Presbyterians were sponsoring Hampden-Sydney College (founded in 1776) in Virginia, and Dickinson College (founded in 1783) in central Pennsylvania. In addition, wherever Presbyterians went, they invariably established schools whose chief purpose was to provide the classical education considered to be the basis for a competent ministry. This means that from Kentucky to western Pennsylvania to Indiana, Presbyterians were often involved in erecting academies that would later be turned into liberal arts colleges, much in the same way that the Tennents' Log College evolved into the College of New Jersey (later Princeton University). Even so, these other schools and academies were small, poorly funded affairs without clear oversight from a presbytery or synod. As such, again as in the case of the Log College, they often provided an education that bore the particular slant of the presiding pastor or teacher. In this case, the multiplicity of colleges and academies may have added to the divisions within the Presbyterian Church rather than supplying it with a measure of coherence and institutional identity.

Another important factor to consider is that the education provided by even the best schools, such as Harvard, Yale, and Princeton (College of New Jersey), was more a classical curriculum than one allowing specialization in theology and the Bible. Students would be exposed to courses that explicitly defended the truth of Christianity against its contemporary critics, or that called them to their duties as Christians. But for the kind of theological training presbyteries required of candidates for licensure and ordination, college graduates usually needed to spend a year or more as an intern with a local pastor who would in turn school them in the rudiments of theology and expose them to the nature of ministerial work. In other words, to expect the liberal arts college, even if identified with a sponsoring church, to produce graduates ready for the ministry was to set the bar too high.

For these reasons, the Presbyterian Church during the first decade of the nineteenth century began to explore the possibility of founding a seminary. Historically, the seminary had been the educational form that Roman Catholics used to train their priests. In the early nineteenth century when Protestants began to look for schools that would be devoted to the training of pastors, they modified the seminary structure to suit their own needs.

As early as 1800, Ashbel Green, a Philadelphia pastor and graduate of the College of New Jersey, hatched among colleagues and friends the idea of a school devoted to the training of ministers. Five years later he sent an overture to General Assembly with the urgent appeal, "Give us ministers." The Assembly's response was essentially to urge presbyteries and synods to "use their utmost endeavors" to increase the number of worthy candidates for the ministry. In 1808, another Philadelphia pastor, Archibald Alexander, in his sermon before the General Assembly as retiring moderator, issued a plea for greater attention to ministerial training, remarking that the existing colleges were "little adapted to introduce a youth to the study of the sacred Scriptures." Finally, in 1809, requests such as these paid the dividend of the General Assembly forming a committee to study formal theological education. What may have spurred the Presbyterian Church was the formation in 1808 of Andover Seminary in Massachusetts by Congregationalists alarmed at the takeover of Harvard by Unitarians.

106

The immediate issue before the church was not whether to have a seminary but how many and where. Some on the committee advocated one central institution, while others wanted several schools located regionally, either one in the North and one in the South, or one in each of the four synods. The plan that eventually prevailed in 1811 was one that called for the establishment of one seminary under the control of the General Assembly, that it be located in Princeton, New Jersey, and that it appoint three professors. That institution began its instruction *Alexander* in the fall of 1812 as Princeton Theological Seminary, with only one professor at first, Archibald Alexander. In 1813 the Assembly approved *miller* the call of a second professor, Samuel Miller, who taught ecclesiastical history and church polity. Not until 1822 would the original plan for *Hodge* three faculty be realized when the Assembly appointed Charles Hodge to teach the biblical languages and courses in the Old and New Testaments. The aim of the school was to train "a learned, orthodox, pious, and evangelical Ministry."

Princeton would not long remain the only theological seminary for ministers in the Presbyterian Church U.S.A. It would be the oldest, the one with direct ties to and supervision from the General Assembly, and so the seminary seemingly with the most clout. But within twenty years of its founding at least six other Presbyterian seminaries were founded, usually with the particular needs of a region of the church in mind. In 1818 the presbyteries of central New York State joined hands to form Auburn Theological Seminary. The Synod of Virginia followed suit in 1824 with plans for Union Theological Seminary, located in Richmond, a venture that in 1826 required the financial support and hence the oversight of the General Assembly. At roughly the same time, plans for a seminary to serve the Synod of the Carolinas were unveiled and they were eventually responsible for the seminary in Columbia, South Carolina. Western Theological Seminary, in Pittsburgh, was in 1826 the cooperative endeavor of the Synods of Pittsburgh, Ohio, and Kentucky. The latter two synods also joined with Presbyterians from Indiana to found Danville (Kentucky) Theological Seminary in 1827, and a year later Lane Theological Seminary, in Cincinnati. A late bloomer in this crop of Presbyterian seminaries was Union Theological Seminary in New York City, founded in 1836, without official ties to a presbytery or synod but with the support and governance of individual Presbyterians who served on its board of directors.

Although Princeton was soon to lose its status as the Presbyterian Church's sole theological institution, its founding in 1812 did represent a turning point in the life of the American church. The church's aim in establishing a seminary was to respond to the desperate need for ministers, and especially learned ones. As Presbyterians left the settled East Coast for the interior of the continent, not only could pastors seldom keep up, but the ones who did were sometimes inexperienced or held novel views. Indeed, the history of the Presbyterian Church in the decades after the founding of the American nation is one of a multiplicity of voices and techniques for establishing and nurturing new congregations. Consequently, the need for a seminary was great, so great that seven others soon emerged.

But in establishing Princeton, the Presbyterian Church received more than an agency that would provide theological education for aspiring ministers, or a model for other seminaries to follow. With the coming of the seminary the Presbyterian Church also obtained, perhaps unintentionally, a denominational self-consciousness. These schools not only became objects by which to nurture support for and identification with a Presbyterian cause. By adopting a set curriculum and hiring specific professors, these seminaries also would be responsible for cultivating a theological outlook that in turn would shape the character and ethos of the surrounding congregations, presbyteries, and synods. In other words, the seminaries, which were designed to supply the stream of churches surging in the West, would actually end up channeling that flow of religious energy into well-defined vessels that would contribute directly to the formation of a self-conscious American Presbyterian identity.

6

Revivalism and Division (Again)

Charles Grandison Finney (1792–1875) began his controversial career as revivalist, theologian, and philosopher with the blessing of the Presbyterian Church in the U.S.A. Finney, a native of Connecticut, was with his family part of a wave of migration of New Englanders who streamed west through New York State, some settling finally in the Northwest Territory. His parents stopped in the village of Henderson, New York, where they attended the local Baptist church. Although reared in a devout home, Finney did not convert until the age of twenty-nine. He had returned from New Jersey, where he was teaching school, to work as a clerk in an attorney's office. A local revival was the spark that triggered his conversion. Under the conviction of his sin, and sensing a call to the ministry, Finney prayed that if God would save him, he would leave his current occupation and become a preacher.

To keep that promise, Finney sought the care and training of the local Presbyterians in upstate New York. In 1822 he came under the care of the Presbytery of St. Lawrence and began theological study with the local

Presbyterian pastor, George W. Gale. (The establishment of Presbyterian seminaries did not mean that degrees from them were a requirement for licensure and ordination.) Gale had studied at Princeton Seminary with one of the first classes of students to attend the denomination's seminary. Any suggestion that Finney pursue a course of study there, however, received his disapproval.

Later in life Finney would observe that the "grand defect" of seminaries was that their graduates were not "fit to go into a revival." Seminaries shut students "out from intercourse with the common people" and trained ministers in "irrelevant matters." He also deduced that any man "filled with the Spirit" was worth more than five hundred educated ministers. But Finney's case against Princeton or her sister institutions was not merely functional. He was not at all sympathetic to the theology taught at places such as Princeton.

In 1823, his mentor, Gale, needed a leave of absence and persuaded the presbytery to call Finney to be his replacement until the congregation could find a successor. When examined for licensure by presbytery and asked if he received the Westminster Confession, Finney responded that he had never examined it "with any attention" but did receive it "for the substance of doctrine, so far as I understand it."

The answer proved to be sufficient for the Presbytery of St. Lawrence, an indication of the different standards that prevailed throughout the Presbyterian Church. To be fair, Finney's instructor, even though a Princeton Seminary student, had not thought to expose his pupil to the theology of the Westminster Standards. In fact, Gale's own theological convictions sided more with the revival-inspired New Divinity of Jonathan Edwards's disciples than with the scholastic theology of Francis Turretin that Archibald Alexander used in the classroom at Princeton. This suggests that seminary education went only so far in generating theological coherence within the Presbyterian Church. Even so, not everyone in the congregation where Finney preached was satisfied with his manner or content.

By the summer of 1824 presbytery persuaded Finney to take a call as a missionary evangelist for the local Female Missionary Society (an organization designed to enlist women for lay evangelism), a position for which he was ordained in the same year. His work as an itinerant Presbyterian evangelist was the springboard for the career of a man who, in the words of the church historian, Mark A. Noll, ranks with Andrew Jackson, Abraham Lincoln, and Andrew Carnegie as "the most important public figures in nineteenth-century America."

If Finney was also the *"crucial* figure in white American evangelicalism after Jonathan Edwards," as Noll adds, he was also the most disruptive minister in the Presbyterian Church during the first half of the nineteenth century. The revivals he led became the source of a repeat of colonial era disputes in which the extremes of religious fervor had split the Presbyterian Church into the Old and New Side factions. But at the beginning of his ministry, and before his work polarized American Presbyterians, Finney represented the breadth of teaching in the denomination and the reason why some were beginning to reconsider the union with New England Congregationalists.

When Revivals Become Great

The Plan of Union, which in 1801 brought Presbyterians and Congregationalists into close cooperation and fellowship in western New York State and beyond, was not the only factor that opened the Presbyterian Church to the talents of a man like Finney. Even before the evangelist's ordination as a Presbyterian itinerant, the denomination had been witnessing religious awakenings, which practically everyone referred to as revivals, with a degree of frequency that almost made extraordinary spiritual stirrings look ordinary.

In the General Assembly minutes of 1816, revivals were a constant theme. Specific mention was made of awakenings in Pennsylvania—Philadelphia, Basking Ridge, and Norristown; New York—New York City, Troy, and Albany; among the New York presbyteries of Long Island, Hudson, Oneida, Onondaga, Champlain, Geneva, and Cayuga; and in Virginia's Winchester Presbytery. In 1817 the evidence of revivals was equally obvious. The Presbytery of Jersey reported fifteen hundred conversions within its bounds from revivals during the previous year. The city of Troy, though its numbers were not as impressive, counted five hundred new church members through awakenings among its Presbyterian congregations.

And so the reports to General Assemblies in subsequent years continued, all the way up to 1824, when Finney became a Presbyterian minister. E. H. Gillett estimates that between 1816 and 1826 "not less than fifty thousand must have been added to the Church, as the fruits of the revivals which had been enjoyed." He also credits these revivals with adding to the numerical growth of the Presbyterian Church's presbyteries and pastors. During the same decade (1816–26), the number of presbyteries within the whole denomination increased from forty-three to eighty-six. Meanwhile, the number of pastors jumped from 543 to more than 1,140.

The prevalence of revivalism in the Presbyterian Church should not, however, diminish the significance of Finney or the polarizing influence he would have. Just as in the so-called Great Awakening of the colonial period, the work and notoriety of one man—Whitefield in the eighteenth century—seemed to symbolize and encapsulate all the local revivals that were in place before his arrival on the religious scene, so in the so-called Second Great Awakening (from the late 1820s to the 1830s) Finney emerged as the spokesman and celebrity for a period marked by religious fervor and moral crusades. His initial success occurred among the towns in western New York where Presbyterians and Congregationalists were laboring to plant churches.

Finney's 1826 revival in Utica, New York, was notable for the methods that characterized his revivals, what became known as the "new measures." Those methods included praying for people by name, visiting towns without invitations from the local preachers, the immediate admission of converts to church membership, protracted nightly meetings, and exhortations by female preachers. Arguably the most controversial of Finney's techniques was the "anxious bench," a seat at the front of the church or pavilion to which at the end of his sermon he called listeners who were feeling convicted of their sinfulness and need for salvation. Here the "anxious" could receive counsel and prayer for their doubts and fears. The bench became synonymous with the altar call of the camp meeting, which was another mechanism for calling troubled souls forward to receive spiritual guidance and to signal commitment to Christ.

Finney also benefited, as Whitefield had, from publicity in the press, either in advertising his travels or in reporting on the amazing results of his labors. By 1830 Finney's methods had turned him into a religious celebrity. Late in that year he arrived in Rochester for a series of revival meetings. He cooperated closely with local churches, preaching at both First and Third Presbyterian Churches. But unlike previous revivals where the evangelist might speak for the better part of a week, the Rochester revival lasted for six months, involving the congregations not only in the city but also in the surrounding small towns. The membership rolls of the participating churches swelled so much that scholars estimate that Protestant churches in the Northeastern United States added more than one hundred thousand new members in 1831 alone, with Rochester being the epicenter of these developments.

Finney's methods, however, were not the most serious challenge to the Presbyterian Church. After all, his innovations were not necessarily any more radical or novel than those of the colonial revivalists; by some reckonings, Whitefield's pulpit antics may have been more dramatic and potentially more manipulative than Finney's. Where Finney would draw fire was over a theory of revivals that flew directly in the face of the Westminster Standards' Calvinism.

On the one hand, he pleaded with sinners in a way that made it seem the person under conviction, as opposed to God, was sovereign in the process of coming to faith. Finney denied that "the human *constitution* was morally depraved," argued that the Bible nowhere taught the "theological *fiction* of *imputation*" of Adam's sin to the human race (except for Christ), refused to accept that persons were "utterly unable to comply with the terms of the Gospel, to repent, to believe, or to do anything that God required them to do," and rejected the notion that "God had condemned men for their sinful *nature*."

Furthermore, Finney affirmed a universal atonement, but also that Christ's death did not put God under "obligation to save *anybody*." This was an understanding, as many scholars have noted, well suited to a democratic ear of popular government in which people were encouraged to believe they were sovereign and so had as much right to vote for God as they did for public officials. On the other hand, Finney also conceived of revivals in a way well adapted for the scientific cultural ideals nurtured by the Enlightenment. He believed that the execution of a revival was a scientific enterprise, thoroughly predictable according to the spiritual laws of the universe. As he taught in his *Lectures on Revivals of Religion* (1846), "a revival is not a miracle, or dependent on a miracle in any sense. It is a purely philosophic [i.e., scientific] result of the right use of the constituted means."

What may have prevented Presbyterian Church leaders from seeing all the problems of Finney's teaching and preaching (aside from the fact that his sermons and lectures would not be published until well after his initial notoriety) was that the revivalist supported a variety of social reforms that were attractive to many Presbyterians. For instance, part of the success of Finney's Rochester crusade of 1830–31 was his decision to tie choosing Christ to support for the local temperance society. In late December, the evangelist recruited one of his prize converts, Theodore Dwight Weld, who was emerging as a renowned temperance advocate, to give lectures. Weld informed his audience at Rochester's First Presbyterian Church of alcohol's insidious responsibility for violent crime, poverty, domestic disputes, and lawlessness.

The link between revivalism and temperance was simply one aspect of a deeper connection between the Second Great Awakening's notion of conversion and the holy life and godly society that genuine conversion inevitably fueled. As a result, a variety of reform endeavors sprung up that the revivals energized. Protestants, with Presbyterians often playing a significant role, formed voluntary societies for advancing education, wholesome literature, Sunday schools, the observance of the Lord's Day, missions, Bible and tract distribution, as well as temperance, the abolition of slavery, prison reform, and even healthy diets. One prominent historian of the Second Great Awakening argued that it was the singular organizing mechanism of a nation that was young and lacking in the sorts of civil associations necessary for a well-ordered society, especially in the rapidly expanding West. Many of these endeavors preceded Finney's evangelism, but his national notoriety gave them a significant boost.

The Presbyterian Church had no official policy on participation in these voluntary societies. Because they were voluntary, and because the Presbyterian Church was largely decentralized in its denominational structures, individual Presbyterians, sessions, presbyteries, and synods might choose to support or become involved with these social reforms and religious agencies. A pastoral letter from the General Assembly of 1817 to the churches about the work of home missions was indicative of the attitude that many held about the outpouring of interest in promoting true religion and wholesome morality throughout the United States. It read:

Embrace every opportunity, to the extent of the ability which God has given you, to form and vigorously support *missionary associations*, Bible societies, plans for the distribution of religious tracts, and exertions for extending the benefits of knowledge, and especially spiritual knowledge, to all ages and classes of persons around you. . . . We are persuaded that all those periods and Churches which have been favored with special revivals of religion have also been distinguished by visible union and concert in prayer. We entreat you, brethren, to cherish this union and concert.

The letter did acknowledge that because of the differences among the Protestant denominations in the United States, the cooperation and support being recommended might generate controversy over points of doctrine or polity. "That differences of opinion, acknowledged on all hands to be of a minor class, may and ought to be tolerated among those who are agreed in great and leading views of truth, is a principle on which the godly have so long so generally acted that it seems unnecessary, at the present day, to seek arguments for its support."

Written six years before Finney's ordination and twelve before his celebrated Rochester crusade, this letter indicated the Presbyterian Church's initial reaction to the revivals of the Second Great Awakening. At the start the results were almost entirely positive. Church members were being added, presbyteries were being created, and the influence of Protestant Christianity appeared to be at a high water mark. No wonder, then, that Charles Finney, arguably the foremost Arminian theologian of nineteenth-century America, began his work and ministry under the auspices of the Presbyterian Church. Yet, ironically, the popularity of his methods and teaching would also prompt Presbyterian leaders to rethink the diversity of the American Protestation and raise questions about the benefits of nineteenth-century revivals.

Theological Crisis — *emerging consensus in NE Congregationalism*

Finney's theological convictions were not his own. They were in fact part of the emerging theological consensus in New England Congregationalism. That some of his ideas about the atonement, the imputation of Adam's sin, and freedom of the will, which clearly contravened

115

Calvinism, went by the name of "consistent Calvinism" made Finney's teaching all the more a problem for American Presbyterians.

The modifications in New England Calvinism between Jonathan Edwards and Finney were often subtle. Still, the intervening years between Edwards's death in 1758 and Finney's career had provided sufficient space for an interest in revivalism rightly understood to evolve into revivalism with the right to determine theological understanding. Edwards himself had admirably defended Calvinistic teaching and the revivals, though his views on the imputation of Adam's sin were sometimes fuzzy (he did not write a systematic theology), and his distinction between natural and moral inability could be used later to deny original sin.

Edwards's disciples, known as the New Divinity school, or as Hopkinsianism, named after Samuel Hopkins, further modified New England Calvinism to weaken even more than Edwards implicitly had the forensic character of the atonement and the legal penalty that all people inherit because of Adam's sin.

An attenuated estimate of sin and the exemplary nature of Christ's death on the cross continued to make inroads in New England theology in the work of Finney's contemporary, Nathaniel William Taylor, professor of theology at Yale Divinity School. His "New Haven Theology" asserted that "sin consists in the sinning," a further departure from the Reformed understanding of original sin. Taylor's exceptions to the imputation of Adam's sin would eventually affect his understanding of the imputation of Christ's righteousness since the two doctrines usually went hand in hand. At the end of his life Taylor wrote *The Moral Government of God* (1858) in which he questioned the vicarious atonement, insisting that Christ did not die in place of the elect but did so to show God's displeasure with sin (e.g., the governmental theory of the atonement). Finney may have drawn the flack for these views because of his celebrity, but he was no more innovative than several schools of New England theology before him.

With the rise of Presbyterian seminaries such as Princeton and the emergence of a class of theological "experts" whose task was to analyze ideas, it was likely that some formal assessment and critique of the New England theology would surface. But because of the Plan of Union, which gave Hopkins's and Taylor's views a foothold in the Presbyterian

Church, critique and opposition were all the more likely in settings outside the academy.

Indeed, hostility to Hopkinsianism was evident as early as 1813 when Pine Street Presbyterian Church in Philadelphia called a pastor to replace Archibald Alexander, who had recently moved to Princeton to teach at the seminary. The man called was Ezra Stiles Ely, an itinerant evangelist in New York City and the author of the controversial book, *The Contrast,* in which he placed side by side the views of representative Hopkinsians with orthodox theologians, to the obvious discredit of the former. Some members of Pine Street Church opposed Ely's call, and they left to form another congregation. The incident prompted the Presbytery of Philadelphia to resolve not to license any candidates who held Hopkinsian tenets.

The process also raised suspicions about T. H. Skinner, the pastor of Philadelphia's Second Church, who was known to be cordial to the New Divinity. Likewise, the Synod of Philadelphia also sent a pastoral letter to its presbyteries advising them not to call any ministers who might be suspected of holding "any of the opinions usually called Hopkinsian." In fact, Synod had grouped the New England teaching with Arianism, Socinianism, and Arminianism as "the means by which the enemy of souls would, if possible, deceive the very elect."

When the General Assembly received a request to look into the affairs that had prompted this letter, the Assembly's report cautioned against divisiveness. Although the Synod's zeal "to promote strict conformity to our public standards" was commendable, its manner in expressing this zeal was "offensive to other denominations" and might "introduce a spirit of jealousy and suspicion against ministers in good standing."

But the Assembly's report did not end the matter. Two members of the Synod of Philadelphia registered formal protests against the Assembly's statements. One of them read, "We do not believe that the doctrines called Hopkinsianism are innocent, or that they are so trivial as not to require the interference of the Synod in the manner adopted in their records to prevent their propagation." The second objected on the grounds that the "distinguishing doctrines of Hopkinsianism" were inconsistent with "our public standards" and "essentially contradictory to sound orthodox doctrines," and that their proclamation constituted a "violation of ordination vows."

Though not as direct, opposition to Hopkinsianism also surfaced in 1817 among Presbyterians in New York City. The occasion for this antagonism was the call of Gardiner Spring to pastor the Brick Presbyterian Church—a man about whom some presbyters had reservations. Spring's father was an acknowledged proponent of the New Divinity. Even though guilt by association was insufficient to block Spring's ordination, local Presbyterian ministers were able to rally support against a city missionary of the Young Men's Missionary Society because of his sympathies with New England theology. By a vote of 160 to 90, the members of the society disapproved of the appointment of S. H. Cox, whom Spring believed should not be subjected to a theological investigation. When members of the Society examined the Brick Church minister, who had substituted himself for the position denied to Cox, they declared Spring's views to be unsound.

These initial forms of opposition to New England theology turned out to be relatively minor compared with the controversy that emerged over Albert Barnes's preaching about a decade later. Born in 1798 in upstate New York and a graduate of Princeton Theological Seminary, Barnes received his first call to the Presbyterian church in Morristown, New Jersey. He was a proponent of the revivals that characterized the period—something that his education at Princeton did not change—and he held theological convictions that supported the zeal and reform that the awakenings nurtured.

In 1829 he delivered a provocative sermon, "The Way of Salvation," which was eventually published and generated close scrutiny from those wary of New England's consistent Calvinism. In the sermon Barnes showed all the signs of moving in the same direction as Hopkins and Taylor. For instance, on the question of original sin and the guilt passed on from Adam to all his descendants, Barnes declared that Christianity did not hold that the sinner is "personally answerable for the transgressions of Adam" or that "God has given a law which man has not power to obey." If that were the case then Christianity would be "most clearly unjust." "The law requiring love to God, supreme and unqualified," he explained, "is supposed to be equitable; fully within the reach of every mortal, if there [is] first a willing mind."

Barnes also spoke with a New England inflection when he addressed the topic of the atonement. Christ's death, he said, "was for all men" and opened a way for pardon. It had "no particular reference to any class of men." In fact, Barnes judged that Christ "died for all." He did not go as far as Finney in asserting the significance of human agency or free will. He still affirmed that "those who are saved, will be saved because God does it by the renewing of the Holy Ghost." Nevertheless, Barnes was clearly moving in a similar direction as the New Divinity and the New Haven Theology.

When Barnes received a call to Philadelphia's First Presbyterian Church in 1830, his contested views came under close scrutiny. Ashbel Green opposed the call even though the Presbytery of Philadelphia received Barnes without examining him. Those opposed to Barnes eventually appealed the matter to the Synod of Philadelphia, which directed the presbytery to study the matter. In the same year as his call, the Presbytery of Philadelphia condemned Barnes's sermon, "The Way of Salvation," but stopped short of condemning the minister who gave it. Barnes was not content with the distinction and appealed the ruling to the General Assembly of 1831.

In effect, "The Way of Salvation" had alerted many in the Presbyterian Church to the dangers posed by the New England theology. As the editor for the *Christian Spectator* put it, "The real question is *whether New England Calvinism shall any longer be tolerated in the Presbyterian Church of this country.*" Barnes himself would later acknowledge his debt to New England: "We loved the great features of New England Theology. . . . We had supposed that they had done much not only to defend the great system of Calvinism and to place it where it could not be assailed with advantage." Its theologians had also "done something to give the ancient system a more liberal cast; to divest it of some of its harsh and rigid features . . . to show how in its essential features it accorded with the true laws of the mind . . ."

The controversy over Barnes was indeed a turning point in the development of a self-conscious Presbyterian understanding of the boundaries involved in the Calvinistic scheme of salvation taught in the Westminster Standards.

According to Ashbel Green, at the 1831 Assembly, "There occurred such disorder and confusion as we have never witnessed in the General Assembly . . ." Barnes's appeal to the General Assembly resulted mostly in the vindication of the Philadelphia pastor. The Assembly ruled that

"The Way of Salvation" had "a number of unguarded and objectionable passages" but also that Barnes's explanations were adequate. It also advised the Presbytery of Philadelphia to stop its pursuit of the matter. After the Assembly, Green's reaction was ominously threatening. "Unless in the passing year," he wrote, "there is a general waking up of the *old school presbyterians*, to a sense of their danger and their duty, their influence in the General Assembly will forever be subordinate and under control."

Although Barnes received a generally propitious verdict, soon other ministers found themselves under scrutiny for harboring views close to those of the New England theology, perhaps spurred on by Green's warning.

One instance occurred nearby in the Presbytery of Carlisle in 1832, where ministers took issue with the teaching of George Duffield on the nature of regeneration. In his 1832 book, *Spiritual Life: or, Regeneration*, Duffield had generally expressed the New Haven understanding of human depravity. Sin consisted "in the misdirection and inappropriate exercise of his faculties; not in *wrong faculties inherited.*" This did not mean that Duffield thought sinfulness was unlikely. Instead, it was "*morally certain*" that persons would sin. Still, while asserting the priority of the Holy Spirit in regeneration, Duffield conceived of divine initiative in such a way that it functioned as a fillip that prompted men and women to moral motivation and behavior. The emerging "old school" Presbyterians in the Presbytery of Carlisle were in the minority, and the most they could secure was a warning against the harmful implications of Duffield's teaching. Like Barnes, Duffield would remain in good standing, able to continue his ministry.

Farther afield, the Presbytery of Cincinnati in 1835 received charges against Lyman Beecher, one of New England's best-known pastors, for holding similar views to Barnes and Duffield, again rooted in conceptions hatched in New Haven. This trial gained national attention partly because of Beecher's own reputation. A Presbyterian pastor on Long Island for a little over a decade, and then a Congregationalist minister in Litchfield, Connecticut, for another fifteen years before becoming pastor of Park Street Church in Boston, Beecher was a prominent figure in the creation of voluntary agencies that implemented the moral reforms of the Second Great Awakening. (He was the father of Henry Ward Beecher, one of the most popular ministers in the last half of the nineteenth century, and of Harriet Beecher Stowe, the author of *Uncle Tom's Cabin*.) He played an important role in the founding of both the American Bible Society and the American Temperance Society.

In 1835 the board of Lane Seminary in Cincinnati called Beecher to preside over the school in southern Ohio. But his transfer to the Presbytery of Cincinnati met resistance from "old school" Presbyterians who accused Beecher of holding New Haven conceptions of depravity, moral ability, and regeneration. Although he had used terminology similar to Taylor's—Beecher and Taylor had been in close proximity and were friends during his time in Litchfield—in his defense the Lane president argued that his views were essentially those of Jonathan Edwards. This proved satisfactory to the emerging "old school" party, rendering the judgment from one that Beecher's expressions were "comparatively orthodox."

Although practically all of those accused of Hopkinsianism or the New Haven Theology escaped conviction, the cumulative effect of these trials was twofold. On the one hand, it cultivated a Presbyterian party of opposition to the spread of the New England theology that conceived of itself as "old school" or traditionalist. This party was emerging as the one that would question both the means and ends of the revivals and moral reforms of the Second Great Awakening. On the other hand, the opposition to the New England theology signaled a heightened awareness of the distinctive teachings of Calvinism and their importance to the ministry of the Presbyterian Church.

Such developments led the likes of Finney to leave the Presbyterian fold. In 1835 the revivalist began work as a professor of moral philosophy at Oberlin College, and did so with an expression of good riddance to his former Presbyterian peers. In the same year that he took up residence in Ohio, he said, "No doubt there is a jubilee in hell every year, about the time of the meeting of the General Assembly." Had he remained Presbyterian a year or two longer, he might have revised the statement to increase the frequency of such celebrations.

The Old School-New School Split

In 1834, thanks to their increasing frustration with the actions of the General Assembly and the spread of the New England theology within the Presbyterian Church, the would-be Old School Presbyterians wrote a memorial for the consideration of the General Assembly. The *Western Memorial,* as it was called, carried with it the signatures of only eighteen ministers and ninety-nine ruling elders. But despite the small number of signers, this document summarized the convictions of the Old School Presbyterians, a group that would achieve a wide constituency in the church within several years. It was also basically a repudiation of the cooperative spirit that had entangled the Presbyterian Church with New England Congregationalists through the 1801 Plan of Union.

The *Memorial* had three parts. The first listed ten items of concern, all of which indicated the growing hostility to the Plan of Union's consequences. Several of these points were generic, such as a warning about the increasing number of divisions within the church at large. The others broke down essentially into the categories of doctrine and church polity. Under the former, the *Memorial* mentioned specifics ranging from the creation of new presbyteries where creedal subscription was not practiced to individual ministers, such as Barnes, Duffield, and Beecher, whose views were unsound. The examples cited to demonstrate the abuse of Presbyterian polity ranged from another construction of two presbyteries in Philadelphia to offset the antagonism over Barnes, to the unwholesome practice of allowing an interdenominational agency such as the American Home Missionary Society to perform the Presbyterian Church's work in planting and establishing new congregations.

One of the points in this first part led directly to the *Memorial's* second list of matters deserving immediate attention. The tenth heading in the first section referred to "doctrinal errors" which were then enumerated in what for all intents and purposes was a theological section. Here the authors of the *Memorial* took issue with teaching that undermined or denied nine points of Calvinist orthodoxy: Adam as the "federal representative" of the human race; the imputation of Adam's sin; the inheritance of original sin by infants; human depravity as the product of both original sin (or a corrupt nature) and actual "transgressions"; the inability of fallen men and women to obey God's law; the impossibility of regeneration apart from the Holy Spirit's miraculous work of changing a heart of stone into one of flesh; the vicarious sacrifice of Christ's death on the cross; the forensic or legal character of the atonement; and the efficacy of Christ's atonement being limited to the elect.

122

The last section of the *Memorial* urged the Assembly of 1834 to take six specific actions. The first was to abrogate the Plan of Union. Then followed a plea to prevent presbyteries from ordaining ministers who would then work within the bounds of another presbytery. Third, the *Memorial* called on the Assembly to transfer the supervision of home missions from interdenominational voluntary associations to the direct control of Presbyterian authorities. Next it requested a statement that specified the doctrinal errors that were disrupting the church and that directed presbyteries and synods to take due diligence in rooting them out. Fifth, it urged that the Assembly clarify the procedures for transferring credentials from one presbytery to another and the degree to which a presbytery could examine or criticize the views of the man switching judicatories. Finally, it requested the reunification of the two presbyteries of Philadelphia and the end of establishing presbyteries or synods based on elective affinity rather than geographical distribution. The General Assembly of 1834, however, was not persuaded by the *Memorial* or its defenders' argument. It rejected all of the document's points and supported status quo in the Presbyterian Church.

From this the antagonism between the Old and New Schools was no longer merely a local concern for presbyteries but played itself out at the annual meetings of the General Assembly, the outcomes of which depended on whether the Old or New Schoolers were in the majority.

At the 1835 Assembly, the Old School party arrived better organized and benefiting from a majority of delegates. This owed in part to a pre-Assembly meeting, roughly one month before, in Pittsburgh with representatives from fifty-four presbyteries who drew up a strategy for the upcoming gathering based on their new statement, *The Act and Testimony*. This statement largely repeated the concerns of the *Western Memorial* except for protesting the actions of the 1834 Assembly, which according to *The Act and Testimony* had "corrupted our doctrines" and gave "permanent security to error and to themselves by raising an outcry in the churches against all who love the truth well enough to contend for it."

With a majority of delegates and a group of them well organized to boot, the Old School reversed several of its defeats from the previous year. They managed to adopt measures allowing presbyteries to examine members transferring from other judicatories, rejected the idea of elective affinity and reunited several bodies in the vicinity of Philadelphia, reminded the church of the priority that should be given to denominational agencies for missions, recommended terminating the Plan of Union, warned about Pelagian threats to Calvinist teaching, and urged greater allocation of resources to denominationally administered foreign missions.

In 1836 the New School Presbyterians were delighted to realize that putting teeth in the Old School's affirmation would take more effort than the Presbyterian Church could muster. It helped that the New School was in the majority.[1] What enabled the New School to show its strength was the second trial of Albert Barnes. It had occurred in 1835 soon after the publication of his *Notes on the Epistle to the Romans*, which was part of his popular commentary series. The charges against him in the Presbytery of Philadelphia were almost the same as those at his first trial. In this case, Barnes was suspended from the ministry and could not preach for close to a year while awaiting his appeal to the Assembly of 1836. Although the debates were intense and prolonged at General Assembly, the delegates there, thanks to the majority of those sympathizing with the New School, acquitted Barnes.

In retaliation, the Old School started to prepare in earnest for the next year's Assembly. A newly organized Old School Committee of Correspondence sent out a letter which read, "Fathers, Brethren, Fellow-Christians, whatever else may be dark, this is clear, *we* CANNOT CONTINUE *in the same body*." Most of the communications coming from this committee were confidential and sent only to like-minded ministers and ruling elders. Instead of meeting early as was the case in 1835, the Old School decided to meet in Philadelphia only a few days before the 1837 Assembly that was scheduled to convene there. Here they deliberated on the best strategy, depending on whether they were in the majority or minority.

1. It should be noted that the church members, pastors, congregations, presbyteries, and synod in the Presbyterian Church at this time were not easily identified as either Old or New School. In his biography of his father, Charles Hodge, Archibald Alexander Hodge counted four different groups in the church, two being at opposite ends and clearly identified by the Old and New School labels, with the other two being more moderate, though having affinities with either the Old or New School. In effect, the majority of the denomination was in the middle, with the Old School party (the strict Calvinists) in hot pursuit to rid the church of the New School (the compromised Calvinists).

As it turned out, the Old School had a fairly clear majority when the Assembly finally convened and voted on a measure to abrogate the 1801 Plan of Union. The measure passed by a vote of 143 to 110. In addition, the Assembly adopted a statement that specified sixteen doctrinal errors that had been agitating the church for the past two decades, thus finally achieving the theological clarity that the New Englanders had obscured. And most dramatically, the General Assembly exscinded four synods of churches formed under the Plan of Union—those of Western Reserve (Ohio), Utica (New York), Geneva (New York), and Genesee (New York). The total number of churches involved in this action was stunning. With this vote the Presbyterian Church excluded twenty-eight presbyteries, 509 ministers, and close to sixty thousand communicant members.

The actions of the 1837 Assembly, however, did not settle the matter, since Presbyterian polity generally allows for protestors to be heard. In the year after the devastation of the "exscinding act," the New School began to develop its own strategy. Some recommended abandoning Presbyterianism altogether for Congregationalism. But those who attended a meeting in Auburn, New York, during the summer of 1837 were not willing to take defeat so readily. This group decided to declare the acts of the 1837 Assembly to be "null and void" and called on those bodies affected by the exscinding act "to retain their present organization and connection, without seeking any other." They also drew up an Auburn Declaration, which rebutted the doctrinal charges brought against the New School, and which affirmed generally the Calvinism of the Westminster Standards, without addressing the question of discipline for those such as Barnes or Duffield whose writings conflicted with those affirmations.

In 1838, the drawn-out dispute between the Old and New School Presbyterians came to something of a sordid ending. At the 1838 Assembly, scheduled to meet at Seventh Church in Philadelphia, the Old School arrived first, took all the seats closest to the front of the church, and locked the doors near the front, thus forcing the New School to find seats at the back. When one of the members from the exscinded synods tried to have his name recognized as being present for the Assembly, the retiring Old School moderator from the 1837 Assembly bellowed, "Sir, we do not know you." At that point pandemonium broke out. Some New School member read protests, while Old School Presbyterians

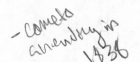

shouted for order. Eventually the New School formed its own Assembly at the back of Seventh Church, thus furnishing one of the first instances in Presbyterian history of concurrent General Assemblies in the same building. Eventually, the New School took its deliberations to another location but still claimed to be the Presbyterian Church in the U.S.A. The Plan of Union that had added substantially to the growth of the church had now prompted a division between the Old School and New School Presbyterian churches.

The Meaning of Division

Since 1838 historians of American Presbyterianism have offered a variety of explanations for the hostile separation of the Old and New Schools. Clearly the Plan of Union was an overriding issue that accounted for several factors. Most important, theology was a substantial cause for the division, even though the chief opponent of the Old School, Barnes, was a graduate of Princeton Seminary. No matter where individual pastors may have studied, the trends of the New England theology clearly ran contrary to the teachings of the Westminster Standards. Since the Plan of Union opened the Presbyterian Church to the spread of New England's views, putting a stopper on that supply of unsound teaching was crucial to the Old School.

Another significant factor was the influence of revivalism and the link between the New England theology and the Second Great Awakening. To the extent that Presbyterians were worried about effects on their denomination of the New England theology, and to the extent that they could blame the excesses of emotionalism and enthusiasm on the ideas gaining popularity in New England, ending the Plan of Union became a means of correcting the problem. In addition, the Plan obviously introduced significant irregularities in church government because of the mingling of Presbyterian and Congregationalist polities, thus providing yet another reason to end the arrangement and blame New England for the Presbyterian Church's woes.

Also a factor was the moral activism that the Second Great Awakening encouraged and which drew strength from New England Congregationalism. Revivalists such as Finney in the 1830s began to crusade against slavery and castigated it as a sin. In the South that message was hardly welcome. Since the Old School was stronger in the region that depended on slavery than in the North, the economic motives for removing the New England presence in the church made obvious sense.

Although each of these circumstances played a significant part in the 1837–38 division, another feature is often overlooked. It is the emergence of self-conscious Presbyterianism for both the Old and the New Schools. Prior to the debates over theology and church polity that began to shake the Presbyterian Church in the 1820s, the denomination lacked a clear identity. This accounts in part for the union with Congregationalists, but was also evident in the indiscriminate embrace of camp meetings and revivals. In other words, prior to 1830 the Presbyterian Church in the U.S.A. was one voice in the generic mix of English-speaking, Reformed-leaning American Protestantism. But the formation of seminaries, and especially the crucible of theological controversy, changed the Presbyterian Church from simply one other denomination contributing to the religious well-being of the United States to a church that needed to decide exactly what its boundaries were according to the character of its theology and witness. The division of 1837–38 may have been too high a price to pay for such denominational clarity. But it did transform American Presbyterian identity.

7

The Flowering of American Presbyterianism

The standard vocabulary used to refer to the division of 1837 and 1838 is to speak in terms of Old School and New School Presbyterians. In point of fact, the two General Assemblies to emerge from the split did not apply those labels to themselves. Instead, the New School called its gathering the Constitutional Assembly, while the Old School referred to its meeting as the Reforming Assembly.

These were interesting choices if only because the reputation of each side does not readily coincide with these terms. As the "newer" or more progressive branch of American Presbyterianism, the New School might have preferred *reform* to *constitutional* if only because the ways of the church were in need of revision. Likewise, as the conservator of Presbyterianism's "older" habits, *constitutional* would likely have served the Old School's purposes more than *reform*, which connoted modification. Nevertheless, the terms stuck and were indicative of the emergence of self-conscious reflection by both parties on the nature of American Presbyterianism.

As it turned out, this process of reflection would also engage the civil courts of Pennsylvania. In 1839 the New School initiated proceedings against the Old School for unlawfully expelling them from the Presbyterian Church in the U.S.A. The Constitutional Assembly (New School) believed that it was still entitled to the legal status of the church's Act of Incorporation of 1799. After three weeks of argument, the Court of the Eastern District of Pennsylvania ruled in favor of the New School. From the perspective of the judge, the Constitutional Assembly, the one excluded from Seventh Church in 1837, was in fact the true "General Assembly of the Presbyterian Church." But that was not the courts' final word. On appeal to the Pennsylvania Supreme Court, the Old School gained vindication for its actions at the Reforming Assembly. There the judge ruled that the exscinding acts of 1837 were "certainly constitutional and strictly just" and that the commissioners from the excluded synods "were not entitled to seats in the Assembly, and that their names were properly excluded from the roll."

By having to justify their separate existence, both to themselves and to the courts, the New and Old Schools were forced to engage the question of their own identities. What was true Presbyterianism? What distinguished the New from the Old School varieties of Presbyterianism? Did American Presbyterianism possess characteristics that were peculiar to it? And did either the New or Old School embody those American features better than the other? These were questions that had rarely occurred to American Presbyterians prior to the split in 1837 and 1838. As such, the division and competition between the Old and New Schools actually produced more zeal for being Presbyterian than the American church had mustered during its first 130 years of existence. Indeed, the reality of two rival American Presbyterian denominations, despite the blow to desires for Christian unity, accomplished more good for Presbyterianism in the United States than a united denomination.

New School Presbyterianism

Prior to the division of 1837 and 1838, New School Presbyterianism was not a well-defined set of convictions but generally the pose of American Presbyterians who were caught up in the progress of the American nation and wanted the church to lend a large helping hand.

Indicative of this outlook were the two best-known New School Presbyterians, Lyman Beecher (1775–1863) and Albert Barnes (1798–1870). The point here is not that New School Presbyterians grossly made the nation a priority in their understanding of Christian ministry. Still, they were guilty of not necessarily recognizing the dangers inherent in a religion that fused the ecclesiastical and civil spheres.

In Beecher's conception of his own calling as a minister, the moral welfare of the nation was a chief concern. He drew upon both the older Puritan conceit of the national covenant between God and New England, and the recent American republican position that recognized the necessity of a virtuous citizenry for a free and ordered society. In this convergence of ideas, Beecher returned over and over again to the standards of the Old Testament and the logic inherent in Israel's past. The success of the American nation, like Israel's, depended on the people's faithfulness to God. Apart from the true religion, the United States would face the same sort of judgments and penalties that had afflicted Israel during times of apostasy.

This mindset was responsible both for Beecher's support and encouragement of revivals and for the moral crusades that were crucial to the success of the Second Great Awakening. According to the New Englander, the revivals of the early nineteenth century "seem to indicate the purpose of God to give a prominent place to this nation in the glorious work of renovating the earth." But individual conversions were insufficient to prevent the United States from apostasy and ruin. For instance, Beecher believed that Sabbath observance was essential to the protection of American liberty. "Europe never will be qualified for liberty until she keeps her Sabbaths in a better manner," while the United States would soon retrogress "after the influence of her Sabbaths has passed away."

Even more zealous was Beecher for the elimination of alcohol consumption in America. "Intemperance," he wrote, "is the sin of our land . . . and if anything shall defeat the hopes of the world, which hang upon our experiment with civil liberty, it is that river of fire . . ." What Beecher regarded as intemperate was the daily use of ardent spirits "IN ANY FORM OR ANY DEGREE." This notion became so prevalent among New School Presbyterians that during the 1830s they initiated an effort to have congregations switch from wine to grape juice in the observance of the Lord's Supper. Likewise, in 1840 the New School General Assembly

130

passed a rule requiring total abstinence from all beverages that could possibly lead to drunkenness.

Albert Barnes did not come from the New England stock that Beecher did, but was no less prone to see the progress of the American nation in essentially religious categories. Barnes conceived of the church's mission as essentially one of providing moral guidance to society. For instance, in 1857 he wrote that the church "owes an important duty to society and to God"; its mission was not simply to secure and sanctify "its own members" or to engage in missions and the distribution of religious literature. Instead, "On all that is wrong in social life, in the modes of intercourse, in the habits of training the young, and in the prevailing sentiments in the community that have grown out of existing institutions, God may have planted the church there to exert a definite moral influence—a work for himself." In turn, Barnes was an active member and supporter of temperance societies, practically shutting down the liquor trade in Morristown while a pastor there, and promoting "dry banquets" in Philadelphia for working men during celebrations of Independence Day. The Sabbath was another important reform that Barnes supported, and like Beecher he linked his advocacy to preserving the health of the nation and avoiding the licentiousness that so often afflicted free societies.

If these were the general features of New Presbyterianism before the split with the Old School—revivalism, reform, and nationalism—after the division New School Presbyterians entered a phase more Presbyterian than evangelical. The reason stems in part from the dilemma facing the New School. George M. Marsden explains that New School Presbyterians wanted to reject the perceived wooden traditionalism of the Old School while claiming still to be Presbyterian and biblical. "They sought a distinct theological identity for their denomination without repudiating their heritage."

A good indication of the dynamics of this dilemma came from Barnes on two occasions. The first, an 1846 essay prepared for the *American Biblical Repository* on "The Relation of Theology to Preaching," identified three kinds of theology that should not be preached. The first was a view of God without any recognition of the mystery and darker side of human existence. Barnes may have had in mind the pantheistic tendencies of the New England Transcendentalists. The second kind of theology to be avoided was one that subsumed expository preaching to liturgy and formality, such as was the case with Rome. The final type of doctrine that should not be preached was Old School Presbyterianism. According to Barnes, "It contains dogmas so abhorrent to the obvious teachings of the Bible; so repellent to the common sense of mankind; so at variance with what are found to be just principles of philosophy, so fitted to retard a work of grace; and so utterly contradictory to what man is constrained to preach when his heart is full . . . that he *cannot* preach them." This was essentially the position of the generic evangelical Protestantism of the period, opposed to errors on the left (Unitarianism) and the right (Roman Catholicism), attempting to be biblical, but also firmly rejecting traditional expressions of Protestantism (such as the Old School) that divided Protestants.

By 1852, when Barnes made the second of his definitive statements, he was sounding more Presbyterian than evangelical. At that year's New School Assembly, Barnes preached a sermon attempting to define "Our Position."

First, he explained to the delegates, was the New School's commitment to American Presbyterianism: "we had supposed that the terms of adhesion to the Presbyterian Church allowed a reasonable latitude of construction, so as to admit all who held sincerely the great Calvinistic system as distinguished from Arminianism, Pelagianism, and Socinianism." Second, the New School stood for cooperation with like-minded Christians in benevolent endeavors: "We supposed that organizations might be formed not strictly ecclesiastical for the promotion of the common objects of Christianity. . . . Our preferences were for a cooperative Christianity in distinction from ecclesiastical exclusiveness . . ." Finally, the New School was significantly indebted to New England Calvinism: "we were especially disposed to make common cause as far as we could do with all the Puritan family and particularly with our New England brethren" since many American Presbyterians were "descended from New England." Consequently, while wanting to distance themselves from the Old School's rigidity and remain open to collaboration with other Christians, the New School, as Barnes elaborated its position, still ranked "Presbyterianness" as its most important feature.

New School Presbyterian self-consciousness was evident not only in the remarks of its leaders. In 1845, for instance, the New School Synod of New York and New Jersey appointed a committee to investigate the publications of the American Tract Society, an agency that during the Second Great Awakening had enjoyed the full blessing of Congregationalists and Presbyterians for producing wholesome reading material for churches and families. The Society had a fairly good record of reprinting standard practical works from such Puritans as John Flavel and Jonathan Edwards. But the synodical committee found that the Tract Society was revising the contents of these works. The explicit reason for the changes was to render them more readable for a contemporary audience. But the Presbyterians on the committee objected that these revisions also altered "the doctrines of God's absolute sovereignty in saving men, in predestination, elections, perseverance—of the nature and the extent of the atonement, of man's ability, and of infant baptism . . ." In some cases the text was "materially modified, and in others wholly excluded."

Of course, these were the very doctrines that had prompted the split of 1837 and 1838. But in this instance the synodical committee took a view similar to the Old School when it declared that these doctrines were "of vital importance to the system of truth to which they belong."

George Duffield, the pastor on trial in 1832 for deficient views on regeneration, also adopted a heightened Calvinistic stance when in 1848 he reviewed Charles Finney's *Lectures on Systematic Theology*. In the review Duffield remarked on his long-standing regard for the revivalist. But with a note of regret Duffield admitted that Finney's book gave "more reason for censure than we had suspected." The New School Presbyterian faulted Finney for embracing the doctrine of the freedom of the will and that of Christian perfection, thus departing from "the faith he once held in common with the Presbyterian Church."

Beyond theological critique, the New School's maturing self-understanding also involved institutional adjustments. Probably the greatest example of the New School's development as a self-conscious Presbyterian denomination was its diminishing ties, whether formal or informal, with New England Congregationalists. During the 1840s New England Congregationalists began to found their own theological journals, such as the *New Englander* and *Bibliotheca Sacra*, rather than rely on the New School–sponsored *American Biblical Repository*. A few years later the New School started another journal of its own, the *Presbyterian*

Quarterly Review, founded in 1853, another sign of the denomination's increasing Presbyterian identity.

At the same time, a number of New School pastors, with roots and ties to New England, left their calls in the Presbyterian Church to take pulpits or teaching posts in New England. Lyman Beecher, for instance, in 1850 left the presidency of Lane Seminary to retire and did so by moving to Brooklyn where his son, Henry Ward Beecher, pastored a Congregationalist church. Furthermore, the New School Presbyterian church gradually ceased to be an attractive outlet for the graduates of New England's seminaries, such as Andover and Yale. The number of graduates from these schools taking calls as Presbyterians declined significantly in the years between 1838 and 1861, especially after 1853 (for reasons see below).

At the formal level, New School Presbyterians also gradually pulled back from cooperative ventures with New England's Congregationalists. Within a decade after the division of 1837 and 1838, the New School had switched from conducting its home missions through the Congregationalist-dominated American Home Missionary Society to forming in 1847 its own Standing Committee on Home Missions. Some of this had to do with Congregationalists themselves, who were increasingly willing to plant churches without New School Presbyterian assistance. Still, by 1850 the New School recognized the need, calling it a "command obligatory to our branch of the church," to plant congregations that were New School in identity and association.

This trend toward denominational isolation from New England's Congregationalists culminated in 1852 when the Albany Convention of the Congregationalist Churches did what the Old School had executed in 1837, namely, the abrogation of the 1801 Plan of Union. According to the complaint of one Congregationalist churchman at the Albany gathering, the New School Presbyterians "have milked our Congregational cows, but they have made nothing but Presbyterian butter and cheese." New Englanders believed that the Plan of Union had always favored Presbyterians and now were interested in protecting their own ecclesiastical assets.

But New School Presbyterians felt betrayed. The editor of the New School's *Presbyterian Quarterly Review* wrote, "This from New England! These are the men who were to stand by us, shoulder to shoulder. Et tu

Brute!" By 1855 any semblance of cooperation between the New School and New England had evaporated. That was, in fact, the last year that the two denominations exchanged fraternal delegates. In effect, roughly fifteen years after the Old School had pulled the plug on collaboration with New England, the New School had decided on similar action.

Even so, the observation of similar outcomes does not do justice to the different temperaments of the New and Old School Presbyterians. The former had taken longer to reject New England Congregationalism and to recognize the implications of Presbyterian theology and practice. But they also required more evidence to reach those conclusions. By the mid-1850s the outcomes of Finney's teaching on sanctification were clear, and evidence was mounting that Nathaniel Taylor's New Haven Theology was not going to be a resting point for the New England theology but would in fact be a path to even greater modifications of Calvinism. Furthermore, New School Presbyterians took longer than the Old School to see the tensions between Presbyterian theological convictions and the American Protestant search for a doctrinal lowest common denominator to sustain interdenominational cooperation and moral reform. All of this is to say that the New School came to its Presbyterian identity mainly through the gate of Calvinism. Still, its theological instincts were not to be assertive but to speak softly.

These theological impulses came through in a series of tracts that the New School denomination, at the direction of the General Assembly, prepared during the 1850s on its doctrines and government.

The first in the series was *The Extent of the Atonement* by the late James Richards (1767–1843), a professor of theology at Auburn Seminary, who had served as moderator of the Presbyterian Church before the division and on Princeton Seminary's board of directors. Richards avoided the Old School position on limited atonement and contended that Christ's death made salvation available to all, unless of course "we wish to be more Calvinistic than John Calvin himself." To justify this interpretation, Richards distinguished between the ultimate design and practical effect of the atonement. Its ultimate purpose was to save the elect, but its practical effect was to *"open a way for the salvation of all."* The consequence for preaching was that *"a salvation offered, implies a salvation provided."*

The second pamphlet in the series came from Albert Barnes, on the topic of justification, *How Shall Man Be Just with God?* Similar to the Richards pamphlet, this one also tried to steer a middle course between the more difficult teachings of Calvinism and the more robust affirmation of human ability taught by the American experiment with political liberty. As such, Barnes's treatment of the imputation of Christ's righteousness became essentially God's purpose "to treat those who are themselves guilty, as if they were righteousness." But this need not be a mysterious or apparently arbitrary transaction. Instead, Barnes likened it to everyday experiences such as the characteristics of a father being attributed to his children, or credit being extended to the owner of a business because of the financial capacities of stockholders.

In a similar vein, the third pamphlet in the series addressed another doctrine peculiar to Calvinism, the perseverance of the saints. The author, Eliphalet W. Gilbert, a Princeton Seminary–trained pastor of Western Presbyterian Church in Philadelphia, admitted that this doctrine was not essential to Presbyterian teaching but was nevertheless biblical and therefore important. Its significance was all the more obvious because of its affirmation that "every saint, without exception, shall be saved." As George M. Marsden observed, these New School pamphlets demonstrated the denomination's desire to be biblical and Calvinistic, while presenting theology "in terms that may be applied practically."

Although older leaders of the New School church helped clarify the denomination's understanding of some of the points that had led to the division with the Old School, younger theologians emerged to add depth to New School Presbyterianism. One of the most significant on this score was Henry B. Smith (1815–77), a product of New England seminaries (Andover and Bangor) who taught church history and then systematic theology at Union Seminary (New York) from 1850 until his retirement in 1874. Smith was well suited to the needs of New School Presbyterianism since existentially he bridged the worlds of New England Congregationalism and New York Presbyterianism.

Theologically as well, his aim was to present a mediating theology that featured Christ as the center of the system. In 1836, for instance, while still a seminarian, he admitted that he could not find truth in either the Old or New School position. His only hope was "in the doctrine of redemption," thus making his ambition to "harmonize a system which shall make Christ the central point of all important religious truth." After studying in Germany, where Smith became familiar with the christocentric theology of the evangelical party there, he taught at Amherst College prior to his move to New York City. His German studies were especially important for Smith's effort to find a new synthesis that would move beyond the extremes of Old and New School Presbyterianism. Although he faulted German Protestantism for heading in dangerous directions, he also believed that specific theologians, even Friedrich Schleiermacher, the so-called father of liberal Protestantism, had reinvigorated theological scholarship with an awareness of the centrality of Christ's mediating work. As such, Smith featured Christ's redeeming work as the centerpiece of his theological reflection. "It gives us a fact and not a theory," Smith wrote, "a person and not an abstract doctrine."

Through his influence at Union Seminary, Smith emerged as the leading theological figure among the second generation of New School Presbyterians and signaled the New School's capacity to adjust to theological developments beyond the categories supplied by the debates of the 1830s.

As new as some of Smith's ideas were, his theological impulses were well suited to those of New School Presbyterianism. These Presbyterians were still working within a Calvinistic framework but sought to channel their theology in directions that would blend Reformed doctrine with present-day realities. As such, the New School tended to avoid the seemingly harsher teachings of Calvinism, or smooth its rough edges, to the end of participating in the evangelization and reform of the expanding nation.

Were it not for the division with the Old School, the New School might not have been as deliberate in articulating its understanding of Presbyterianism. To be sure, the Old School continued to voice major reservations about the New School's theological instincts and ecclesiastical practices. Marsden observes that the New School's effort to establish its Presbyterian credentials "never completely dominated" its vigorous support for revivalism and social reform. But during its years as a separate denomination, the New School became proud of its Presbyterian identity in a way that was unexpected during the debates leading up to its break with the Old School.

Old School Presbyterianism

Soon after the division of 1837 and 1838, Charles Hodge, then still the junior member of Princeton Seminary's faculty and at the relatively young age of forty-one, determined to put the Old School-New School controversy in historical perspective. His effort led to the two-volume history of colonial Presbyterianism, colorlessly named *The Constitutional History of the Presbyterian Church in the United States of America* (1839).

Although Princeton had been something of an awkward bystander in the debates of the 1830s, hoping to avoid a split (if only because so many of its graduates were in the New School party), the seminary ultimately came down on the side of the Old School. Hodge's attempt to vindicate his denomination's position helped to articulate the characteristic features of Old School Presbyterianism. On the first page of this history, Hodge, trying to avoid offense, wrote that "the one party is in favour of a stricter adherence to the standards of the church, as to doctrine and order, than the other." Obviously, the stricter party in view was the Old School. And in arguing that the Old School represented better the original features of American Presbyterianism, he emphasized the Scottish as opposed to the New England heritage of his church.

Whether Hodge was right about the historical and ethnic origins of American Presbyterianism, his history of the church was significant for two reasons. First, it showed that the split with the New School also prompted the Old School to become self-conscious about the features that differentiated it from its former brethren. Second, in identifying the Old School as stricter than the New School on "doctrine and order," Hodge gave a handy summary of Old School Presbyterianism.

The strictness of Old School Presbyterianism on doctrine was nowhere better exhibited than in the polemical writings of Hodge himself. Over the course of his career at Princeton (1822–78), Hodge taught more seminary students than any other Presbyterian professor during the nineteenth century, and the bulk of his instruction was summarized in his three-volume *Systematic Theology*, published between 1872 and 1873.

But in addition to his classroom assertions, Hodge was a relentless critic of what he deemed to be departures from the Reformed system of truth, thus exhibiting the trait most associated with Old School Presbyterianism and emerging as one of its chief spokesmen. For instance, when Charles Finney's lectures on systematic theology appeared in 1846, Hodge was quick to pounce, declaring the Oberlin professor to be guilty of bald Pelagianism. He wrote, "the radical principle of Pelagius's system [was] that he assumed moral liberty to consist in the ability, at any moment, to choose between good and evil, or, as Mr. Finney expresses it, 'in the power to choose, in every instance, in accordance with the moral law.' " With remarkable confidence, Hodge responded that it was an "undisputed" historical fact that his idea, which derived moral ability (free will) from moral duty (divine command), "has not been adopted in the confession of any one denominational church in Christendom, but is expressly repudiated by them all."

With similar assurance, Hodge reviewed and pronounced verdicts on departures from Calvinistic teachings on the atonement, original sin, and the imputation of Christ's righteousness. In another review from the 1840s, for example, this time of a pamphlet on the atonement by the New School Presbyterian minister Nathan Beman, Hodge demonstrated the doctrinal precision and self-assurance characteristic of its strict Calvinism:

> The doctrine of the atonement for which we contend as the distinguishing and essential doctrine of the gospel, is, 1. That sin for its own sake deserves the wrath and curse of God. 2. That God is just, immutably determined, from the excellence of his nature, to punish sin. 3. That out of his sovereign and infinite love, in order to redeem us from the law, that is, from its demands and curse, he sent his own Son, in the likeness of sinful flesh, who in his own person fulfilled these demands, and endured that curse in our stead. That his righteousness, or merit, thus wrought out, is imputed to every one that believes, to his justification before God. This is the doctrine of the church catholic, overlaid, corrupted, and made of none effect, in the church of Rome; disembarrassed, reproduced, and exhibited as *the* doctrine of the Reformation; in manifold forms since opposed or rejected, but ever virtually embraced and trusted in by every sincere child of God.

In addition to defending the finer and more difficult points of Calvinism, Old School Presbyterian leaders also devoted careful attention to church polity, the second feature mentioned by Hodge in the introduction to his *Constitutional History*. Here even the usually precise Hodge was not up to the degree of precision pursued by some Old School theologians. James Henley Thornwell (1812–62), for instance, who taught at Columbia Seminary in South Carolina, developed the doctrine of *jure divino* Presbyterianism, which meant that the Presbyterian form of church government was not simply permissible but required by Scripture.

Thornwell and Hodge debated each other on several occasions, which indicated that the Old School by no means thought with one mind. The two issues that generated the most sustained argument were, first, whether ruling elders could participate in the laying on of hands during the ordination of ministers, and second, whether the work of missions should be conducted by boards or commissions. The arguments on both of these subjects resist easy summation. But the heart of Thornwell's position in both cases was the idea that the specifics of true church government were taught in the Bible. He wrote:

> . . . the Church, before she can move, must not only show that she is not prohibited; she must also show that she is actually commanded—she must produce a warrant. Hence, we absolutely denied that she has any discretion in relation to things not commanded. She can proclaim no laws that Christ has not ordained, institute no ceremonies which He has not appointed, create no offices which He has not prescribed, and exact no obedience which He has not enjoined. She does not enter the wide domain which He has left indifferent, and by her authority bind the consciences where He has left it free.

By this logic, Thornwell argued that elders should be part of the laying on of hands during the ordination of ministers and that the church must use a commission to oversee the work of missions. On the first subject, he argued that the Bible makes no distinction between elders who rule and those who don't. All elders rule and the word *presbyter* refers to this in the case of elders and pastors. Obviously, elders did not preach. But the pattern that Thornwell saw in Scripture, especially the case of Timothy's ordination, was one in which all elders, including ruling ones, were involved in the ceremony of ordination.

On the second question, again following his logic that a clear warrant from Scripture was necessary for the church's law and practice, Thornwell reasoned that commissions, as representative bodies of either the General Assembly or synods, were the way to conduct the oversight of missions because only church judicatories had the authority to regulate the church's ministry. As independent agencies, with some ordained officers and some unordained philanthropists and gifted administrators, boards were unbiblical because they were not directly accountable to the church's assemblies. As Thornwell explained in the course of his debate with Hodge, "We hold that her organization is given; he holds that her organization is developed. He holds that any system which shall realize the parity of the clergy, the rights of the people, and the unity of the Church, is a *jure divino* government; we hold that, if these principles are realized in any other way except through Presbyters and Presbyteries, the government is not scriptural."

In the end, Hodge prevailed in these contests. During the early 1840s the Old School church rejected resoundingly a proposal that would have included elders in the laying on of hands. Likewise, throughout the 1840s and 1850s the Old School church regularly heard complaints against its use of boards to oversee the work of missions, both foreign and domestic, and the General Assembly regularly rejected those complaints and expressed general satisfaction with the existing arrangement. Still, the arguments of Old School theologians such as Thornwell are indicative of a tendency within this branch of American Presbyterianism to look for the consistent and integral position required by Reformed convictions and interpretation of Scripture. For the New School, these considerations often looked like nitpicking. But the strictness of the Old School in doctrine and polity was a case of putting practical considerations behind the first-order ones of thinking through exactly the implications of biblical and confessional teaching for the witness and order of the denomination.

A third feature that flowed directly from strictness in polity and doctrine was a teaching that became a hallmark of Old School Presbyterianism. It was the doctrine of the spirituality of the church, an often maligned and misunderstood teaching about the nature of church power

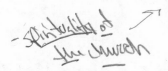

141

and the function of its ministry. In the minds of many later Presbyterians, this doctrine gained an unwholesome reputation because it was so often used by southern Presbyterians to avoid condemning slavery. Here again, Hodge and Thornwell differed, and the former thought the latter's position extreme. But even Hodge articulated a view consistent with the spirituality of the church when in 1861 he said:

> The doctrine of our church on this subject is, that the state has no authority in matters purely spiritual and that the church no authority in matters purely secular or civil. That their provinces in some cases overlie each other . . . is indeed true. . . . Nevertheless, the two institutions are distinct, and their respective duties are different.

This was a conviction consistent, in Hodge's view, with the Westminster Confession's assertion in chapter 31 that synods and councils are not to meddle in civil affairs, except in extraordinary cases or when the magistrate petitions the church's advice. Instead, the church's authority and concerns extended only to matters ecclesiastical and spiritual, hence the doctrine's name, the *spirituality* of the church. This doctrine rested on the Old School commitment to the supremacy and sufficiency of Scripture, the same basis on which Thornwell grounded the idea of *jure divino* Presbyterianism. Hodge himself would echo Thornwell's statement when he also wrote that the church may only "exercise her power in enforcing the word of God, in approving what it commands, and condemning what it forbids."

But arguably the most thoughtful and careful exponent of the spirituality of the church was Stuart Robinson, a Kentucky Presbyterian who ministered in Louisville and taught at Danville Theological Seminary. Robinson is not as well known as Hodge or Thornwell, but his 1858 book, *The Church of God as an Essential Element of the Gospel,* ranks with any of the theological writings produced by an Old School Presbyterian church that was blessed with a bevy of capable theologians. In this book, the purpose of which was to add further weight to the biblical character of Presbyterian church government, Robinson helpfully explained the religious, as opposed to the political, reasons for understanding the church as a spiritual institution, with spiritual means for clearly spiritual ends.

142

The church and the state "serve two distinct ends in the great scheme devised for man as fallen," he wrote. The state was established "to hold in check" sinful human nature and "to furnish a platform, as it were, on which to carry on another and more amazing scheme of mercy . . . ," that is, the work of the church. The church, as such, transcended political arrangements and was "designed to constitute of the families of earth that call upon [God's] name . . . a nation of priests, a peculiar nation, not reckoned among the nations, of whom Jehovah is the God and they are his people." To confuse the purpose of the church with that of the state and to blur their related spheres was not only dangerous for politics, since it would restrict religious liberty. It was even more destructive of the church since it distracted the church from a mission that no other institution or authority was called to execute.

Even if these Old School beliefs about doctrine and church polity were not the unanimous convictions of all Old School ministers, elders and church members, the theological reflection that informed them gave Old School Presbyterianism a reputation as arguably the strictest and most doctrinally precise denomination in the United States. That reputation helps to explain why Charles Hodge, who was not even the most exacting of the Old School's theologians, could say without irony of his denomination that it was "the most conservative Church in the land."

The Old School's conservatism also led Hodge on another occasion to say of the Princeton theology what many observers thought of the Old School at large, that "it is without distinctive meaning" because it never generated "an original idea." Indeed, for the Old School, resisting change and novelty was honorable, not something of which to be ashamed. What Hodge and other Old School Presbyterians seldom realized was that such Presbyterian conservatism was in fact a novelty within the history of American Presbyterianism. Prior to the Old School, American Presbyterians had not been so jealous of their distinct religious heritage and principles. But because of the split with the New School and the need to articulate core beliefs and practices, the Old School church fanned into flame a form of Presbyterianism that was arguably unparalleled in the history of the American church for its self-conscious reflection on the implications of Reformed Protestantism for the witness, teaching, and rule of the church.

The Americanization of Presbyterianism

To put in perspective the flowering of American Presbyterianism in both its Old and New blossoms, a comparison with developments in Scotland during the same period is useful. During the 1830s the kirk experienced a controversy that also split Scottish Presbyterians. The specific issue was the authority of congregations to exercise power in the call of clergy.

As part of the inheritance of the medieval church, Scottish Presbyterians continued to allow landowners and similar persons of patronage to appoint clergy in their parishes. This had been a practice to which the Covenanters and Reformed Presbyterians objected, which kept them out of the established church. It became a point of controversy again in 1834 when the conservatives in the kirk, who enjoyed a majority of commissioners at the General Assembly, passed the Veto Act, which gave parishioners the right to veto pastors appointed by local patrons.

The ensuing controversy lasted a decade and culminated in the formation of the Free Church of Scotland. This denomination, in order to gain the spiritual independence of the church, was willing to give up its status as a state church. Although important Free Church leaders still held on to the usefulness of national religion and an established church, others recognized that for the church to be the church, for it to be sovereign within her own spheres of theology, worship, and polity, she would need to be independent from the oversight and support of the state.

The result—and this is the important point to keep in mind—was a flowering of Presbyterianism in Scotland comparable to the one in the United States. Some of the greatest Presbyterian theologians and churchmen of the nineteenth century—such as William Cunningham, Robert S. Candlish, John Duncan, James Buchanan, and James Bannerman, who taught at the University of Edinburgh's New College—were voices of the Free Church's renowned Presbyterian witness and theology.

The example of Scottish Presbyterians was similar to that of Old and New School Presbyterians in the United States. Interference from the state was, of course, not an issue that hampered American Presbyterians. Still, they demonstrated that the principle of spiritual independence could do wonders for the church. Without the support of the state and the necessary restrictions that accompanied it, New School and Old School Presbyterians were able to participate in a trans-Atlantic invigoration of Presbyterianism.

One important difference between the New and Old Schools is worth noting here. Each church experienced this liberty from state regulation in different ways, even while both were fully committed to the experiment in American politics that allowed churches freedom to govern their affairs and minister the Bible in ways they deemed best.

For the New School, the political ideal of American freedom was a notion they attempted to accommodate in their own self-understanding and denominational identity. They would strive to be Presbyterian in ways that were surprising from the vantage of the 1830s. But their understanding of Presbyterianism was generally hemmed in by the prevailing American idea of liberty and democracy. Its Calvinism would be modified to be less repulsive to Americans accustomed to believing in the freedom of the will. Its church government would not be a system too remote from the experience of Americans who valued democracy and lay participation. In brief, the New School was an Americanized version of Presbyterianism but more self-consciously so.

The Old School, of course, was different. It developed ideas about Calvinism and Presbyterian church government, as well as the mission and nature of the church, that patently ran against the grain of American political sentiments and instincts. They emphasized human sinfulness in ways that made little sense to men and women who believed their own virtue was the bedrock of America's social order. And their precise views about the mission and government of the church obviously struck some as parochial in the worst sense.

But this did not mean that the Old School was any less an Americanized version of Presbyterianism. For the refinements that Old School Presbyterians made to their faith and practice were very much a function of the American order in which churches were free to develop their own views and practices without fear of penalty from governmental authorities.

In fact, as much as the United States may have contributed to a democratized form of Christianity because of its experiment with religious liberty and the separation of church and state, it also made possible the flourishing of theological and ecclesiological convictions that were impossible to European churches because of the state church system. If American Presbyterianism gained a measure of coherence from its generally fluid pattern of evolution throughout the colonial and early national periods, it had much to do, ironically, with a split in the church and the freedom of both sides to develop their distinct understandings of Presbyterian faith and practice.

8

War and Division

The American revisions of the Westminster Standards in 1788 involved a serious reduction in the magistrate's role within the church and her affairs. For that reason, events at the 1861 General Assembly of the Old School Presbyterians were unusual. These did not include any government official calling or presiding over the Assembly, but did yield telegrams between the commissioners meeting in Philadelphia at Seventh Presbyterian Church and members of Abraham Lincoln's Cabinet.

Of course, the year 1861 was significant and readily explains the surprising familiarity of Presbyterian commissioners and White House officials. Meeting only five weeks after South Carolina's secession and the capture of Fort Sumter in Charleston, Old School Presbyterians gathering for the Assembly could not help but have the nation's politics on their minds. If they were reading their newspapers during the sixteen-day meeting, they found plenty to remind them of the growing conflict between North and South. Midway through the Assembly, the popular Colonel Elmer Ephraim Ellsworth, the first casualty of the Civil War, lost his life while cutting down the Confederate Flag in Alexandria,

Virginia. The events of the day meant that this was not going to be a business-as-usual General Assembly.

The specific matter that prompted an exchange of telegrams between the Old School General Assembly and the White House was that of the Gardiner Spring Resolutions, named for the hoary minister from New York City who had pastored at Brick Church since 1810. On the third day of the Assembly, Spring called on the Assembly to appoint a committee to study the "expediency of making some expression of . . . devotion to the Union of these States, and their loyalty to the Government."

The Assembly initially tabled the motion by a relatively close vote. But the subsequent publicity in the local press, which filled Seventh Church to standing-room-only capacity (more than one thousand non-commissioners observed the proceedings), and the death of Ellsworth, provoked Spring to propose another and less timid set of resolutions, thus earning them the name of their resolver. Spring called for a day of fasting and prayer on the upcoming July 1, and for the Assembly to encourage its ministers and churches "to do all in their power to promote and perpetuate the integrity of these United States, and to strengthen, uphold, and encourage the Federal Government."

Once on the floor, these resolutions occupied the attention of the Assembly for the better part of a week. The reason was obvious. The Old School had a large number of churches in the South, and a pledge of allegiance to the federal government put Southerners in an acute dilemma. So subsequent debates and committee proceedings sought a way to soften and modify the Spring Resolutions in a way that would not split the Old School church the way that other prominent Protestant denominations had done over the conflict between the North and the South.

Preserving the union of the Old School church was also the reason for communications between the General Assembly and the White House. During debates, Charles Hodge asserted that he had heard one Cabinet official say that the best thing the Old School Assembly could do for the Union was "to keep unbroken the unity of your Church." Another commissioner also indicated that he had a telegram from White House officials expressing the same opinion. Spring countered that he did not think the Lincoln administration understood the situation. Opponents of the Spring Resolutions then produced two telegrams, one sent to Edward Bates, Lincoln's attorney general, asking whether it was the opinion of members of the Cabinet that the best thing the Assembly could do "to sustain the Government is to preserve the unity of the Presbyterian Church by abstaining from any deliverance on our present troubles." Bates's answer was, "Yes; for myself, decidedly; and I believe for other members of the Cabinet." But then Salmon P. Chase, Lincoln's secretary of the treasury, sent an unexpected telegram that read, "Cannot properly advise, but perceive no valid objection to unequivocal expressions in favor of the Constitution, Union, and freedom."

Equivocation from the White House would have seemed to be all the supporters of the Spring Resolutions needed to gain the support of a majority of the Assembly. Still, the main point of Spring's proposal, namely, declaring the Old School Presbyterian church's support for the federal government, was not so easily secured. First, the Assembly had to dispose of a majority report from a subcommittee that advised abstaining from "any further declaration" on the present state of the country. The minority report from the same committee that expressed the main features of Spring's original resolution, which was submitted by only one person of the nine-member subcommittee, finally prevailed on the floor of the Assembly by a majority of 156 to sixty-six. The specific language of the resolution declared the Old School church's obligation to:

> promote and perpetuate, so far as in us lies, the integrity of these United States, and to strengthen, uphold, and encourage the Federal Government in the exercise of all its functions under our noble Constitution; and to this Constitution, in all its provisions, requirements, and principles, we profess our unabated loyalty.

But because of the obvious difficulty this placed on the Old School Presbyterians in the South, the Assembly added language that clarified that the "Federal Government" referred to was not "any particular administration, or the peculiar opinions of any particular party." Instead, it meant "the central administration . . . appointed and inaugurated according to the forms prescribed in the Constitution of the United States . . ."

Even with this modified language the Spring Resolutions set the Old School church on a course of division. In fact, one New School Presbyterian newspaper could not help note, with a good deal of sarcasm, that the Old School in 1861 had in effect done to its southern synods and presbyteries what it had done in 1837 to the synods of New York and Ohio. It might seem "revolutionary" to insist that no one be allowed a seat at future General Assemblies without "*first taking the oath of allegiance to our Government*," but certainly the "successors of the men of '37 and '38" could overcome "any constitutional scruples they might cherish on the subject." The editor added that "the excision of the rebellious synods of '61 would be a far clearer vindication of the loyalty of the church to the government, than the excision of the four Synods in '37 was of loyalty to the Confession of Faith."

Of course, the Old School had not cut off the synods of the South. But the Spring Resolutions made it inevitable that southern Old School Presbyterians would withdraw and form a regional branch of the Old School church. On December 4, 1861, the southern Old School church held its first General Assembly in Augusta, Georgia, and consisted of ten synods, forty-five presbyteries, 840 ministers, and approximately seventy-two thousand communicant members.

The Old School Presbyterians were one of the last denominations to split along regional and political lines. Despite the New School's derision at the expense of the Old School's woes, the New School had already divided four years earlier between the North and South when, after constant pressure to declare slavery sinful, six New School synods and twenty-one presbyteries in the South formed the United Synod of the Presbyterian Church. Between 1857 and 1861, then, the Presbyterian Church in the U.S.A., already divided between the Old and New School branches, was split again with New School and Old School denominations in both the North and the South. In each case, the moral and political controversies that were dividing the United States overwhelmed the Presbyterian consensus that had developed after 1837. Indeed, the debates that added to the division of American Presbyterianism would be decisive for the witness and aims of Presbyterians not only during the Civil War but also in subsequent decades.

Doubly Divided

The issues that fueled the regional divisions of the New and Old School churches said a great deal about the character of each denomination. For New School Presbyterians, whose roots were in the revivals and moral reforms of the Second Great Awakening, it made sense that slavery would be decisive, since the abolition of trading and owning African-Americans was one of the chief moral crusades of the revivalists and the voluntary associations they inspired. For the Old School, which had the reputation for devoting careful attention to constitutional detail, predictably the political issue of preserving the Union, not slavery, was pivotal to the split between its northern and southern branches. In each case, Presbyterians ended up using theological insight to support political preference.

As early as 1818 the Presbyterian Church took a firm stand opposing slavery. The circumstance that called for the church's attention was the sale of a slave by a slaveholder, both of whom were Presbyterians in good standing, but disagreed on the desirability of the sale—the slave opposing, the master supporting.

In response to this case, the General Assembly declared that the "voluntary enslaving of one part of the human race by another" was a "gross violation of the most precious and sacred rights of human nature," "utterly inconsistent with the law of God, which requires us to love our neighbor as ourselves," and "totally irreconcilable with the spirit and principles of the gospel of Christ." The declaration went on to assert that slavery created "a paradox in the moral system," since it exhibited "rational, accountable, and immortal beings in such circumstances as scarcely to leave them the power of moral action," and as "dependent on the will of others whether they shall receive religious instruction; whether they shall know and worship the true God; whether they shall enjoy the ordinances of the gospel; whether they shall perform the duties and cherish the endearments of husbands and wives, parents and children, neighbors and friends . . ."

The Assembly's statement conceded that the "evils" of slavery were not always evident. Still, the slave was "deprived of his natural right," and "degraded as a human being. . . ." For these reasons, the Assembly advised American Presbyterians "to correct the errors of former times, and as speedily as possible to efface this blot on our holy religion, and to obtain the complete abolition of slavery throughout Christendom, and, if possible, throughout the whole world."

Having denounced slavery in clear terms, though not calling it explicitly a sin that deserved church discipline, the 1818 General Assembly resisted a call for immediate emancipation. Such an act would likely have been radical and disrupted the social order. But the statement did call for a "total abolition of slavery" as quickly as regard for the public welfare "truly and *indispensably* demands."

This declaration, of course, came almost two decades before the division between the Old and New Schools, and so reflected a Presbyterian consensus that was congenial to the northern parts of the church but out of step with southern Presbyterian quarters, which, in 1818, were hardly organized or vocal.

The loss of unanimity on the question of slavery became especially apparent during the controversies of the 1830s when the antislavery movement, through the efforts of such famous abolitionists as William Lloyd Garrison and support from revivalists including Charles Finney, became more radical by demanding immediate emancipation. Some prominent New School Presbyterians, including Lyman Beecher, favored gradual manumission, but others such as Theodore Dwight Weld and Albert Barnes pushed for more decisive action.

Many commissioners to the 1836 General Assembly feared a split in the church over slavery. As it turned out, the abolitionists were not as numerous or as well organized as those fears suggested. Still, during the year leading up to the exscinding acts of 1837, three of the four synods that the Old School eventually expelled had passed resolutions that called for the discipline of slaveholders. The urgent and aggressive nature of some Presbyterian opposition to slavery may very well have helped a majority of southerners to be more willing to condemn the errors of the New England theology (especially its ideas about the freedom of the will as an important factor in opposition to slavery) and to recognize the value of division between the Old and New School Presbyterians.

After the division of 1837 and 1838, Presbyterian opposition to slavery assumed a different and less urgent character. For the New School, slavery was a subject that came up repeatedly at its General Assemblies, from 1838 on. Because of the presence of southern New Schoolers at these meetings, and owing to a desire to keep the church together, the New School during its first years as a denomination left the matter to local synods and presbyteries and refused to make a declaration at the level of the General Assembly. Some in the North grew frustrated with the church's silence, and by 1846 the New School did condemn the institution of slavery. But it neglected to adopt a policy about individual slaveholders, again hoping to maintain the unity of the church. The New School's failure to take a more radical stance was one of the factors that contributed to the Congregationalists' (who were openly abolitionist) decision in 1852 to abandon the Plan of Union and break their remaining ties with Presbyterians.

Yet, just a year later the New School, perhaps stung by Congregationalist criticism, decided to come to some resolution on slavery. In 1853 the General Assembly received a request to form a committee to study the situation in the southern churches with regard to slavery and its effects on Presbyterians. But southerners perceived this suggestion to be inquisitorial in nature, and the motion did not receive adequate support to yield the proposed study. A similar measure came to the Assembly in 1855, this time having enough votes to create the committee.

But the subsequent report, not surprisingly, proved to be divisive and objectionable to the southern New Schoolers. In response, the Presbytery of Lexington in 1857 notified the General Assembly that southern Presbyterians held slaves "from principle" and saw no contradiction from Scripture. The implied threat from Kentucky New Schoolers did not stop the 1857 Assembly from adopting a report, by a vote of 169 to 26, that "disapproved and earnestly condemned" the position of the Presbytery of Lexington, and declared that such "doctrines and practice" would not be tolerated within the New School church.

In response, twenty-two ministers, all from the South, filed a protest, explaining that this action "degraded the whole Southern Church" and would mean the "virtual exscinding of the southern synods and presbyteries," and threatened the "union of these United States." In turn, this protest by the southern New Schoolers became the basis for their withdrawal in 1857 to form the United Synod of the Presbyterian Church. At this point there were three separate expressions of the Presbyterian Church in the U.S.A.

Old School Presbyterians managed to avoid formal division within their church over slavery, but their opinions were nevertheless as divided as their official statements were perplexing. The Old School contained some abolitionists, mainly in the North and West, plus some who defended slavery as a valuable institution and certainly not condemned by Scripture, and others who, while conceding that the Bible did not forbid slavery thought, that the institution as practiced by the South was morally repugnant. Debates among these various positions could be intense at times, but were generally contained at the local level within synods and presbyteries. In 1845 these arguments did percolate up to the General Assembly, which issued a statement that was generally acceptable to all except the radical abolitionists. The question addressed in the Old School Assembly's resolution was simply: "Do the Scriptures teach that the holding of slaves, without regard to circumstances, is a sin, the renunciation of which, should be made a condition of membership in the church of Christ?" The commissioners' answer was equally direct:

> It is impossible to answer this question in the affirmative, without contradicting some of the plainest declarations in the Word of God. That slavery existed in the days of Christ and his Apostles, is an admitted fact. . . . This Assembly cannot, therefore, denounce the holding of slaves as necessarily a heinous and scandalous sin, calculated to bring upon the Church the curse of God, without charging the Apostles of Christ with conniving at such sin, introducing into the church such sinners, and thus bringing upon them the curse of the Almighty.

Old School Presbyterians did not want to be misunderstood, however. They conceded that there was "evil connected with slavery," and that the South tolerated "defective and oppressive laws" to regulate the institution. The Assembly's statement, furthermore, should not be read "as countenancing the idea that masters may regard their servants as mere property, not as human beings, rational, accountable, immortal." The point was that "since Christ and his inspired Apostles did not make the holding of slaves a bar to communion, we, as a court of Christ, have no authority to do so." At the same time, as desirable as it might be to ameliorate the condition of the slaves or to remove slavery from the states, "these objects . . . can never be secured by ecclesiastical legislation" or by "indiscriminate denunciations against the slaveholders" like those common to "modern abolitionists." By a vote of 164 to 12, the Assembly passed two motions, one declaring that slavery was "no bar to Christian communion," and the other that any petitions seeking to constitute slavery a matter of discipline would not be welcome, since it would divide the church.

Six protesters signed a complaint observing that the Old School's resolutions contradicted the General Assembly's 1818 statement that condemned slavery. One commissioner proposed at the convening of the 1846 General Assembly that the Old School take steps that would bridge the differences between the antislavery statement of 1818 and the Assembly's 1845 stance of toleration. The specifics of this recommendation ranged from the Assembly calling for a day of prayer and fasting, and declaring that slavery should end, to forbidding ministers from holding slaves and reaffirming the statement of 1818.

Other commissioners objected that any such action would be easily distorted among the public at large. Still others argued that the 1818 and 1845 statements were not inconsistent because it was plausible to regard slavery as an evil that should be removed but not declare it to be a sin in and of itself. What the 1846 Assembly finally resolved was a clarification that asserted, "the action of the General Assembly of 1845 is not understood by this Assembly to deny or rescind the testimony that has been uttered by the General Assembly previous to that date." The Old School tried awkwardly, then, to maintain that slavery was an evil institution but that slaveholding itself was not a bar to communion in the church.

This was the last action that the Old School General Assembly would take on slavery, even though the issue would not go away. Several synods and presbyteries sent overtures to the Assembly asking for better clarification of the two seemingly contradictory statements—without success. Meanwhile, the politics and morality of slavery continued to affect the affairs of synods and presbyteries. For instance, the Synod of the Northwest engaged in a lengthy dispute throughout the 1850s over the location of a seminary to serve the region. However, the placement of the school was virtually a pawn in a larger contest between opponents and supporters of slavery. But the 1840s were the period of the Old School's most sustained attention to the topic, and the delicate balance its General Assemblies achieved was sufficient to prevent slavery from dividing the church.

What did eventually contribute to the breakup of the Old School was not slavery but controversy over the politics of the United States. The two main political parties available to Presbyterians at the time of the division of 1837 and 1838, the Whigs and Democrats, attracted Old Schoolers to each, largely along regional lines.

The Democrats were largely a party of farmers and other agricultural interests, opposed to the growth and centralization of the government, and skeptical of moral crusades that interfered with personal liberties. The Whigs favored a system of economic and political consolidation that would improve efficiency and strengthen the nation, while also advocating standards of public virtue necessary for a free society to avoid licentiousness.

Old Schoolers could be found on both sides of these political arguments. But in the 1850s, slavery and its expansion into the territories rattled the relative tranquility of this two-party system. The Whigs divided over slavery, with many of the party's southerners eventually aligning with the Democratic Party. In the North, the Republican Party, formed in 1854, eventually attracted former Whigs. But during the 1856 and 1860 presidential contests, as candidates debated the relative powers of the states versus the federal government, as well as the controversial issue of slavery's extension outside the South, various political parties emerged to represent different perspectives on the emerging regional division between the North and the South.

The election of Abraham Lincoln in 1860 on the Republican platform of opposition to the expansion of slavery into the territories may have yielded clarity for the confused state of America's party politics, but it also heightened regional disputes. Many Old Schoolers in the North and in the border states counseled moderation as a means of preserving the Union, still hoping that states would retain their sovereignty and that the federal government would not encroach on states' authority.

But in the deep South, the election of a Republican known for outspoken opposition to slavery (though by no means a radical), and the apparent threat of a federal government that would try to end the southern way of life, caused Old School Presbyterians to follow the lead of southern politicians calling for secession. Indicative of the southern Old School frame of mind was James Henley Thornwell's sermon, delivered only a few weeks after Lincoln's victory, in which he warned, "The Union, which our fathers designed to be perpetual, is on the verge of dissolution." Thornwell added that no matter whether the path to preserving the South's institutions went "through a baptism of blood," "we shall love [Our State] all the more tenderly and the more intensely, the more bitterly she suffers."

By the time of the Old School's General Assembly, the antagonism that Lincoln's election seemed to signal had become real with the political division between North and South. On December 20, 1860, South Carolina seceded from the United States, and five months later the opening battle of the Civil War transpired with the attack on Fort Sumter, on April 12, 1861, in Charleston, South Carolina. In this context, the Spring Resolutions calling on the Old School church to side with the federal government were analogous to throwing gas on a fire already out of control. Consequently, just as slavery had split the New School in 1857 between its northern and southern wings, so now allegiance to the federal government versus the rights of states split the Old School. The bloom that had grown with the flowering of American Presbyterianism had by 1861 almost completely faded.

The Politics of Presbyterian Unity

To say that the Civil War preoccupied the attention of Presbyterians would be an overstatement. Each of the four Presbyterian branches either tried to maintain its agencies and activities—or in the case of the new denominations in the South, the United Synod and the Old School church, attempted to establish new ventures to carry on the work of the church at large. Obviously, the situation at the local level, whether for presbyteries or congregations, differed depending on their proximity to the battle lines. But for churches far from the war, the week-in, week-out work of worship and proclamation carried on.

Possibly the greatest difference between wartime and peace was the diversion of ministers from local congregations to service as military chaplains. Even those pastors not commissioned as chaplains, but close to the battles, would regularly conduct services for soldiers whenever possible. The war did alter church life. At the same time, the Civil War was also responsible for changing the institutional character of each Presbyterian church, prompting Presbyterians to adopt positions so extreme that their churches appeared to be more representative of their regions and the accompanying politics than of a theological tradition or ecclesiastical heritage.

For the southern church, the hardening of political opinions meant a shift on slavery. The simplest way of describing the change is to say that what had once been a permissible institution, a practice clearly not forbidden in Scripture, had become a system that the Bible approved as the basis for a good and orderly society. Thomas Smyth, a pastor in Charleston, South Carolina, referred to "The constitution of society with diversities in rank and condition, including bond and free; and with limitations of rights, so as to secure the most perfect liberty possible to man as sinful and selfish; distinctly pointed out and provided for in God's word—a slaveocracy, God's chosen model and illustration." Or as a North Carolina Presbyterian newspaper had it, "the institution of slavery is divinely recognized and sanctioned. . . . We are upholding and defending a sacred trust, committed to us by the providence of God."

Before the war, southern Presbyterians likely held these same convictions but would have been reluctant to express them so candidly or aggressively in the presence of fellow church members who disagreed. But with the removal of the opposing side in the debate over slavery, southern Presbyterians were free to vent their bluntest statements both about the politics of the institution and its scriptural warrant.

At the same time, the hardening of southern resolve on slavery did not diminish the desire of many ministers and church members for reform of the institution. Several Presbyterian ministers, such as James A. Lyon of Mississippi, introduced arguments that would curtail and eventually end the abuses that often accompanied the institution. He wrote, for instance, that "there is nothing in our legislation, so far as we know, that recognizes marriage between the slaves; or that prohibits fornication, adultery, bigamy, incest, or even rape among them." He concluded this was an "outrage upon the laws of God, both natural and revealed."

In addition to seeking a reform of slaves' domestic relations, Lyon advocated that blacks and whites gather together for worship, and that classes be established for catechizing African-Americans. He also favored a repeal of laws that prohibited slaves from learning to read and write. Lyon's proposals received consideration at the 1862 General Assembly (Old School) and from numerous presbyteries and synods in the South.

Lincoln's Emancipation Proclamation, however, pulled the plug on deliberations to adopt a formal policy on the reform of slavery. Instead, the 1864 Assembly asserted that it was the "peculiar mission of the Southern Church to conserve the institution of slavery, and to make it a blessing both to master and slave." By the time the 1865 Assembly met, the subject was settled, since the South had surrendered and slavery was illegal. 1865

Another important change for southern Presbyterians by the close of the Civil War was the end of the Old School/New School antagonism. Here the South's growing resolve in the defense of its "peculiar" way of life almost completely obscured the original theological and ecclesiastical disagreements that had led to the division of 1837 and 1838. Of the six synods that left the New School church to form the United Synod of the Presbyterian Church in 1857, three were within the bounds of the Confederacy (the other three were in the border states).

The idea of a merger between the South's Old and New School Presbyterians originated as early as the 1861 Assembly of the Old School. But leaders such as Thornwell opposed it on grounds of the Old School's original concerns about Calvinist theology and Presbyterian polity. Thornwell's death in 1862 removed a significant source of opposition, and talk of union gathered momentum at the 1863 Assembly when Old School commissioners appointed a committee, headed by Robert Dabney, to confer with a similar committee appointed by the United Synod. The joint committee proposed the construction of a statement that would "manifest our hearty agreement," "remove suspicions and offenses," and "restore full confidence between brethren."

South Carolinians, led by John B. Adger, adamantly opposed the planned union "except upon a formal and distinct repudiation by [the United Synod] of every one of the new school errors which have been entertained by those with whom they so long continued to maintain the closest fellowship." But other conservatives including Dabney feared that if the union failed, the United Synod would establish its own seminary with professors who would likely propagate defective views.

A union would end the need for a United Synod seminary and encourage all southern Presbyterian candidates for the ministry to attend Old School institutions that Dabney believed to be above reproach theologically. As a result, the Old School Assembly decided in 1864 by a vote of fifty-three to seven to unite with the New School "on the basis of our existing standards" without any other statements or qualifications.

The United Synod was unable to meet as a whole, but the presbyteries in Virginia, Kentucky, and Missouri endorsed the union. In Tennessee only some of the presbyteries approved merger. Others pursued reunion with the northern New School church, which after the Civil War began to send northern ministers to Presbyterian congregations in Eastern Tennessee, where ministers loyal to the South had departed for calls in the now united southern Presbyterian Church. The newly united southern church took the name Presbyterian Church in the U.S.

Northern Presbyterians followed a similar path to reunion, though taking longer. After the departure of southerners in 1857 and 1861, the Old and New School Presbyterians in the North came to like-minded convictions in their condemnation of slavery and support for the federal government.

The case of the Old School was more dramatic since its change of mind involved a repudiation of former arguments. At the Assembly of 1862, the Old School once again affirmed its support for the federal government in terms that suggested sympathy for the rights of states was a form of faithlessness to "all authority, human and divine, to which they [owe] subjection." Old School presbyteries and synods followed suit with affirmations of support for the president and his conduct of the war.

A presbytery in Wisconsin called on its churches to "use their influence, in all lawful ways, to induce our able-bodied young men" to accept Lincoln's petition for three hundred thousand soldiers. Likewise, the Synod of Buffalo declared it a religious duty to support the government even if it meant "laying down our lives in its defence." The support was by no means unanimous throughout the northern Old School church. But it was sufficiently strong that at the 1863 Assembly, despite a lengthy debate about whether to fly the Stars and Stripes above the church where the Assembly met, the American flag flew with the support of a sizeable majority of commissioners.

The Assembly of 1863 was also the occasion when the Old School began to address the vexing question of slavery. At that meeting, the Old School commissioners reaffirmed the language of the 1818 Assembly in condemning slavery, while finessing its previous declarations of 1845 and 1846. Still much more conservative than the rest of the North, the Old School moved to a more mainstream position the following year. The 1864 commissioners issued a statement that declared, "*the time has come, in the providence of God, when it is His will that every vestige of human slavery among us should be effaced, and that every Christian man should address himself with industry and earnestness to his appropriate part in the performance of this great duty.*" The Old School's support for this declaration was almost unanimous. It constituted a significant shift for a church that had previously refused to consider the question.

But the Old School's change of mind was not agreeable to Presbyterians in the border states of Maryland, Missouri, and Kentucky, which had remained part of the Union but whose citizens had strong sympathies with the South. These Presbyterians were not persuaded by the resolutions of the Old School Assemblies and often issued declarations that protested the politicization of their communion.

The difficulty for border-state Presbyterians became particularly acute at the 1865 Old School Assembly, which met almost a month after President Lincoln's assassination. Because of the alarm and indignation many northern Presbyterians felt over the loss of a revered statesman, the terms the Old School established for planting churches and receiving ministers into fellowship were cast in a tone of retaliation.

On the one hand, the Old School laid claim to the entire Confederacy as the territory for its domestic missions and would recognize as part of its fellowship only congregations and members that had remained loyal to the federal government. It directed its presbyteries in considering any southern ministers or ministerial candidates for reception in the church to examine them for their loyalty to the United States and their condemnation of slavery. The Old School even instructed its presbyteries to discipline any Old School minister who may have been sent away "beyond the jurisdiction of the United States" by civil authorities because of his disloyalty to the federal government. These ministers should be suspended from the ministry until the presbyteries obtained "satisfactory evidence of . . . repentance."

Although level-headed participants such as Charles Hodge could observe that the 1865 Assembly had "transcended its power," Presbyterians in Kentucky were not so dispassionate in their reaction. The Presbytery of Louisville at its next meeting issued the *Declaration and Testimony*, a seventy-two-page rebuttal of the Assembly's actions. The substance of the presbytery's objection was the decidedly political nature of the Assembly's resolutions. These were matters that properly belonged to the "civil commonwealth" and were not settled by the teaching of Scripture.

Stuart Robinson, the able defender of the doctrine of the spirituality of the church, undoubtedly had a major role in drafting the presbytery's pamphlet. But beyond objecting to the Assembly's decisions, the *Declaration and Testimony* stated that its signers would not recognize the authority of the Old School church as long as its resolutions were in place, and that they would not support the agencies of the General Assembly, such as missions and theological education. Louisville's statement gained the support of the presbytery and barely missed receiving the Synod of Kentucky's approval. Meanwhile, the *Declaration and Testimony* attracted signatures from members of the Synod of Baltimore, and a significant number of the Synod of Missouri's members.

Rather than attempting to pacify the situation, the General Assembly of 1866 rose to the same level of defiance that Louisville had exhibited. The first order of business was what to do with the commissioners from the Synod of Kentucky. With doubts about their loyalty to the federal government and their views on slavery because of the *Declaration and Testimony*, Kentucky commissioners were denied seats at the Assembly. In further deliberations, the Assembly received a proposal to dissolve the Presbytery of Louisville, create a new one, and force the old members to submit to examinations before being admitted to the new body. Important church leaders recognized the injustice of ruling on these Louisville ministers without giving them a hearing. Consequently, a milder action was proposed that condemned the Louisville statement, deferred final action on it until 1867, and gave its signers a year to consider their course of action.

Back in Kentucky during the following meeting of Synod, the body divided between those loyal to the General Assembly and those who would not abide its resolutions of 1865. The pro-southern synod would in 1867 join the Presbyterian Church in the U.S. A similar situation developed in Missouri where the Synod also split, and the pro-South synod there waited until 1873 to join the southern Presbyterian Church.

Clearly the war to preserve the union of the nation could not maintain the unity of the nation's Presbyterians. But union of sorts did emerge for Presbyterians after the Civil War. Just as American and regional politics had encouraged the merger of the southern New School and Old School Presbyterians in 1864, similar developments harmonized the divided Presbyterians in the North. During the Civil War both the northern Old and New School assemblies had shown interest in union, beginning to exchange fraternal delegates as early as 1862.

As Lewis G. Vander Velde rightly observed in his study of Presbyterians during the Civil War, the Old School's support for the federal government and its denunciation of slavery were responsible for the cessation of New School hostility. In fact, at its 1864 Assembly, the New School offered "heartfelt Christian salutations" to the Old School church and also provided the rationale for union: "the tendencies of modern society, the condition of Protestant Christianity, the increase of infidelity, the progress of Romanism, and the present prospective state of our country, afford powerful arguments against further subdivisions, and in favor of that union and unity of the Church into which it is to grow. . ."

A year later, the New School fraternal delegate to the Old School Assembly could report back to his fellow Presbyterians that although the Old School had been "less prompt than some in reaching their position," they were now "surpassed by none" in "declarations of unfaltering, patriotic, and Christian devotion to the Government and institutions of the country." The withdrawal of the border state synods and presbyteries undoubtedly helped this transformation of the Old School. And when the southern church in 1865 declared that the Old School church of the North was "simply . . . a separate and distinct ecclesiastical body" with no "higher claims on our courtesy" than any other northern Presbyterian church, hopes of reestablishing the pre-war Old School church vanished.

At the 1866 Assemblies of both the northern Old and New School churches, each of which met in St. Louis, the commissioners approved the appointment of committees to recommend the best way forward to reunion. The following year the Plan of Union was presented to each Assembly and received hearty approval from the New School and only mild opposition from some of the older members of the Old School, with a determination by each party to vote on union at the 1868 Assemblies. At this point, the only opposition to reunion surfaced, with Charles Hodge leading the opposition. His main objection was that the New School had a different standard for subscribing to the Westminster Standards, and that this defect was evident in the unwillingness of the New School ever to repudiate the views held by Albert Barnes, Lyman Beecher, and George Duffield. As eloquent as Hodge was, his objections did little to derail the proposed plan.

At the 1868 Assemblies, the New School voted unanimously to send the plan to the presbyteries for their consideration. Hodge's arguments, along with other Old School holdouts, prevented so decisive a victory in the Old School church, but the plan was still approved by vote of 188 to 70. The response from the presbyteries was equally decisive. Of the Old School's 144 presbyteries, only three cast votes against reunion. The New School's presbyteries were unanimously behind the plan.

In 1869 each Assembly ratified the previous year's decision. Again the New School was unanimous, and the opposition in the Old School dwindled from seventy to nine. Having entered the Civil War era divided between the Old and New Schools, American Presbyterians left the period still divided but now according to region, not theology, or polity. The last initials of the two branches of American Presbyterianism were telling: the northern church's name was the Presbyterian Church in the U.S.A., and the southern church was the Presbyterian Church in the U.S.

The Withering of Presbyterianism

With the reunion of the Old and New Schools in the North in 1869, American Protestantism began a period characterized by interdenominational cooperation and church union (see chapter 9). But the division between the North and South would be hardest for Presbyterians to overcome. The northern church would be able to accommodate Cumberland Presbyterians (1906), Welsh Calvinistic Methodists (1920), and the heirs of Presbyterian Seceders in the United Presbyterian Church of North America (1958). But northern and southern Presbyterians could not accept each other until 1983.

Most observers both inside and outside the Presbyterian fold have regarded the separation of American Presbyterianism along regional lines as unfortunate and a detriment to each church's witness. Some of these observations lament any barrier that prevents Christ's followers from being one, especially when they bear the same denominational name. Even worse is a division among Christians based on national politics rather than theological error, idolatrous worship, or a lack of discipline. After 1869 American Presbyterianism still possessed many fine pastors, gifted theologians, courageous missionaries, and influential agencies. But after 1869 American Presbyterianism was captive to the policies of the state in ways that would shift the emphasis more toward being American than being Presbyterian.

Because of the trauma resulting from the Civil War, the loss of close to seven hundred thousand lives, the emancipation of close to four million slaves, the assassination of a president, and the expansion of the federal government's power, changes to American Presbyterianism would have been extraordinarily difficult to avoid. Still, as understandable as it was to be caught up in the politics and morality of the Civil War, equally momentous were the changes to American Presbyterianism.

Prior to the war the Presbyterian churches, both New School and Old School, had flourished in remarkable ways compared with the first 125 years of American Presbyterianism's history. Signs of intellectual maturity, reinvigoration of Presbyterian worship, and attention to the genius of Presbyterian polity were evident, if not in abundance, between 1840 and 1857. To be sure, these aspects of church life would continue to be part of the northern and southern churches' life and witness.

But after 1869 these singularly Presbyterian features would be subordinate to those concerns that united Presbyterians to American Protestants with similar allegiance to the United States. As Vander Velde put it, the "great war" had turned Presbyterian minds "from their ecclesiastical differences to their common interest in the salvation of the Union." As important as the Civil War was, then, for preserving the Union, the war was equally destructive of the Presbyterian faith and practice, both Old and New School, that had flourished during the middle decades of the nineteenth century.

PART 3

1869–2006

9

Ecumenism and Progress

On April 29, 1869, the year of the Old School-New School reunion, Presbyterian missionary Sheldon Jackson stood on the bank of the Missouri River overlooking Sioux City, Iowa. As he gazed westward, the thirty-five-year-old Princeton seminary graduate committed himself to "win the West for Christ." Appointed the "Superintendent for Missions for Western Iowa, Nebraska, Dakota, Idaho, Montana, Wyoming, and Utah," Jackson followed the construction of the transcontinental railroad, fighting "the tidal wave of wickedness, the cesspools of iniquity, and the desperadoes," as he spread the gospel and established churches.

As he later wrote, "it was going out to the churchless, Sabbathless, growing communities on the frontier—to the world, lawless, gambling, saloon-cursed mining camps where gravitate the most abandoned, hardened, and desperate characters of the country." Within a decade he had established almost a hundred churches as well as a number of schools. By 1884, he turned his attention to Alaska, where he founded more churches and schools.

Nicknamed the "Bishop of All Beyond" and the "Apostle to Alaska," Jackson, for his part, credited the reunion of northern Presbyterianism as a vital ingredient to his success. In 1897 the Presbyterian Church honored him for his labors by electing him moderator of the General Assembly.

Jackson's labors in the western frontier symbolize Presbyterian optimism in the late nineteenth century. After the Civil War, America entered the Gilded Age. Industrial development, combined with scientific and technological progress, promised to usher in an age of opportunity as the nation continued to push westward. Reunited Presbyterians saw themselves positioned to serve the spiritual needs of the nation with a spirit of self-confidence, and for good reason. The Reunion Fund, established in 1870 with an ambitious goal of raising $5 million, exceeded expectations with receipts of $7 million in gifts to the church.

As Old School and New School church boards eagerly merged, the church took on greater organizational efficiency that enabled its mission to expand on several fronts, including higher education, Sunday school, and missionary work both domestic and abroad. Presbyterians met the challenges of the age with a confident, can-do spirit. As Sheldon Jackson's success indicates, it was as close to a golden age in missions as American Presbyterians were to experience.

Organizational Consolidation

In the years following the Presbyterian reunion in the North, the former differences between the Old and New Schools assumed declining significance. In George Marsden's words, "Disputes over moral depravity, limited atonement, and mediate imputation lost much of their urgency in the midst of national crisis." The perils posed to Christian civilization in America (Sabbath desecration, intemperate use of alcohol, and assaults to the stability of the Christian home) not only sustained the Presbyterian reunion; beyond that it urged greater Presbyterian cooperation with other American Protestants.

It was therefore for the welfare of the country that Presbyterians joined the Evangelical Alliance (formed in 1867) and the Presbyterian Alliance (in 1875). The Evangelical Alliance was founded originally in London in 1846 but failed to gain an American branch until almost three decades later. Its purpose was to bring "individual Christians into closer fellowship and cooperation on the basis of the spiritual union which already exists in the vital relation of Christ to the members of his body." The timing of the Alliance's American arrival was more than coincidental. Thanks to a perceived threat to American institutions that the Civil War had exposed, Protestants believed closer cooperation was necessary to preserve the religious foundation of the republic.

The leaders of the Evangelical Alliance in America included many prominent Presbyterians. In fact, the reunion of the Old and New Schools greatly facilitated support for the Alliance because many of the impulses behind Presbyterian union were also at work in evangelical cooperation. As the committee on the reunion of the Old and New Schools put it, "the welfare of the whole country, and the kingdom of our Lord in all the earth" required merger of the two denominations as well as cooperation among Protestants.

Founded a few years later, in 1875, the Presbyterian Alliance was designed to accomplish under Presbyterian auspices what the Evangelical Alliance was doing for all Protestants. But the Presbyterian organization was also devised to include those Presbyterian and Reformed denominations that might balk at cooperation with non-Presbyterians. The Presbyterian Alliance was a way then to bring these reluctant denominations to the broader task of fighting atheism, religious infidelity, immorality, materialism, and Roman Catholicism.

The motivation behind the Presbyterian and Evangelical Alliances was for what James McCosh, another Scottish Presbyterian minister summoned to America to preside over the College of New Jersey, called "the moral improvement of mankind." These motives only intensified during the decades after the Civil War, when industrialization and urbanization seemed to threaten the social and religious order that Protestants had previously helped to establish before the war.

Adding to this sense of urgency was the increasing number of Roman Catholics arriving in the United States to live in the growing cities and work in the nation's new factories. Protestants had already cultivated a firm bias against Roman Catholics, both for theological and political reasons, but the postwar immigration fanned the flames of anti-Catholicism. Papal pronouncements against democracy and religious liberty in the *Syllabus of Errors* (1864) and the claim of papal infallibility at the First Vatican Council demonstrated the dangers of Protestant divisions and the need for forming a united Protestant front against what many regarded as "the Man of Sin." Altogether, the dangers of materialism, skepticism, infidelity, and Catholicism persuaded Presbyterians to work with other Protestants on the basis of their common convictions.

Lefferts A. Loetscher's characterization of the reunion of the Old and New Schools sums up well the sentiments that led to so many cooperative endeavors among Presbyterians specifically and Protestants more generally. "Reflecting the spirit of the times," he wrote, "the Church was becoming increasingly responsive to everything that made for effectiveness of action, and correspondingly allergic to any theoretical considerations that might hamper its vigorous activism."

Reinforcing this mandate was a growing awareness of the Presbyterian Church's national identity. The United States was "the land of the future" because Protestant convictions were thoroughly incorporated in the life and spirit of the country. The nation itself, for James McCosh, embodied precisely what the Evangelical Alliance was trying to accomplish, namely, a pervasive unity of evangelical spirit. For that reason he urged his fellow Presbyterians to support the Alliance to "combine the scattered energies of Christendom all over the world."

Presbyterians provided more than support; they also supplied much of its administrative staffing. William E. Dodge Sr., an active New School Presbyterian elder, presided over the American Evangelical Alliance, and Samuel Irenaeus Prime, an Old School minister and editor of the influential *New York Observer*, shaped the direction of the new cooperative venture. Presbyterian involvement in these interdenominational endeavors prompted one contemporary to conclude that Presbyterians were "leaders in the matter from the first."

These early stages of Presbyterian interest in ecumenical activities had two important effects on the northern Presbyterian Church. First, ecumenism reshaped Presbyterian notions of the mission of the church. In the face of a nation that appeared to be veering away from Christian control, Presbyterians began to set aside theological differences over soteriology, the sacraments, and church order, and they rallied to the nation-state as an area of common endeavor and sure means of preserving Protestant hegemony. Plans for Protestant cooperative campaigns lacked systematic treatments of the doctrine of the church and unity in Christ. Instead, what emerged were general notions that all Christians should be one, linked with efforts to ease Protestant fears about the threats to the stability of American society.

Put another way, the late-nineteenth-century ecumenical impulse was a manifestation of the social gospel, whether it deserved to be designated by capital letters or not. Of course, substantial numbers of Presbyterians continued to believe in the necessity of individual conversion and regeneration. But often the salvation of individuals was a means toward the end of shoring up public order. More important, the areas in which Protestants agreed to cooperate overwhelmingly concerned matters of public morality. Observance of the Sabbath, consumption of alcohol, labor and management issues, and the dangers of infidelity, materialism, and Roman Catholicism were all issues that had a direct bearing on public life and became the criteria for judging whether or not the nation was Christian.

In turn these concerns moved Presbyterians to conceive of the work of the church more as social than spiritual. It was the New School's idea of the church prevailing over the Old School's. Public morality and civic righteousness pushed aside Word and sacrament. Practical results rather than doctrinal standards became the measurement of churches. The culmination of this outlook was the founding in 1908 of the Federal Council of Churches, which also depended heavily on Presbyterian leadership. At the inaugural meeting in Philadelphia's Academy of Music, the council elected William H. Roberts, the stated clerk of the PCUSA, as the chairman of the executive committee.

Second, ecumenism and its accompanying social and political concerns contributed to the bureaucratization and consolidation of the northern church. In fact, a significant factor in Protestant cooperation was the ideal of efficiency. If redundancy of Presbyterian, Baptist, and Methodist efforts was one reason for greater cooperation among the churches, the same principles within the church led to the consolidation of synodal and presbyterial efforts in central offices. As the American historian Samuel Haber wrote, the words "Efficient and good came closer to meaning the same thing [in the progressive era] than in any other period of American history."

Between 1870 and 1936 what James H. Moorhead, professor of church history at Princeton Seminary, called the "mystique of organizational efficiency" bedazzled Presbyterians even while the church went from a small set of national offices to an organizational behemoth. Scientific planning and business-like management began to characterize the boards and agencies of the church as the size of these institutions mushroomed.

For example, the Board of Domestic Missions doubled, with specialized ministries such as urban, rural, and Jewish missions. Presbyterian agencies inaugurated new programs to apply the gospel to all areas of life and improve the standard of living both in the United States and around the world, with the goal of building a Christian civilization. In order to coordinate these operations more effectively, the northern church greatly enlarged the powers and duties of the stated clerk, establishing it as a full-time position in 1894.

Thus the growth of church agencies transformed what had been a small collection of ministries rooted in the work of local churches, presbyteries, and synods into a corporate juggernaut where denominational agencies increasingly defined the identity and mission of the church. With the growth in the church bureaucracy, the identity of the Presbyterian Church after the war was shaped less and less by Old School and New School debates.

It is common to interpret the late nineteenth and early twentieth centuries as a time when Presbyterians polarized into two theologically antagonistic camps, one conservative and one modernist. The picture is more complicated than that, and Presbyterians actually experienced a remarkable degree of consolidation even as the theological fault lines were deepening. Former Old School and New School Presbyterians generally embraced these developments, and the "broadening church" that emerged was less the result of harmonizing competing visions than a testimony to the success of organizational efficiency and consolidation.

The accord between the two camps can be seen in the manner in which moderators were elected in the first dozen years after the reunion, carefully alternating between Old and New School appointments. By the time the practice ended with the election of consecutive New Schoolers, the distinct beliefs of the two schools were fading into Presbyterian history.

To be sure, there were times when the marriage was put to a severe test. Less successful, for example, was the effort to collaborate in a united theological journal. *The Presbyterian Review* began publication in 1880 as a joint effort between the Old School and the New School, with A. A. Hodge of Princeton and Charles Briggs of Union carefully appointed as co-editors. The ten-year history of the journal was often stormy, especially by 1888 when Briggs's antagonist, Benjamin B. Warfield, assumed the task of being his co-editor. The journal ceased publication a year later.

Southern Presbyterian Dissent

At the time that former northern Old Schoolers were giving overwhelming support to Protestant interdenominational alliances, this expansion of the mission and work of the church drew criticism. Several conservatives protested the diminishing regard for Presbyterian theology and the growth of a social definition of the church's mission. This criticism emerged primarily among southern Presbyterians. Their objections to evangelical cooperation involved political differences, of course, but they also revealed a divergent understanding of the church.

Southern Presbyterians took the lead in arguing for the wisdom of separate denominations. Toleration of diversity was accomplished easily enough by recognizing the difference between the visible and invisible church. While all believers were one spiritually in Christ and, therefore, members of the invisible church, they were not all members of the same institution. These Presbyterian critics of ecumenism were willing to recognize the legitimacy of other non-Presbyterian communions, even if in error, a principle they believed taught by the Reformation. In fact, one of the charges often hurled against interdenominational cooperation and ecumenism was that Protestants, in responding to the threat of Roman Catholicism, were merely creating their own pope. As Robert L. Dabney, professor of theology at Union Seminary (Richmond), wrote of the Presbyterian Alliance, "there is little difference between a pope in the singular and in the plural number. The essential doctrines of popery will appear."

Southern Presbyterian dissent registered an important point, namely, that the inclusive spirit which so often motivated Protestant ecumenism usually carried with it intolerance of those who dissented from union or cooperative enterprises, hence, the comparisons with the papacy.

Indeed, southern Presbyterian critics predicted the trajectory that would characterize Protestant ecumenism in the next century. With great insight, Dabney wrote that "the same argument which demands that Presbyterian churches must be unified in a visible centre, will necessarily be extended to all others recognized as true churches, though non-Presbyterian. . . . Thus will come about a still wider confederation, not Pan-Presbyterian, but Pan-Protestant; and the necessary condition of its existence will be precisely that combination of loose, unfaithful, *doctrinal* broad churchism, with tyrannical enforcement of outward union and uniformity, which now characterizes popery."

For Presbyterian opponents of church union, institutional cooperation and affiliation went hand in hand with organizational infallibility and the means to coerce or bind the conscience. For the only way to ensure such unity was through a power, usually centralized, that would exclude differences and enforce harmony. "The suppression of the truth, and the binding of the conscience," according to one critic, "are necessary consequences of every attempt to realise organic unity." Appeals to a broad doctrinal consensus were of little avail in persuading these Presbyterians of the benefits of union, because such a form of agreement was so broad as to prevent "differences of opinion from existing" and "men from thinking."

Protestant unity would ultimately result in the abolition of parties in the church and the prohibition of their views. Thus, Protestant ecumenism was, from these critics' perspective, a direct betrayal of Protestant convictions about the authority of Scripture and freedom of conscience. Conversely, the Presbyterian defense of denominationalism stemmed not merely from southern bitterness but from Protestant convictions about church power and the lordship of Christ.

This critique included two additional points that were telling for the Presbyterian controversies that would emerge after the First World War.

First, southerners identified the same sentiments animating both the Evangelical Alliance and the reunion of Old and New School Presbyterians in the North, namely, doctrinal indifferentism. According to one writer, "the broader the basis of union, the more lax and imperfect becomes the system of discipline and of doctrine." So too, Dabney argued that the kind of union proposed by the Evangelical Alliance and similar ecumenical efforts would inevitably result in "the Sadducean indifference to truth." Again with remarkable foresight, he also detected within the

176

union movement what would become the substance of liberal Protestant theology: under the guise of merely "adjusting" "old dogmas" to new philosophies, a minister subscribed to a Calvinistic creed all the while advancing " 'as explanation of it,' a false philosophy, which every intelligent Pelagian and even Socinian hailed as his own."

Underlying Dabney's critique of Protestant ecumenism was the idea that the church's primary responsibility was to bear witness to Christ and the gospel, thus the importance of sound preaching, correct teaching, and high standards for ordination. A minister, Dabney insisted, was bound to "declare 'the whole counsel of God' as he conscientiously understands it."

Second, opponents of church union argued that Presbyterian ecumenism undermined the corporate witness of the church. Ministers were bound to declare the counsel of God according to their honest conviction. Because the ministerial commission to proclaim the whole counsel of God was through the visible church, ministers were obligated to uphold the confessional standards of their denomination. A minister stands in the pulpit not as an individual but as an ordained minister from a particular communion.

"The public," Dabney wrote, "hears [the minister's] church in him." Therefore, officers had a duty to keep those out of the ministry who did not consent to the church's teaching. If they did not, if they lent any part of their "official weight or countenance to aid" in the proclamation of religious error, "contradicting in any point more or less essential that code of redeeming truth which Christ has committed" to them, they were guilty of being unfaithful to Christ. This is why a number of southern Presbyterians were so reluctant to enter into fellowship with non-Presbyterians or even with other, less rigorous Presbyterians, such as the northern church. Doctrinal laxity would compromise the corporate witness of the church and thereby render the church faithless.

Thus, two different understandings of the church were at work in deliberations about church unity and ecumenical relations, with the South maintaining the perspective characteristic of the Old School, and the North showing the triumph of the New School.

Advocates of interdenominational cooperation usually regarded the task of the church increasingly in social terms. The church was an agent of bringing Christian civilization to the United States, and beyond that to the world. The social understanding of the church sanctioned the cooperation of Protestants who had disparate views of the sacraments, sanctification, church government, ordination, and the decrees of God. Whether to baptize infants or adults made little difference when the mounting tensions between labor and management threatened national unity.

The other understanding held that the church was a spiritual institution. Its concerns went well beyond those of any particular nation, ethnic group, or class. The church's task was to proclaim the gospel, the good news that prepared souls less for this world but more for the world to come. This stress on the witness-bearing character of the church and its ministry required special vigilance in the oversight of the church's messengers. For this reason the effort to find the lowest common theological denominator among Protestants or even Presbyterians diminished what was the God-given duty of the church. Rather than overlooking differences about baptism, for instance, in order to join with Baptists in civic reform, Presbyterian confessionalists made infant baptism a mark of the church and its supporting theology a reason for opposing cooperative endeavors among evangelical Protestants.

Presbyterians and Progress

Accompanying and reinforcing the organizational consolidation and ecumenism of this period was the Presbyterian attraction, especially in the North, to the cultural ideal of progress. Presbyterians' first responses to this form of thought emerged in the context of evolution, when Charles Darwin published *The Origin of Species* in 1859.

Initially, Presbyterian reaction to Darwin was mixed, and he found critics and defenders. In "What is Darwinism?" Charles Hodge attacked Darwinism because it inevitably entailed a denial of both design and teleology in creation. "We cannot see how the theory of evolution can be reconciled with the declarations of Scripture."

At the same time, James McCosh at the college next to Princeton Seminary encouraged a qualified acceptance of Darwin's theories. "There is a wonderful correspondence or parallelism between Genesis and genealogy," he wrote, "between the written record and the record in stone." He went on to acknowledge "the need of a power above evolution to account for the beneficence of evolution." As teachers in the same town and worshipers in the same church, Hodge and McCosh are often cited as two contrasting Presbyterian reactions, the former denouncing Darwinism as atheism and the latter cautiously endorsing it as the divine method of providence.

There was less difference here, however, than a crude comparison of Hodge's and McCosh's statements suggested. Like McCosh, Hodge embraced concordist interpretations of the Genesis creation account. That is, he strove to harmonize his own interpretations of the Bible with the leading scientific results, even to the point of accommodating geological findings that concluded that the earth was much older than the six millennia that many theologians believed.

Hodge's successors at Princeton, including his son, A. A. Hodge, and Benjamin B. Warfield warmed up to evolutionary theory by dividing the science of evolution from the philosophy of evolution, and so defending a providential account of evolution as opposed to one ruled by randomness and chance. In 1886 the younger Hodge wrote that "we have no sympathy with those who maintain that scientific theories of evolution are necessarily atheistic." Warfield put it even more boldly when he claimed that Calvin's doctrine of creation, as it entailed God's work through secondary causes, was "not only evolutionism but pure evolutionism."

The ultimate effect of Darwinism on Presbyterians was subtler than debates over human origins and the harmony of biology and Genesis. For many Protestants in America, Presbyterians included, Darwin had become the denomination's Galileo, and his theories became the test for the willingness of the church to embrace change. Under the spell of Darwinism, Presbyterianism became synonymous with progress, and Presbyterian adjustment to the new science became a matter of denominational pride. As evolutionary theories gained greater acceptance in American colleges and universities, it was Presbyterians especially who embraced these claims. One Presbyterian minister observed that Presbyterians regarded intellectual progress with sympathy and encouragement: "no one can charge Presbyterians with standing in the way of any advance in knowledge." Presbyterianism itself was subject to evolution, he added, because it was progressing from one state to a more desired state.

The author of that assertion, Andrew C. Zenos, a professor of church history at the Presbyterian Theological Seminary of Chicago (formerly an Old School institution), conceded that Presbyterians had not always embraced a progressive spirit. One example was an antiquated insistence on "divine right" Presbyterianism, which falsely assumed that Presbyterian polity was biblically revealed, and thus had reached a fixed and final state. Zenos was pleased to see northern Presbyterians abandon that claim, thus opening themselves up to further development with "the hope of advancement of freedom and the abounding of the richer life."

Zenos's assessment came almost seventy years after the publication of Darwin's original findings, but it showed that evolution functioned more often as a metaphor for cultural advance than for a specific scientific discovery. Here the conclusion that Zenos attached to his 1937 book, *Presbyterianism in America*, shows how for several generations of Presbyterians after the Civil War, evolution underwrote progress and became synonymous with right-thinking Presbyterianism:

> The conclusion of the matter is that progressiveness is an essential part of the heritage of Presbyterians. It is a denial of Presbyterianism to assume an uncompromising and implacable attitude of hostility toward movement. Progressivism presupposes liberty, open mindedness, and catholicity. Any undue effort to close the doors and limit and regulate action by tradition and precedent alone is unpresbyterian in its essence. Progressivism entails risks. But it is wiser and more loyal to take these risks than to deny progress.

This attitude toward progress was also in sync with the ecumenical ideals of the age. By arguing at least implicitly for the malleability of Presbyterian identity, even to the point of embracing an infelicitous analogy of Presbyterianism as "plastic," Zenos's version of progress became a useful means for overcoming the divisions that might impede cooperation between Presbyterians and other Protestants. Divine right rhetoric, then, was a small price to pay for progressives. The language of Presbyterian singularity, accordingly, died in the North, but continued in the South, where Presbyterianism continued to uphold the spirituality of the church and a more sober estimate of where the American nation was going.

Conservatives in the church would clash with the progressive paradigm toward the end of the century when in 1881 A. A. Hodge and B. B. Warfield co-published an article in the *Presbyterian Review* on "Inspiration." The article, which defended the notion of the inerrancy of the "original autographs" of Scripture, generated two sets of responses. Conservatives saw it as faithfully articulating the Westminster Confession's teaching on infallibility in the light of new challenges from biblical higher criticism. Progressives viewed the article as a defensive innovation, and an embarrassment to the church. Although the doctrine of biblical inerrancy received the endorsement of the denomination in the "Portland Deliverance" at its 1892 General Assembly, it was viewed by a significant part of the church as alien to the true genius of Presbyterianism, which was its adaptability to modern times. A claim to an errorless Bible, by an appeal to inaccessible original autographs, and locating the identity of the church in "fixed, unchanging truth" did not appeal to the progressive spirit in the church.

Just as important, the Hodge-Warfield approach was out of step with the pragmatic spirit of the age. Debates over inerrancy were disruptive and hindered the "positive" work of the church. In response to the Portland Deliverance, a "Plea for Peace and Work," signed by 235 ministers of the church in 1893, argued that new tests of orthodoxy, such as biblical inerrancy, "would only frustrate the church, especially in its missionary enthusiasm and progress." The Plea cited Presbyterian history in making its case. "We remember that our Church has been twice rent asunder by issues which have been recognized shortly afterwards as unnecessary. We dread the possibility of having such a painful experience repeated in our times. We are persuaded that the great body of the Church, laymen and ministers, have little sympathy with the extremes of dogmatic conflict, and are already weary of the strife of tongues, and are longing for peace and united work." In short, the Plea argued, theology divides, and evangelism unites.

Confessional Revision

The greatest apostle for Presbyterian progress was Charles A. Briggs (1841–1913). As professor of Hebrew and cognate languages at Union Theological Seminary in New York, Briggs actively promoted higher-critical approaches to the Bible. He was a leading advocate of Protestant church union, for which cause he gave the very evidence of Dabney's fear of doctrinal indifference. In 1887, Briggs argued that a "great barrier to the reunion of Christendom is *subscription to elaborate creeds*." He pursued both higher criticism and ecumenism in the interest of religious progress. "Progress in religion, in doctrine, and in life," he wrote, "is demanded of our age of the world more than any other age."

But there was an obstacle preventing Presbyterians from embracing fully the spirit of its age, and that was their rigid commitment to a theology of the past. So Briggs also went about promoting revision to the Westminster Confession, especially in his 1889 book, *Whither? A Theological Question for the Times*. Briggs's argument was twofold. On the one hand, he defended the Confession from its contemporary supporters, who had distorted the spirit of its teaching. American Presbyterianism, he charged, had departed from the Westminster Standards and substituted a false orthodoxy in its place. That false teaching—what he labeled "orthodoxism"—was coming from Princeton Seminary, principally the Hodge-Warfield formulation of inerrancy. Briggs wrote,

> Orthodoxism assumes to know the truth and is unwilling to learn; it is haughty and arrogant, assuming the divine prerogatives of infallibility and inerrancy; it hates the truth that is unfamiliar to it, and prosecutes it to the uttermost. But orthodoxy loves the truth. It is ever anxious to learn, for it knows how greatly the truth of God transcends human knowledge. . . . It is meek, lowly, and reverent. It is full of charity and love. It does not recognize an infallible pope; it does not bow to an infallible theologian.

Though critical of the alleged innovations from Union's Old School rival, Briggs didn't prescribe a recovery of the Westminster Confession stripped of a Princetonian gloss. Presbyterians must acknowledge the inadequacies and errors of the confession, and since progress was of the essence of genuine Presbyterianism, the confession itself encouraged its adjustment "to the higher knowledge of our times and the still higher knowledge that the coming period of progress in theology will give us." To fail to take this step was to retreat to errors of Rome and to abandon the very principles of the Reformation.

Briggs was tapping into a growing consensus in the church, growing at least since the reunion of 1869, to soften the harder Calvinistic edges of the confession. In the words of Benjamin J. Lake, "some of the time-honored rigidity in the Westminster Confession seemed obsolete to many Presbyterians." Typically, Presbyterian rigidity was spelled, "predestination."

But if Briggs's proposals outraged conservatives, the spirit and the terms of the 1869 reunion dissuaded efforts to discipline him. That reticence ended in 1891, however, on the occasion of Briggs's inaugural address on "The Authority of Holy Scripture." Delivered upon his induction to the chair of biblical studies at Union and immediately following his re-subscribing to the Westminster Standards, this lecture was a broadside against the verbal inspiration and inerrancy of Scripture. "I shall venture to affirm that, so far as I can see, there are errors in the Scriptures that no one has been able to explain away; and the theory that they are not in the original text is a sheer assumption."

Conservative reaction was swift. Sixty-three presbyteries presented overtures calling for General Assembly action. The 1891 Assembly voted overwhelmingly (449 to 60) to veto Briggs's appointment at Union, and the 1893 Assembly found him guilty of heresy and suspended him from the ministry. Union's board of directors refused to accept the decision, and so it divorced itself from any denominational oversight and retained Briggs on its faculty.

The Briggs trial prompted the initial defeat of a plan for confessional revision in 1893. Briggs himself eventually left for the Episcopalian church, but the push for revision continued. Thirty-four presbyteries overtured for revision in 1900, and that Assembly appointed a study committee of fifty, which included a former president, Benjamin Harrison, and a former Supreme Court justice, John Harlan. One who was invited but declined to serve was Benjamin Warfield. "It is an inexpressible grief," he wrote, to see the church "spending its energies in a vain attempt to lower its testimony to suit the every changing sentiment of the world around it." Once again, Warfield's anti-progressive lament would meet opposition. In an era where change was a sign of health, his dissent sounded, in the words of an opponent, as a call for the "harmony of standing still." Briggs may have left the Presbyterian fold, but clearly his spirit lived on.

Despite some support for a major overhaul, a compromise prevailed that effected minor revisions to the confession. In 1903 the northern church added two chapters on "The Holy Spirit" and "The Love of God and Missions." Both were crafted in language that was vaguely biblical and not distinctively Reformed. In addition, the church revised chapter 16, paragraph 7, which described the works of the unregenerate. Where these works were formerly described as "sinful and cannot please God," the revised language described them as "praiseworthy."

Perhaps of greatest significance was the inclusion of a "Declaratory Statement" that sought to explain the confession's doctrine of election. In words that many accused of being deliberately ambiguous, the statement offered an "avowal . . . of certain inferences" about predestination that seemed to imply human agency was powerless in salvation. Accordingly, the revisions softened the Westminster Standards' Calvinism for many who found it offensive and contradictory to the freedom of the will.

Most Presbyterians enthusiastically embraced these changes. It was a preservation of "generic Calvinism" in the judgment of many. Henry Van Dyke, a Presbyterian academic who taught literature at the College of New Jersey, carefully framed the results within the mainstream of Calvinist orthodoxy: "These two truths," he wrote, "God's *sovereignty* in the bestowal of his grace, and his *infinite love for all men,* are the hinges and turning points of all Christian theology. The *anti*-Calvinist decries the first. The *hyper*-Calvinist or Supralapsarian decries the second, holding that God creates some men on purpose to damn them, for his glory. The true Calvinist believes both and insists that they are consistent." The nation's press, which followed the denomination's politics, echoed Van Dyke's assessment. According to the *Philadelphia Public Ledger*, the new version of the confession left its basic Calvinism intact while able "to render it instantly so much more congenial to the modern mind."

Years later, Princeton historian Lefferts Loetscher was more candid when he described the alterations as a "change to Arminianism." By these revisions, he wrote, "the Remonstrants of the Synod of Dort . . . finally won recognition" in the American Presbyterianism. Evidence for Loetscher's interpretation can be found in the reunion that took place on the heels of revision, when the Arminian prodigals of the Cumberland Presbyterian Church reunited with the northern Presbyterians in 1906.

A majority of the Cumberland Presbyterians had little hesitation joining the Presbyterian Church U.S.A. once it had removed fatalism from
its confession, though a sizeable majority of the Cumberland Church
balked at the merger.

Two years later, the forces of church union and interdenominational
cooperation culminated in the formation of the Federal Council of
Churches, an agency in which Presbyterians played prominent leadership roles, and which achieved even closer links than those established
by either the Evangelical or Presbyterian Alliances.

Federal Council of Churches

By the time of the confessional revision of 1903 and the reunion
that it precipitated, northern conservatives began to utter the kinds
of complaints about church union that southerners had long voiced.
Indeed, the merger between the Cumberland and northern mainline
Presbyterian churches made southern Presbyterian criticisms of church
union look prophetic.

A principal factor in the union of 1906 was the 1885 decision that
had allowed the Cumberland Presbyterian Church to affiliate with the
Presbyterian Alliance. And the kind of doctrinal indifferentism that
southerners had detected in the Presbyterian Alliance provoked among
northern conservatives, especially the faculty at Princeton Seminary,
a similar set of criticisms against church cooperation. Accordingly,
Warfield, who earlier questioned whether the so-called liberality of
church union was actually a form of tyranny, wrote of the proposed
union with the Cumberland church that "differences as to the nature
of the Gospel . . . constitute the primary ground of righteous separation." If differences between the two were minimized—in this case the
differences between Calvinism and Arminianism—these denominations would be committing "treason to the very life of the church of
God." So, too, William Brenton Greene Jr., professor of apologetics,
recognized that the motive of "greater efficiency" in Protestant ecumenism, especially the merger with Cumberland Presbyterians, was
slowly eating away the theological integrity of the Presbyterian Church.
"Broad churchism" produced intellectual suicide, hostility to truth,
and "indifference to God."

The confessional revisions of 1903 paved the way for an even
broader conception of ecumenism and interdenominational cooperation. But that was not its only consequence. Equally significant was

185

the effect it generated among conservatives, who began at this time to adopt new strategies for fighting the rise of liberalism in the Presbyterian church.

Beginning with the 1892 Portland Deliverance, resistance to modernism in the Presbyterian Church took the form of defending the "necessary and essential" elements of the church's teaching, especially the so-called "fundamentals" of the faith. In the Portland Deliverance, and in the 1910, 1916, and 1923 General Assemblies of the northern church, conservative Presbyterians reaffirmed inerrancy, the virgin birth, the vicarious atonement, the resurrection, and the supernatural character of Christ's work. By doing so, they sought to italicize certain doctrines as the Bible's truly nonnegotiables, rather than the Standards themselves, as containing the system of doctrine found in the Scriptures.

When Union Divides

Presbyterian involvement in and reaction to ecumenical and interdenominational endeavors between 1870 and 1920 demonstrate that ecumenicity actually had a reverse effect by increasing antagonism among Presbyterians. The ecumenical impulse birthed and reinforced a progressive and pragmatic spirit in the church that substantially redefined its mission. So instead of looking at this period as the opening round of battles between the so-called modernists and fundamentalists, we'll consider the ecclesiological differences that arose between those favoring church union and those favoring doctrinal precision. This perspective may provide, in the end, a more fruitful way for understanding subsequent Presbyterian history.

It is important to underscore that the ecumenical impulse was not limited to those who would come to embrace theological modernism. Some conservative Presbyterians were also establishing ecumenical connections, especially with other Protestants who were also adamant about defending the "fundamentals" of the faith. In doing so, they began to defend the faith in more broadly evangelical terms and were also responsible for undermining the distinct cadence and pronunciation of Presbyterian doctrine and church government.

Decades later, when Presbyterian conservatives invoked the language of doctrinal indifferentism and the corporate witness of the church

186

against their liberal adversaries, they would discover that evangelicals had as much trouble with certain parts of the Westminster Confession as modernists did with other parts. Thanks to Protestant cooperation and the spirit of the ecumenical age, confessional language was atrophying. And the Westminster Confession itself, let alone the Larger and Shorter Catechisms, was becoming obsolete both on the left and the right.

- confessional language atrophying

10

The Presbyterian Conflict (North)

According to chapter 23 of the Westminster Confession of Faith, among the powers that the civil magistrate possesses is lawfully to "wage war upon just and necessary occasions." Since colonial times, when Presbyterians encountered French hostility along the western frontier during the French and Indian War, they have defended the notion of just war, often coming vigorously to the defense of America's wars.

This pattern continued into the twentieth century. When the Spanish-American War erupted in 1898, ministers such as Henry Van Dyke of Brick Presbyterian Church in New York preached and prayed for an American victory. Van Dyke's pro-war pamphlet, *The Cross at War*, was widely distributed, and the General Assembly in that year pronounced its blessing on the American cause.

A few years later, when Europe descended into the Great War, American Presbyterians were nearly unanimous in affirming their support of the Allies. The 1913 General Assembly validated American involvement in the war against Germany (though expressing it more

1898
Spanish American WW

188

gently than Presbyterian revivalist Billy Sunday, who thundered that if one turned hell upside-down, one would find the words, "Made in Germany"). Presbyterians joined other Protestants in attaching profound religious significance to the Great War, and they were eager to embrace the Presbyterian president, Woodrow Wilson, and his crusade to make the world safe for democracy. This battle pitched the civilized world against barbarians, and the task of the church was to help America fulfill its moral purpose in the world.

There were very few dissenters. One of them was Princeton Seminary professor J. Gresham Machen, who expressed skepticism about Presbyterian war rhetoric. The American alliance with Britain was dangerous, and the war effort, including military conscription, was eroding civil liberties. He regretted that Princeton had become a "hot-bed of patriotic enthusiasm and military ardor," which made him feel like a "man without a country." Nor was Machen impressed by estimates of America's cultural progress that placed the United States at the vanguard of western civilization. "The improvement appears in the physical conditions of life," he observed, "but in the spiritual realm there is a corresponding loss." Where others saw improved standards of living, Machen saw only dreary homogenization and cultural decline.

If Machen joined secular intellectuals in claiming that America's hollow idealism died on European battlefields, other Presbyterians were unfazed. The task of postwar recovery underscored the importance of the church's "peace and work" platform. The Presbyterian Church U.S.A. heartily endorsed Wilson's ill-fated proposal for a League of Nations, which only furthered its ecumenical impulse, because the unity in the civil realm underscored the importance of unity in the ecclesiastical realm.

Robert Speer, the longtime secretary for the Presbyterian Board of Foreign Missions, believed, according to his biographer, that Christian unity "was the great lesson of the war." And Harry Emerson Fosdick, the Baptist supply pastor at First Presbyterian Church in New York City, writing in the *Atlantic Monthly* in 1919, claimed that America's returning soldiers would not accept the traditions of yesterday's Christianity. The church especially owed it to those who fought on America's behalf to offer a message that accommodated itself to the spirit of the age.

189

"Peace and work" may have been the mantra as Presbyterians turned their attention from European warfare to domestic challenges. Ironically, however, the issues before them would convert peace advocates into protagonists in a large-scale ecclesiastical battle. The conflict that would unfold has become commonly known as the "fundamentalist-modernist controversy," as Presbyterians debated the centrality and importance of the "fundamentals" of the Christian faith. Describing it in this way is to suggest that the Presbyterian struggle was a subset of a common battle that eventually consumed all quarters of American Protestantism. But that language is misleading, because it underestimates the ecumenical spirit and the social-crusading ambition of both liberal and fundamentalist Protestants. In both camps a pervasive obsession with preserving Christian America existed (though their prescriptions would differ) and some confessionally savvy Presbyterians saw interdenominational activity on both the left and the right as undermining the ministry of the church.

Plan of Union

Indeed, the Presbyterian controversy came out in the open less because of debates over fundamentals than response to an ecumenical overture, the 1920 proposed "Philadelphia Plan" for Protestant church union. This initiative was the culmination of Protestant ecumenism over the previous half-century, and it revealed how divergent were the doctrines of the church within Presbyterian circles. "The time has come," reported the Committee on Bills and Overtures to the 1918 General Assembly, "for organic church union of the evangelical churches of America." The chair of the committee that brought this recommendation was J. Wilbur Chapman, an associate of evangelist Dwight L. Moody, indicative that the pro-union coalition extended to revivalists and liberals alike.

Nearing the end of his life, Princeton's B. B. Warfield campaigned against its passage. He wrote, "The creed on the basis of which we are invited to form a union . . . contains nothing distinctively evangelical at all," let alone Presbyterian. "So far as the conservation and propagation of evangelical religion is concerned, we might as well form a union on our common acceptance of the law of gravitation."

190

Warfield's colleague Machen was equally opposed. Machen argued that the plan proposed the union of many churches based on a pre-amble laden with vague, shallow, and modernist language. It entailed the abandonment of the Westminster Standards and the relegation of historic Christianity to nonessentials. While Presbyterians joined all churches in proclaiming the gospel of Christ, they were constrained to do so "in harmony with the Westminster Standards." Machen's protest was an extension of the conservative Presbyterian argument, both against organizational unity and for denominational diversity. His defense of historic Protestantism, *Christianity and Liberalism* (1923), emerged from his Presbyterian scruples against the plan of union.

That the presbyteries eventually rejected the plan was of little comfort to Machen, because the failed overture had received an alarmingly large show of support. Even more grievous was the endorsement that two of his Princeton colleagues, President J. Ross Stevenson and Charles Erdman, gave to the plan. Coupled with his grief over the passing of Warfield in 1921, Machen mourned that "Old Princeton" had died with Warfield, and feared that the controversy now threatened to divide even the seminary. Still, the plan served to organize conservative opposition, and as Machen entered the controversy he established greater contacts with conservative leaders, especially in the Presbytery of Philadelphia.

Presbytery of New York

If Philadelphia was a center of conservative strength, its rival was the Presbytery of New York, where Henry Sloane Coffin (1877–1954) was actively promoting what he called "liberal evangelicalism." Coffin's rhetoric cleverly preempted claims that the terms were oxymoronic. Instead he argued that they aptly described Presbyterian mission for a progressive age. In a 1915 address at Union Seminary, he defined liberal evangelicalism simply as offering the gospel in a persuasive manner to contemporary listeners.

Under Coffin's leadership, New York Presbyterians pressed the liberal agenda in the church. The presbytery sanctioned the services of the liberal Baptist, Harry Emerson Fosdick, as the pulpit supply of First Presbyterian Church in New York City. Fosdick rallied liberals with progressive rhetoric such as he expressed in his famous sermon on May

21, 1922, "Shall the Fundamentalists Win?" Though dismissive of the fundamentals as outdated thinking, Fosdick claimed to be broadminded enough to welcome fundamentalists in the church. The sermon was a plea for tolerance on the part of both camps, but most Presbyterians at the time were dubious about his hopes for peaceful coexistence and believed instead that conservative strength would prevail in ousting liberals from the church. Fosdick himself, in his autobiography published in 1956, confessed that the sermon was a failure and that his plea for goodwill only provoked an explosion of ill will. He took comfort, however, in the subsequent vindication of history: "the controversy, despite the noise it made, was an ephemeral affair . . . trivial in comparison with the real issues of the day."

Clarence Macartney (1879–1957), pastor of Arch Street Presbyterian Church in Philadelphia (where he was as prominent a pulpiteer in his city as Fosdick was in New York), quickly rejoined in a sermon titled, "Shall Unbelief Win?" Macartney defended the fundamentals point by point, demonstrating the "impossibility and the non-desirability" of the reconciliation that Fosdick sought. Macartney concluded the sermon on a revealing note. After scoffing at Fosdick's allusion to a fundamentalist conspiracy within the Presbyterian Church, he disavowed any intention to excommunicate the modernists from the church through ecclesiastical trial. "I am convinced that the far more useful course to pursue is to declare the whole counsel of God so clearly and so fearlessly that the whole world may know there is a difference between what is Christianity and what is not Christianity." Macartney's words would describe much of the conservative strategy over the course of the next decade.

A year later, the New York Presbytery took the provocative step of ordaining two graduates of Union Seminary, Cedric A. Lehman and Henry P. Van Dusen, who could not affirm the virgin birth of Christ. The action was in open rebellion to recent General Assembly deliverances that identified the virgin birth among the necessary and essential elements of Christian doctrine. Together with its defense of Fosdick, this was brazen defiance and a seemingly easy target, to which conservatives took careful aim. The 1923 General Assembly, acting on a complaint against the New York Presbytery, directed it to see that First Presbyterian Church conform to Presbyterian standards. At the same time the Assembly reaffirmed the importance of the five fundamentals: the inerrancy of Scripture, the virgin birth of Christ, the vicarious atonement, Jesus' resurrection, and his miracles.

New York liberals retaliated by convening a gathering of ministers in Auburn, New York, in December 1923 that produced "An Affirmation designed to safeguard the unity and liberty of the Presbyterian Church in the United States of America." The Auburn Affirmation contained a twofold argument. First, it challenged the authority of General Assembly deliverances to proclaim certain doctrines as necessary and essential beliefs for Presbyterian ministers. This was a constitutional point on which many conservatives agreed and by itself was hardly a controversial claim. The Affirmation caused a stir by going on to identify the five fundamentals merely as theories about the Bible's message. Robert Hastings Nichols of Auburn Seminary, one of the document's principal authors, was eager to claim Presbyterian precedent on their side: both the Adopting Act of 1729 and the terms of reunion in 1869 and 1906 allowed for the *No* doctrinal differences that it claimed to be protecting.

Within a year, the Auburn Affirmation secured the signatures of nearly thirteen hundred Presbyterian ministers. It also provoked a variety of conservative protests. These reactions, however, were by no means unified. In fact the emergence of a more aggressive liberalism revealed that important differences and conflicting agendas existed among Presbyterian conservatives.

William Jennings Bryan (1860–1925), who grew up in the Arminian Cumberland Presbyterian Church, was a Presbyterian elder who ran for president on three occasions and served as Woodrow Wilson's secretary of state. After retiring from politics he became a leading Presbyterian fundamentalist, and he was influential in the passage of the Eighteenth Amendment that outlawed alcohol in 1920.

As Bryan observed the decline in morality in American culture and the rise of the apostasy of Presbyterian liberalism, he traced both of them to a common source: the triumph of Darwinism. After narrowly losing election as moderator at the 1923 Assembly, Bryan spent his capital with long and passionate speeches against the wickedness of evolution. He also proposed motions supporting the federal government's prohibition on the sale and distribution of alcohol. Bryan's stance at the 1923 Assembly was a disappointment to other conservatives who regarded the question of human origins and total abstinence as a distraction from the central issues before the church.

J. Gresham Machen took a decidedly different approach. Machen described historic Christianity and modernism as two different religions, in his book, *Christianity and Liberalism,* and he urged that "a separation between the two parties in the church [was] the crying need of the hour." In making his case, however, he did not employ Bryan's anti-evolution rhetoric. Instead he attacked the social gospel dimension of Protestant ecumenism from the point of view of the spirituality of the church. Machen opposed liberalism on the grounds of the corporate witness of the church and his assessment that liberalism was indifferent to doctrine. Machen contended, as conservative Presbyterians had before him, that the work of the church was to proclaim the gospel in all its detail—that is, the whole counsel of God.

Machen went on to challenge the liberals' claim to defend and protect Presbyterian liberty. The liberal Protestant conception of brotherhood, Machen argued, was one of the most intolerant that could be found because it ignored important differences between people, claiming in effect that such differences did not matter. A similar intolerance was at work, he believed, in the talk about the unity of the church. When liberals urge conservatives to unite in the same denomination, they are arguing that "doctrinal differences are trifles." But the heart of conservatism, Machen wrote, was that doctrinal differences were "matters of supreme moment." To suppose that conservatives could ignore theology was in fact "the extreme of narrowness." Thus Machen, like Presbyterian confessionalists before him, championed ecclesiastical pluralism both to preserve Presbyterianism and to protect genuine Christian liberty.

Clarence Macartney, who by this time was pastoring First Presbyterian Church in Pittsburgh, preached a sermon in 1924 on "The Irrepressible Conflict," where he described the Presbyterian situation in Machen-like terms, comprised of two groups "who hold views as to Christ and the Scriptures so divergent and so irreconcilable as to constitute two different religions." The only possible outcome was collision and conflict.

Macartney himself would serve as the moderator of the 1924 Assembly. While that Assembly took action against the Presbytery of New York's handling of Fosdick, it treated the conflict as an administrative matter, namely, the problem of having a Baptist preaching in a Presbyterian pulpit. In line with Macartney's nonbelligerent approach, the Assembly took no action against the Auburn Affirmation and its signers.

The Special Commission

Presbyterians expected a showdown at the next General Assembly, meeting in 1925 at Columbus, Ohio. As many commissioners were convinced of the creedal infidelity of the Presbytery of New York, Henry Sloane Coffin was prepared to lead a highly orchestrated liberal exodus from the church when the Assembly's Judicial Commission ruled, as expected, that the presbytery erred in ordaining ministers who did not affirm the virgin birth. However the Assembly's moderator, Charles Erdman of Princeton Seminary, preempted Coffin's parade by prevailing upon the Assembly to establish a special commission "to study the present spiritual condition of our Church and the causes making for unrest, and to report to the next General Assembly, to the end that the purity, peace, unity, and progress of the Church may be assured."

Erdman went on to appoint a committee of fifteen, comprised mainly of Presbyterian moderates. The best known and most influential of the committee was his close friend, Robert E. Speer, secretary of the Board of Foreign Missions, who would later clash with Machen over the latter's charge that modernism had infected the church's Board of Foreign Missions.

In the ensuing year, the special commission heard the testimony of several voices in the church. Machen argued before the commission that the cause of the unrest among Presbyterians was "reducible to the one great underlying cause," which was the presence of modernism in the church. Modernism was countenanced in the church because of its pragmatic commitment to "the indifferentist slogan of 'peace and work.'" Machen pleaded with the commission to affirm the true, spiritual nature of the mission of the church. The boards and agencies of the church, which were failing to sound a clear evangelical note, must determine whether their calling was spiritual or social: were they entrusted with bringing sinners to new birth or saving mankind through the principles of Christian civilization?

Coffin's testimony countered that the differences were due to "misapprehension." Continuing to fight this battle would "plunge the church into calamitous litigation and hinder us from doing our work and building the kingdom of God. It is ruinous," he continued, "to divide existing forces. We ought to work harmoniously together and emphasize those things in which we agree."

When the commission presented its unanimous report to the General Assembly in 1926, it repudiated Machen's contention that mutually exclusive religions were at war in the church. Instead it asserted that the "Presbyterian system admits diversity of views where the core of truth is identical," agreeing with Coffin that there was "evangelical unity" in the church. "The church has flourished best," it concluded, "and showed most clearly the good hand of God upon it, when it laid aside its tendencies to stress these differences, and put the emphasis on the spirit of unity." The effect was to grant freedom to the Presbytery of New York to reject the virgin birth of Christ as an essential tenet of the church, and a complete vindication of the Auburn Affirmation, ending all efforts to bring its signers to trial.

The approval of the special commission made clear that American Presbyterians stood for toleration and for progress, marking a turning point in the church and decline of conservative strength. Armed with the findings of the special commission, liberals gained control of important denominational agencies and a right to equal standing within the courts of the church. No conservative would be elected as moderator of the General Assembly, and liberals began increasingly to staff the boards and agencies of the church.

The final report of the commission, approved in 1927, emphasized that Presbyterian unity required the end of "all slander and misrepresentation" within the church. The focus of attention, then, fell on one particular source of recent unrest: the factions within the faculty of Princeton Seminary. The General Assembly appointed a committee to supervise the reorganization of the seminary. The reorganization in 1929 brought two signers of the Auburn Affirmation onto its new thirty-member board. Convinced that this would lead the school inevitably to embrace theological liberalism, Machen resigned from Princeton and formed Westminster Seminary in Philadelphia.

196

Missions Controversy

In the next decade the controversy within the northern Presbyterian Church shifted to the final battlefront, the conflict over foreign missions. Conservatives generally believed that the Presbyterian Board of Foreign Missions was the least tainted of the Presbyterian boards. Still they welcomed this development, hoping that the cause of foreign missions would awaken the church to the genuine crisis of modernism and thus succeed in bringing the controversy to a head.

The spotlight fell on missions in 1930 when the Laymen's Foreign Missions Inquiry undertook an ambitious study of Protestant foreign missions, underwritten by generous support from the liberal Baptist philanthropist John D. Rockefeller Jr. The findings of the inquiry were entrusted to a commission chaired by William Ernest Hocking of Harvard University, which released its summary and analysis in the 1932 book, *Re-Thinking Missions.*

Hocking and his associates argued that Protestant missions were "at a fork in the road" and needed to shift from a "religion of fear" to a "religion of beneficence." This required abandoning Christianity's exclusive claims and actively participating with other faiths in an emerging new world religion. Predictably, the report was lauded in liberal circles, especially by novelist and Presbyterian missionary Pearl Buck, who hailed the study as a "masterpiece" that should be translated into every language and adopted by every mission board.

But *Re-Thinking Missions* pressed the progressive mission agenda far beyond the comfort zone of Presbyterian moderates. The report was an embarrassment to Robert Speer. Ever the moderate, Speer sought to craft a balanced assessment that commended many of the report's recommendations while rejecting its theological basis. "The very essence of Christianity" was missing from that basis, Speer noted. "It is a profound mistake," he added, to imagine that the report's conception of Christianity "will vivify the missionary enterprise and supply it with new motive and power." Among conservatives, Macartney welcomed the report as an unambiguous confirmation of his worst fears of modernism. The authors, he wrote, "have scattered the fog" and "torn off from the face of Modernism its mask and disguise." With the publication of this book, Macartney was convinced that the slumbering church would at last awaken to the threat of liberalism. The furor created by the book would fall far short of his hopes, but it was enough to force the resignation of Pearl Buck as a Presbyterian missionary.

Machen used the study to launch an offensive against Speer and the foreign missions board. He was disturbed that Speer had not repudiated the study in more forthright language, especially in light of the presence of two board members on the Layman's Committee. He prepared an overture to the 1933 General Assembly that encouraged the election of conservatives to the board. The overture included a warning of "the great danger that lurks in union enterprises at home as well as abroad." Once again, Machen located the controversy in the context of the problem of Presbyterian ecumenicity.

As the debate came before the presbytery and eventually the General Assembly of 1933, Machen conceded that he was taking on a beloved figure in the church. Speer had "truly amazing power over the hearts of men," he noted, and Machen himself once "stood under the spell of his eloquence." Still, Machen and other conservatives overestimated the will of the Presbyterians to debate the matter. Three decades earlier, Speer wrote the "time when the Church had to fight doctrinally for her life . . . went by long ago" and to trifle with doctrinal matters now was "playing with details while men die." When Machen presented an overture to the 1933 General Assembly, the sense prevailed at the Assembly that his criticism had become personal, and the debate became a referendum on Speer's long and illustrious career as a foreign missionary statesman. When Speer rose to present his report to the Assembly, he was greeted with a long standing ovation, and Machen's overture went down to an overwhelming defeat.

The church having refused to protect the integrity of the composition of its missions board, Machen formed the Independent Board for Presbyterian Foreign Missions, which in turn elected him president. If Machen took this step to bring about a final resolution of the controversy, Stated Clerk Lewis Mudge proved willing to oblige him. Charging Machen with subverting Presbyterian law by undertaking "administrative functions within the church without official sanction," Mudge orchestrated the General Assembly's "Mandate of 1934" which ordered Presbyterian ministers to resign their Independent Board membership. Presbyteries were instructed to bring noncompliant ministers to trial.

Mudge's power as stated clerk was a shock in many quarters in the church. Macartney, though himself no supporter of the Independent Board, decried the action as "unscriptural and unpresbyterian." Even the liberal Coffin regretted that the Assembly had acted "unwisely." No one struck a sharper blow than the southern Presbyterian theologian, William Childs Robinson, when he drew a chilling analogy between the northern Presbyterian establishment and Nazi Germany:

> Those who enjoy a bit of irony may notice that the same General Assembly of 1934, which laid its iron mandate to bind the conscience of Dr. Machen, passed a resolution commending the German Protestants for refusing to obey those actions of the Nazi church which contravene a minister's exclusive allegiance to the Word of God. With a much more vague and less adequate understanding of what the Word of God is, Karl Barth is indeed challenging the German church with the same issue that the Machen case has raised in the U.S.A. church. Is the voice of the church the ultimate; or is it only penultimate, with the Word of God ultimate? Is not the Word of God above the church judging her? . . . Shall we stand for the authority of the Word of God in Germany; and the authority of the voice of the Church in America? Or shall we return to the sole Headship of Christ in His church, and the sufficiency of His Word as a rule of faith and practice?

For his part, Machen made clear that he had no intention of resigning, ignoring the counsel of Macartney and others to moderate his stance. In March of 1935, the Presbytery of New Brunswick convicted him and suspended him from the ministry.

Separatist Presbyterians

As Machen prepared to appeal the decision that would eventually result in his humiliation of being defrocked, other conservative Presbyterians, by now soundly defeated in the church, debated whether the biblical mandate was to "go out from their midst and be separate" (2 Cor. 6:17) or "strengthen what remains and is about to die" (Rev. 3:2).

Ultimately, only a fraction of the conservative voices would join Machen. Some abandoned Presbyterian identity altogether and chose ecclesiastical independency. Others stayed in the mainline church, but even that step represented a form of separatism. The stories of two conservative Presbyterians function as good examples. Wilbur Smith, a Presbyterian minister in Coatesville, Pennsylvania, resigned from the Independent Board rather than face discipline. Smith, who would go on to teach at Moody Bible Institute and eventually at Fuller Seminary, maintained his membership in the Presbyterian Church precisely because it would maximize his independence. He would later observe that staying in the church afforded him freedom as "if I were the pastor of a church entirely independent of any ecclesiastical organization."

The controversy also took its toll on Clarence Macartney, who expressed a similar battle-weary exhaustion. He remained in the pulpit of First Presbyterian Church in Pittsburgh until his retirement in 1957, but stayed on the Presbyterian periphery. He waved the ecclesiastical white flag in a *Christian Century* article, where he wrote: "I value less the whole ecclesiastical structure, and feel that more and more for the true witness to the gospel and the Kingdom of God we must depend upon the particular local church, the individual minister, and the individual Christian."

Indeed, the "reform-from-within" strategy showed little willingness to establish a concrete agenda for the renewal of the Presbyterian Church. The Presbyterian League of Faith, organized in 1931 to voice the concerns of conservative Presbyterians, enlisted a membership of as many as twelve hundred ministers, a number that established at least symbolic symmetry to the "Auburn Affirmation." But despite a pledge to maintain its "militant testimony," even after the exodus of Machen, its voice in the church was so quiet that one liberal reassuringly described the Presbyterian Church in 1939 in this way: "all is now quiet on the theological front. . . . The conservatives are not so conservative, or at least not so militant" having been "reduced to a weedy segment of their former battalions."

Meanwhile, on June 11, 1936, after the General Assembly sustained the verdict against Machen, he led in the formation of the Presbyterian Church of America (which changed its name to the Orthodox Presbyterian Church in 1939). Machen rejoiced that he and his comrades had "become members, at last, of a true Presbyterian church." But what did those words mean? For Machen and the leadership of the new church, which came primarily from the faculty of Westminster

200

Seminary, it meant the maintenance of Presbyterian conservatism against the theological minimalism both of the liberal mainline Presbyterian Church and the emerging evangelical movement. But initially Orthodox Presbyterians were more united in their opposition to modernism than they were in their understanding of the genius of American Presbyterianism. Consequently, the church continued to use the "Auburn Affirmation" polemically as the major evidence of Presbyterian doctrinal decay.

But OPC was a small church which continued to shrink from defections of those with conflicting agendas. Many fundamentalists in the church, already accustomed to functional independency, left the denomination shortly after Machen's early death on January 1, 1937, to form the Bible Presbyterian Church. As George Marsden observed, the threefold concerns that prompted the exodus of the Bible Presbyterians—doctrine (the millennium question), morality (the abstinence question), and polity (whether the Independent Board was to remain independent) bore remarkable resemblance to the New School-Old School division of 1837. Armed with a conservative political agenda, the New School impulse of the Bible Presbyterians, under the leadership of Carl McIntire, found expression in social action (combating such evils as alcohol and Communism) and interchurch cooperation (as McIntire formed his own empire in the American Council of Christian Churches and the International Council of Christian Churches).

The OPC continued to suffer losses of ministers and churches who found greater affinity with American evangelicalism than Presbyterian confessionalism. Carl Henry captured the anti-denominational spirit of American neo-evangelicalism when he decried the Presbyterian options as either the "condemnatory spirit and one-sided propaganda of the 'come-out-ers' " or the "machine-loyalty of the 'stay-in-ers.' " Under the leadership of Harold Ockenga (like McIntire a former student of Machen), neo-evangelicals also sought ecumenical expression through the founding of the National Association of Evangelicals. Soon that movement, through the prominence of Billy Graham, who was reared in the Associate Reformed Presbyterian Church, became the place where conservative Protestants looked for help in combating the consequences of theological liberalism.

Assessments of the Controversy

Typically, historians have described the Presbyterian controversy in terms of the clash of premodern and modern outlooks or habits of mind. On the one side, liberals expressed willingness to accommodate contemporary intellectual currents in their restatement of the faith. In contrast, fundamentalists stressed a static conception of truth and so opposed any effort to modify Christian teaching in order to harmonize it with modern learning or democratic ideals. Though conservatives seemed to have the stronger support in the battle, especially before 1925, victory in the controversy went to the liberals who went from endangered species to leadership and control of the Presbyterian Church.

The controversy has also been interpreted as a rhetorical battle. To be sure, liberal evangelicals including Coffin mastered the vocabulary of liberty, diversity, and peace, while militant conservatives employed the less winsome language of strife and warfare. But the sharpest of conservative rhetoric was hardly a match for the ruthlessness of the Presbyterian establishment, especially in its final disposition of Machen when the judicial committee of the Presbytery of New Brunswick ruled that all of his arguments in defense of the Independent Board, including the question of the constitutionality of the Mandate of 1934, were out of order. Moreover, conservatives arguably lost this conflict less because of their belligerence than their _unwillingness_ to fight. By following the advice of Clarence Macartney, the conservative party in the church, in the analysis of Westminster Seminary church historian Clair Davis, "lost its nerve and changed its strategy from trials to lay rallies and adoptions of General Assembly resolutions."

Others have emphasized that the controversy and its aftermath was a testimony to Presbyterian moderation. After all, the church convicted Briggs and Machen within the space of a half-century, demonstrating its desire to protect its vital center, and wary of extremes at the far ends of the theological spectrum. According to Lefferts Loetscher, the moderation that triumphed in 1927 and 1933 was the moderation that prevailed in the 1869 Presbyterian reunion. Those unwilling to accept that settlement were put on the defensive and eventually silenced or removed from the church. But the ambiguity that characterized the theological boundaries of Presbyterianism was a testament less to moderation than

202

to diversity. With the Westminster Standards becoming optional among ministerial membership in the church, a broad and often incoherent pluralism became the defining mark of American Presbyterianism in the twentieth century. As Bradley J. Longfield concluded in his study of the Presbyterian controversy, "it appears that Machen's fears about the secularization of the church without distinct doctrinal boundaries were well founded."

As small as the exodus turned out to be (five thousand members from a two-million-member church), the controversy left mainline Presbyterianism scarred for a long time. For many years, according to Loetscher, memories of the conflict would "largely inhibit frank and realistic discussion" of theological issues among Presbyterians. In his words, " 'the less theology the better' seems to be the lurking implication—at least so far as the Church's statistical growth is concerned."

But reckoning fully with the Presbyterian controversy involves going beyond theological method or rhetoric. On a deeper level this was the outworking of the struggle between rival conceptions of the nature and work of the church, begun in the previous century.

Some conservatives (such as Bryan) were anti-creedal and pietists who were crusading for a social gospel, albeit of a more conservative version than the New School idea embraced to varying degrees by Coffin, Speer, and Erdman, that the church had a special role to play in the reform of society and the maintenance of national moral standards.

Others, like Macartney, though committed to historic Presbyterianism, declined to use the assemblies of the church to enforce the church's constitution. Among the major voices of the controversy, Machen stood nearly alone in upholding the integrity of the church to proclaim the Reformed faith in its fullness and significance. As eagerly as conservatives may have purchased his *Christianity and Liberalism* in 1923, a decade later Machen's defense of Reformed doctrine and Presbyterian ecclesiology fell on deaf ears among conservative Presbyterians who were fearful of splitting the church, some even mindful of the Presbyterian reunion of 1869 and not wanting to repeat an earlier difficult period of the church's past.

In coming to terms with this story, therefore, it is necessary to distinguish between the pietists and the confessional conservatives. Two groups were at odds in the Presbyterian controversy. The Presbyterians who were

— Pietists and confessionalists

either uncomfortable with or opposed to the external forms that made Presbyterianism distinct included evangelicals such as Speer and Erdman, who stressed conversion over doctrine, and liberals such as Coffin, who emphasized religious experience over creeds and confessions.

Their adversaries, the confessional conservatives, recognized that Presbyterianism could not be separated from distinct Presbyterian teachings and practices without also raising the possibility that the same could be done for Christianity in general. As such, the Presbyterian controversy not only involved the "irrepressible conflict" between naturalism and supernaturalism, but also revealed significant diversity among the defenders of supernatural Christianity. Just as much as the contest contrasted Christianity and liberalism as different religions, it demonstrated that pietism and confessionalism were two very different kinds of Presbyterianism.

11

Presbyterian Consolidation

Why was it necessary for the Presbyterian separatists to form a new denomination, and why did they not seek ecclesiastical refuge with other Presbyterians? A look at Machen's ecclesiastical options provides a review of the Presbyterian scene in the first half of the twentieth century.

The southern Presbyterian Church, whose story will be the focus of our next chapter, may have presented a personal temptation for Machen to consider. Machen was born in Baltimore, and he grew up in the South. He lectured at Union Seminary in Virginia and was offered a teaching post there. Yet for him to turn to the South would abandon the conservative cause within the northern church, because the Mason-Dixon line still distinguished Presbyterian communions.

There was another reason for Machen's reluctance. As early as the 1930s, the perception was gaining strength that the southern church also was succumbing to modernism. To be sure, there were few self-proclaimed modernists in the church then. But there were signs of developing sympathy. In 1931, church historian Ernest Trice Thompson published an article in the *Union Seminary Review* on the question, "Is the Northern Church Theologically Sound?" As he surveyed the previous half century in northern Presbyterian history, including the Briggs heresy trial, the confessional revision of 1903, the signing of the Auburn Affirmation, and the reorganization of Princeton Seminary, Thompson pronounced on the northern church a clean bill of spiritual health, concluding it "fundamentally sound in the faith, and is just as likely to remain so as our own." This was hardly a welcome mat for confessional Presbyterians.

Perhaps a more plausible option might have been with American Presbyterians outside the mainline tradition. The Associate Reformed Synod of the South, which withdrew from the Associate Reformed Synod in 1822, was arguably the most conservative Presbyterian body in the United States in the early twentieth century. But it was even more regionally defined than the PCUS, with most of its twenty thousand members in the Carolinas, and the practice of exclusive psalmody was still a distinctive feature of its worship.

In the North, the union of the Associate Synod and the Associate Reformed Synod formed the United Presbyterian Church of North America in 1858. The union was effected on the basis of the Westminster Confession and Catechisms and the "Testimony of 1858," which consisted of eighteen articles on matters where the Westminster Standards were either silent or judged to be deficient. This included declarations against slaveholding and membership in secret societies, and the practice of exclusive psalmody and public covenanting.

Despite these historic distinctives from the mainline Presbyterian tradition, the denomination throughout its history was active in pursuing ecumenical discussions with no fewer than six different Presbyterian and Reformed denominations. That ecumenical interest, however, may itself have ended the prospects for Orthodox Presbyterians, because one of those bodies with which the conversations were most active was the PCUSA (a union that would consummate in 1958). Thus, progressives in the UPCNA would likely have regarded talks with OPC as regressive and subversive of its greater ecumenical ambitions. For their part, the confessionalists who formed the OPC would have eliminated the UPCNA as a denominational option when the latter, under the leadership of John McNaugher, crafted and approved a new Confessional Statement in 1925.

John McNaugher (1857–1947) was a powerful figure in the denomination. Born a year before its formation in 1858, his life spanned nearly its entire history, and he served for thirty-four years as the president of Pittsburgh Seminary. The Confessional Statement was a briefer summary *The Confessional Statement* of the Reformed faith, consisting of forty-four articles that incorporated the essentials of the Westminster Standards in contemporary language. In the words of one minister, its chief virtue was its brevity that would "command the approval of the busy men of today," implying that a weakness of the Westminster Standards was its wordiness that would not meet the demands of efficiency in an industrial age.

But Westminster was not merely antiquated. It was in need of substantial revision, because its ultra-Calvinism, according to McNaugher, placed a one-sided emphasis on the sovereignty of God. So, for example, the new statement described predestination in positive language that did not include the damnation of the reprobate. Here and elsewhere when the Confessional Statement deviated from Westminster Standards, its preface explained that the new articles were to prevail.

The Confessional Statement also replaced the Testimony of 1858, bringing to a close in that denomination the practice of national covenanting and (even more striking) the end of exclusive psalmody in public worship. The 1858 testimony had prescribed psalms "to the exclusion of the devotional compositions of uninspired men" in public worship. In the 1925 Confessional Statement, a compromise at the point of adoption rendered it silent on hymnody, as it merely "accredited" the psalms "for permanent use" in the church. That silence spoke loudly, however, and exclusive psalmody was officially dead within a year when the denomination approved a new hymnbook. In 1940 the church revised its Confessional Statement to remove any ambiguity about the propriety of hymns, as it endorsed "meritorious evangelical hymns in which are expressed the experiences, privileges, and duties of the Christian life."

The softening of Calvinistic orthodoxy and the abandonment of psalmody were radical turns for the conservative United Presbyterians to make, steeped as they were in the Convenanter tradition that would seem firmly equipped to resist modernization. The Testimony of 1858, after all, in addressing matters on which the Westminster Standards were silent, appeared to tighten the boundaries of confessional identity.

But that very tradition can serve to ease a transition into theological modernism. Testimonies that update a church's constitution can subtly cultivate the sense of creedal obsolescence. When the practice of testimonies becomes the means of addressing confessional concerns, rather than confessional revision, the church begins to value its contemporary teaching or its "living voice" over the practices of the past. Unwittingly, the Testimony of 1858 unleashed a confessional hermeneutic that led to its own demise and that of the authority of Westminster as well. The Confessional Statement of 1925 took an additional step that foreshadowed later confessional developments in American Presbyterianism. In its approval United Presbyterians introduced a diverse "book" of standards with internal inconsistencies.

The consequences of these actions were likely overlooked at the time. Of far greater immediate significance for the church than the modified Calvinism of the new statement was the introduction of hymnody. As the practice of psalm singing died out, so too did any rationale for United Presbyterians to remain a separate denomination. This was a small price to pay for a church eager to assimilate into the Presbyterian mainstream.

Neo-Orthodoxy

Meanwhile, the mainline Presbyterian Church seemed to survive the turmoil of the Presbyterian controversy reasonably well. The PCUSA began to enjoy a period of ecclesiastical tranquility, which lasted for about thirty years. Although the Presbyterian separatists predicted the decline of the mainline church, that fate was delayed at least for a generation by a theological movement that provided a fragile theological consensus for the Presbyterian Church.

The oasis for American Presbyterians came from the Swiss theologian, Karl Barth. In the wake of the devastation of World War I and the Great Depression, liberalism's cultural optimism proved to be a shallow and superficial hope that left the church ill-equipped to address a world shattered by violence, economic upheaval, and moral ambiguity. Barth's rediscovery of Reformed orthodoxy, with particular emphasis on the transcendence of God and the sinfulness of humanity, provided what many Presbyterians welcomed as a middle ground between fundamentalism and modernism. "Neo-orthodoxy" was a faith that looked both ways: it was rooted in the Protestant Reformation and yet relevant to a modern age. It affirmed the authority of the Bible, but also the findings of biblical higher criticism, and thus rejected the doctrine of biblical inerrancy. The creeds of the church, as well, were valuable statements of faith, though time-bound and historically conditioned.

No one was more influential in introducing neo-orthodoxy to American Presbyterians than John Mackay (1889–1983), a native of Scotland, who in 1936 was appointed president of Princeton Seminary (where he served until 1959). Mackay sought to go beyond the fundamentalist-liberal impasse by hiring several neo-orthodox faculty, including Elmer G. Homrighausen and Emil Brunner.

In *The Presbyterian Way of Life,* autobiographical reflections that he penned in 1960, Mackay described the "Presbyterian soul" in neo-orthodox terms. At the heart of Presbyterianism, he argued, is a "greatheartedness" that recognizes "it is a right and duty of a living church to restate and interpret its faith as occasion may require." Out of the fires of purification a new solidarity emerged after 1936. Presbyterians met the demands of their time by following "the example of that great neo-Calvinist, Karl Barth." Mackay's enthusiasm indicates that, although Barth may have chastised the zeal of liberalism in the Presbyterian Church, he was no obstacle for its progressive impulse.

Princeton was not alone in experiencing a Barthian rebirth. Union Seminary in New York, although independent of Presbyterian control, was flourishing at this time as well with arguably the most prestigious theological faculty in America, which included Reinhold Niebuhr and Paul Tillich. Its version of American neo-orthodoxy, signaled by Niebuhr's publication of *Moral Man and Immoral Society,* was as influential on the Presbyterian Church as the instruction from Princeton.

Of course, separatist Presbyterians sought to disturb the peace. Cornelius Van Til, an Orthodox Presbyterian professor at Westminster Seminary, was relentless in insisting that Barth was no "neo-Calvinist" but represented a radical break from Calvin and the Reformed tradition. As the titles of Van Til's first book, *The New Modernism* (1947), and a subsequent study, *Christianity and Barthianism* (1963), suggest, Van Til's strategy was to link the "new modernism" of Barth with the old—that is, the liberalism that J. Gresham Machen had exposed in his 1923 book,

Christianity and Liberalism. "If the late J. Gresham Machen spoke of the necessity of making a choice between liberalism and Christianity," he wrote, "we should be doing scant justice to his memory if we did less today with respect to the new Modernism and Christianity."

Van Til became a popular author among Presbyterian conservatives and fundamentalists, few of whom may actually have read his books, but all of whom were grateful for his heavy lifting. He was also joined by a few critics on the left, who were less than impressed with neo-orthodoxy's ambiguity on the relationship of the church with its culture. Sidney Ahlstrom of Yale Divinity School dismissed neo-orthodoxy as "putting down only a very thin sheet of dogmatic asphalt" over liberal thought.

Despite the criticism, by the 1950s neo-orthodoxy was firmly established as the prevailing theological mindset of northern Presbyterians. It became the majority opinion of the church's college and seminary faculties. Barthian stress on the proclamation of the Word produced a homiletical revival in the church, a welcomed respite from the stifling moralisms of theological modernism. A renewed appreciation for ancient creeds, along with a more theocentric approach to worship, contributed to liturgical renewal among Presbyterians as well, if at the expense of a Reformed attentiveness to the regulative principle of worship (i.e., that worship is regulated by what God commands in his Word).

At the same time, the postwar baby boom and the growth of suburban life ushered American culture and its mainline churches into a period of unprecedented growth and prosperity. Presbyterian church buildings and membership increased at a pace that exceeded population growth in the United States. Sunday school attendance and benevolence giving rose to their highest levels in denominational history.

If Presbyterians at mid-century looked for a symbol for their revival in the "flourishing fifties," they found it less in a Swiss theologian than in an American war hero and president. Though Dwight D. Eisenhower showed little interest in religion in his Kansas Mennonite upbringing, his religious habits changed dramatically upon his election in 1953, when he joined the PCUSA and became an active member of National Presbyterian Church in Washington, DC. His presidency established many of the rituals of American civil religion, including the addition of the phrase, "under God," in the Pledge of Allegiance, the annual Day of Prayer and Presidential Prayer Breakfasts, as well as the highly

publicized White House visits by prominent religious figures such as Billy Graham. By the time he left office, he was lauded as among the most religious presidents in American history.

There was nothing distinctively Presbyterian in any of these initiatives, and Eisenhower's era is generally associated with superficial and highly individualistic piety. His most famous religious utterance may be his infelicitous assessment that the American government "makes no sense unless it is founded on a deeply felt religious faith—and I don't care what it is." While there is scholarly doubt that he actually uttered those words, they are compatible with a religious legacy that conflated religious conviction with American patriotism. In Martin Marty's words, Americans in the Eisenhower years displayed "a very fervent faith in a very vague religion."

There were more substantive examples of Presbyterian public piety in the 1950s, such as Eisenhower's secretary of state, John Foster Dulles. The son of a liberal Presbyterian minister, Dulles was an active Presbyterian ruling elder. His training in international law led to his appointment as chairman in the 1940s of the Federal Council of Churches' Committee on a Just and Durable Peace, which weaned churches from support of American isolationism and into active involvement with the Allied effort of World War II.

Within a few years of his appointment by Eisenhower as secretary of state, however, Dulles's ecclesiastical supporters turned skeptical. His "Just and Durable Peace" formula turned into nuclear brinkmanship and massive retaliation as Dulles became the architect of America's Cold War against Soviet Communism. Reinhold Niebuhr and other critics grew disillusioned as they watched Dulles's realism yield to American self-righteousness and imperialism in his foreign policy rhetoric. Of course, Presbyterians were careful to distance themselves from the worst of American political chauvinism. In their "Letter to Presbyterians" in 1953, Eugene Carson Blake and John Mackay condemned the anti-Communist fearmongering of McCarthyism.

As Presbyterian leaders roused mid-century Presbyterians to the prophetic calling of a countercultural spirituality, Presbyterianism still found comfort in the priestly enclaves of middle-class Protestant pietism. The affinities between mainline ecumenism and evangelical revivalism were particularly evident in the Presbyterian reaction to the rising career of evangelist Billy Graham. To be sure, Graham had his critics among the Protestant mainline. No one pursued him more doggedly than Reinhold Niebuhr, who dismissed him as a "domesticated and tailored leftover" of the circuit-riding days of frontier revivalism. Together with the teaching of Norman Vincent Peale, the prophet of positive thinking from Marble Collegiate Church in New York, Graham's pietistic individualism, according to Niebuhr, displayed the "blandness that befits the Eisenhower era."

But Niebuhr became the exception as the mainline warmed up to Graham. John Mackay dismissed Niebuhr's criticism as unfair, and in 1953 he invited Graham to speak at Princeton Seminary, after which he observed that the evangelist's visit improved the spiritual life of the campus more than anything else during his presidency. And when the New York Council of Churches sponsored the 1957 New York City crusade, Henry P. Van Dusen, now president of Union Seminary, was among the most enthusiastic supporters of the "readily digestible form" in which Graham presented the gospel.

The mainline Protestant revival in which Presbyterians joined, for all its neo-orthodox qualification, was in many respects a superficial phenomenon, filled with the idealism of the liberalism from which it was never weaned. Graham and Peale were symbols that its success was found less in the substance of the message than in the power of personality. The Barthian consensus proved neither durable, nor long-lasting, as the American culture transitioned into the turmoil of the 1960s.

Northern Presbyterians Unite

"To be ecumenical is as Presbyterian as predestination," observed Presbyterian author and activist Robert McAfee Brown (1920–2001). American Presbyterianism relentlessly pursued an ecumenical agenda throughout the twentieth century. As the Evangelical Alliance gave way to the Federal Council of Churches in 1908, which in turn evolved into the National Council of Churches in 1950, American Presbyterians supplied key leadership roles. They were equally visible on the international ecumenical scene, in the formation in 1875 of the Presbyterian Alliance (which became the World Alliance of Reformed Churches in 1970) and in 1948 the World Council of Churches, even as they

212

embraced the secular ecumenism of the League of Nations and the United Nations (1945).

For all their talk of church union, mainline Presbyterians went over half a century, from 1906 to 1958, before executing a successful union. This was not for want of trying. At the end of the Presbyterian controversy, mainline Presbyterians poured their energy into union negotiations, which were complicated because of the many parties involved.

From 1937 to 1955, the PCUSA discussed merger at different times with the southern Presbyterians, the United Presbyterians, and, from 1937 to 1946, even with the Protestant Episcopal Church. During parts of that time span, the PCUS and the UPCNA each conducted negotiations with the Reformed Church in America (RCA) and explored union with the Associate Reformed Presbyterian Church (ARP). In almost every case the delicate conversations aroused suspicions among liberals or conservatives within the participating churches, depending on the ecumenical dialogue partner.

Presbyterians finally succeeded in 1958 when they united with the United Presbyterian Church of North America, a denomination that in its one hundred years of existence grew from fifty-five thousand to two hundred thousand members. The UPCNA was a conservative church that was expanding beyond its parochial Covenanter past, evidenced by its membership in the National and World Councils of Churches. One historian of the church observed that the United Presbyterians' growing emphasis on missions and social work had the healthy effect, throughout the course of the twentieth century, of reducing the time and energy exerted on the discipline of its ministers.

The merger united the churches under the name of the United Presbyterian Church in the U.S.A. (UPCUSA), and for the third time Pittsburgh was the city for the grand reunion of Presbyterianism. As in 1858 and 1869, the prominent geography of the city, with the Allegheny and Monongahela rivers converging to form the mighty Ohio River, served as a convenient metaphor for the occasion. In this case, however, the metaphor may have been a stretch, because the merger met with heightened fears among conservatives in the UPCNA, especially over the steps that the PCUSA was taking in the ordination of women.

Beginning in the late nineteenth century, women's roles in the PCUSA gradually expanded as the church incrementally rejected the

213

1832 General Assembly deliverance outlawing the revivalist innovation of women speaking in the church. With their steadily increasing participation in Sunday schools, missionary societies, and benevolent societies, women secured the right, by the end of the century, to speak in the church at the discretion of the Session.

Presbyterians further expanded women's roles in the twentieth century, approving their ordination as deacons in 1922 and as ruling elders in 1930. Finally, in 1956, on the eve of union with United Presbyterians, the PCUSA opened the office of minister to women. Opportunities for women in the PCUSA were evolving faster than in the UPCNA, which approved women deacons as early as 1906, but never proceeded beyond that to open the offices of elder and minister to women. The merger took place when Presbyterians were satisfied with the assurance that the new denomination would permit, but not require, women ministers in the congregations of churches.

Another factor that played into the success of the merger was the low bar set by the UPCNA constitution. The plan of union merely required a simple majority of the presbyteries for approval, which proved instrumental as United Presbyterian enthusiasm waned while the merger approached. In five votes on union that took place between 1948 and 1957 (two were unofficial), the percentage of favorable votes steadily declined, from 90 percent in 1948 to a mere 57 percent in 1957. Clearly a growing number of presbyters were skeptical about the loss of identity in succumbing to the ecumenical demands of the mid-twentieth century. Despite the fanfare of the Pittsburgh celebration, the United Presbyterians did not greet the union on a strong note of enthusiasm.

Consultation on Church Union

Presbyterian appetites were not satiated with the marriage that produced the UPCUSA. Eugene Carson Blake (1906–85) opened a new chapter for Presbyterian ecumenicity in the 1960s. Blake symbolized the new decade as much as Eisenhower represented the previous one. A product of a revivalist Presbyterian home in the Midwest, Blake pastored Presbyterian churches in New York City, Albany, and California before he became denominational stated clerk in 1951.

While the stated clerk's position expanded of his predecessors, it was under Blake's fifteen-year tenure that the position truly grew as the denominational spokesman and powerbroker. He eventually left the post in 1966 to become the general secretary of the World Council of Churches. But Blake's administrative skills did not establish his reputation. His activism in the civil rights movement included a well-publicized arrest on July 4, 1963 (when he joined an effort to integrate a Baltimore amusement park). He also joined Martin Luther King Jr. in his march on Washington on August 28, 1963, penitently speaking on behalf of the denomination when he said, "We are late, but we are here." Blake seamlessly filled the contradictory roles of organization man and rebel, issuing tough-minded calls for the church to renew its "prophetic voice," with personal charm to see that it was done decently and in order.

On December 4, 1960, Blake preached a sermon at Grace Episcopal Cathedral in San Francisco, at the invitation of Bishop James Pike. There he unfolded a bold plan to unite the four largest mainline American denominations: the Protestant Episcopal Church, the United Methodist Church, the United Church of Christ, and the UPCUSA. The urgency of Blake's appeal was laced with a measure of desperation. The election of John F. Kennedy, America's first Roman Catholic president, in the previous month prompted concern among the Protestant mainline over whether the clock was ticking on their hegemony in American public life. For Protestants to recover their leadership in American public life, cooperation had to overcome competition. "Never before," said Blake, "have so many Americans agreed that the Christian churches, divided as they are, cannot be trusted to bring to the American people an objective and authentic word of God on a political issue. Americans more than ever see the churches of Jesus Christ as competing social groups pulling and hauling, propagandizing, and pressuring for their own organizational advantages."

Blake's impassioned appeal earned him a cover on *Time* magazine, which may have overstated his words as a "landmark in Protestant history." Blake's ambitious proposal sought to go beyond the coordination of mainline churches to their consolidation into an organically united church of more than twenty million members. Following up on Blake's appeal, the 1961 General Assembly sent invitations to the southern

Presbyterians, United Methodists, Episcopalians, and UCC, and in the spring of 1962 the first meetings of the "Consultation on Church Union" (COCU) were held.

Eventually renamed Churches of Christ Uniting, COCU never achieved Blake's vision for a united church that was "truly catholic and truly Reformed." Still, what is otherwise a footnote to American Presbyterian history is noteworthy at least for indicating how far the stated clerk of the denomination was willing to push the ecumenical mandate. Blake could propose a church both ecumenical and Reformed only by stretching the definition of Reformed beyond anything recognizable from the Reformed tradition. Blake did not direct Presbyterians to the theology of the Reformers. To be Reformed entailed a desire for ongoing reform, an egalitarian and democratic spirit that would reject all social inequalities, and commitment to diversity in religious faith and practice.

In 1949, Blake foreshadowed his agenda in his remarks to the graduates of Princeton Seminary: "Any Presbyterian church that does not look to the progress and prosperity of the whole church, that does not ally itself with every other truly Christian church to win a world for Jesus Christ is not a Presbyterian church. It has become a Presbyterian sect. We have in our tradition great treasures to cherish and to offer the coming great church. But if we narrowly follow the path of rigidity now advocated by some Presbyterians, we will find our treasure corrupted and our opportunity gone."

In fulfilling their mission of serving the world, Blake argued that mainline Presbyterians must abandon their preference for Reformed faith and practice. Presbyterianism, along with the rest of Christendom, was about to evolve into something far greater, and the true spirit of Presbyterianism required an ecumenical appetite that would stop at nothing short of Presbyterian obsolescence. As he put it in an interview toward the end of his life, "There is *no future* for a sectarian church, whether it is Protestant, Roman Catholic or Orthodox—*no future—period!*"

Confession of 1967

The attention that Presbyterians devoted to Blake's proposal did not deflect them from the task of working out the details of the 1958 union, which included the challenge of confessional revision. Soon into its work, the revision committee determined that the flaws of the Westminster Confession were too great for the task of revision. Chief among them was its focus on a divine decree that separated the elect and the reprobate. What the church needed to confess was not its separateness from the world but its mission of reconciliation in and for the world. Instead, the committee requested and received a broader mandate to review more thoroughly the American Presbyterian confessional tradition. By 1965 it presented three proposals that would establish a new confessional identity for mainline Presbyterians. 3 Proposals

First, the committee drafted a brief contemporary expression of Reformed theology. In the Confession of 1967 (named for the year it 1967 was adopted) neo-orthodoxy was given confessional standing in the church. The confession affirmed God's transcendence over creation, humanity's fall into sin, and the call to faith as a response to God's grace in Jesus Christ. The confession carefully described the Bible as the word of God in lower case, to subordinate it to the incarnate Word of God, to whom Scripture was a faithful witness. Moreover, the confession endorsed modern biblical scholarship, and so instructed Presbyterians to read the Bible historically and not literally, liberated from the doctrine of inerrancy.

Second, the Confession of 1967 did not replace the Westminster Confession but joined it and several other confessions in a "Book of Confessions." (This was following in the precedent established by the United Presbyterians in the 1925 adoption of their Confessional Statement.) The UPCUSA now subscribed to a multiple confessional base from the ancient church (Nicene and Apostles' Creeds), the Reformation (Scots Confession, Heidelberg Catechism, Second Helvetic Confession, and Westminster Confession and Shorter Catechism), and the modern church (Barmen Declaration and Confession of 1967). The Larger Catechism was dropped, both because it had fallen out of use and because it was judged the most rigid and legalistic of the Westminster documents. Presbyterians united them in one book to remind the church of the cloud of witnesses from its Reformed past, and also to remind it that no single creed could capture the fullness of the Reformed faith, because each of them was a product of particular historical circumstances.

The church solved, or at least attempted to resolve, whatever paradoxes or contradictions these various confessional voices generated, by adopting the third confessional proposal that accompanied the new confession. The denomination revised its ordination vows for ministers and elders. It jettisoned the language from the founding of American Presbyterianism, which required an affirmative response to the question, "Do you sincerely receive and adopt the Confession of Faith and Catechisms of this Church as containing the system of doctrine taught in Holy Scripture?" Instead it required candidates to reply to the question, "Do you sincerely receive and adopt the essential tenets of the Reformed faith as expressed in the confession of our church as authentic and reliable expositions of what Scripture leads us to believe and do, and will you be instructed and led by those confessions as you lead the people of God?"

With the passage of these changes, the UPCUSA arguably abandoned its confessional identity, because the confession no longer bound the officers of the church by determining what was within or beyond the pale of Reformed orthodoxy. The new role of the confessions (as Presbyterians learned to express their standards in the plural) was to instruct, to lead, and to guide. If Presbyterians sympathetically studied how the faith was once confessed in these windows into their Reformed heritage, they would become better equipped to confess their faith today. In the words of Edmund Clowney of Westminster Seminary, mainline Presbyterians created a creedal museum and put the Westminster Standards under glass. Presbyterians further weakened the binding power of Scripture and the confessions by changes in the ordination process. Officer candidates no longer took vows; they answered constitutional questions.

Cornelius Van Til welcomed the Confession of 1967 as proof of his thirty-year claim that Barth had infiltrated the UPCUSA as the new modernism. Indeed, neo-orthodoxy proved to be more triumphant in the Presbyterian church than liberalism. All liberalism managed to do was minimize the Church's faith in the Westminster Standards, but it never succeeded in the church to the point of crafting a new confession. The triumph of neo-orthodoxy was the inevitability of the broadening church that could not protect historic Calvinism from modernism old or new. For Van Til, employing the rhetorical overkill that baffled some readers, the Confession of 1967, insofar as it was fathered by Barth, entailed the rejection, not only of the Westminster Standards, but of all that the historic Christian creeds affirm. The Book of Confessions, consequently, was a Book of Discord, a collection of mutually exclusive gospels.

The Lightness of Being Presbyterian

The Confession of 1967 was organized around the theme of reconciliation: "God's reconciling work in Jesus Christ and the mission of reconciliation to which he has called his church are at the heart of the gospel in any age. Our generation stands in peculiar need of reconciliation in Christ." Specifically, the confession called the church to this mission four ways: race relations, modern warfare, economic justice, and sexual relations. Rather than promote healing in either the church or society, the UPCUSA, by the passing of the Confession of 1967, witnessed the end of its period of ecclesiastical peace and a rise of theological antagonism and denominational strife.

One reason for the end of the truce was that by 1967 liberals in the church were dismissing the Confession of 1967 as "early Barth." The neo-orthodox movement was waning in influence and giving way to a plurality of contextual and issue-oriented theological ventures. Presbyterians advocated feminist theology, black theology, and theologies of liberation and process.

Second, many conservatives complained that the confession and its advocates made the case for reconciliation in blatantly political terms, and they accused the bureaucracy of the church of sounding like spokespersons for the Democratic Party.

In reaction to the Confession of 1967, conservatives organized special interest groups, such as Presbyterians United for Biblical Concerns and the Presbyterian Lay Committee. Added to these, eventually, were organizations on the theological and political left. As loyalty and giving shifted to these organizations, Presbyterians identified themselves less by their denominational affiliation than by the interest group that they supported. Diversity in the church devolved into theological fragmentation as special interest groups increased their lobbying efforts. One denominational official observed that the UPCUSA was marked less by theological diversity "than its avoidance of the challenges of that diversity."

On a deeper level, the PCUSA was suffering less from turmoil than trivialization, in the words of John Frye's terse assessment of the new confession and its aftermath, *The Trivialization of the United Presbyterian Church.* The call to social activism had transformed Presbyterians into a church of "pure doing" where anything it did was mission, by definition. This extended from the scandalous, such as the grant of ten thousand dollars to the defense fund of the radical Black Panther Angela Davis from the UPCUSA's Committee on Church and Race, to mundane chores such as the purchase of choir robes or communion cups. In short, the Confession of 1967 baptized everything Presbyterians did with the confessional legitimacy of reconciliation. When all of life was mission and every member a minister, Presbyterians lost their consciousness of special office and holy vocations.

Although the church continued to proclaim the theme that "theology matters," the task of maintaining and defending the Reformed faith receded from the mission of the mainline Presbyterian Church. As Presbyterians consolidated into greater organizational efficiency, there was growing awareness within the church that they were united in every way but theology, which descended into fragmentation, strife, and incoherence.

Presbyterian Separatists

If observers of American Presbyterianism wanted counter-evidence for Blake's claim that sectarian Presbyterianism had no future, they might have noted two important developments, no matter how small the denominations in which they took place. The first was in the South, the second was in the North.

In the case of the former, the post-Barthian phase of the UPCUSA contrasted significantly with another American Presbyterian encounter with neo-orthodoxy. The Associate Reformed Synod of the South in the twentieth century abandoned exclusive psalmody like the northern synod, but the southern church, which became known as the Associate Reformed Presbyterian Church, established firmer limits to its theological assimilation. While it was influenced to a significant degree by neo-orthodoxy, especially in the 1960s, in the last quarter century it self-consciously rejected Barthianism and reaffirmed its commitment

220

to biblical inerrancy and confessional Presbyterianism. The story of the ARP suggested that it was possible to move back to the theological right after having shifted left.

The second example of a future within sectarian Presbyterianism came in 1964. During that year the first merger among the twentieth-century Presbyterian splinter denominations took place when the eight-thousand-member Evangelical Presbyterian Church united with the two-thousand-member Reformed Presbyterian Church (General Synod) to form the Reformed Presbyterian Church, Evangelical Synod. *RPCES* This was a union of very different strands of the American Presbyterian tapestry. The EPC (not to be confused with the church of the same name formed in 1981) separated from the Orthodox Presbyterians in 1937 under Carl McIntire's leadership but changed its name in 1956 when McIntire and his followers defected from its company. The RPC(GS) was a 141-year-old denomination in the Covenanter tradition.

While the marriage of these two traditions did not produce psalm-singing chiliasts, certain features of their past found expression in the united church. The RPCES revised the Larger Catechism to make it more hospitable to premillennial interpretations of prophecy. The plan of union also included resolutions that warned against the use of alcohol and tobacco, as well as the evils of television, movies, dancing, and gambling. Although those resolutions were the basis for the merger, they carried no binding legislative power.

The story of these Presbyterian separatists went largely unnoticed amid the consolidation and growing turmoil of the mainline. Still they testified that sideline Presbyterianism might still have theological and ecumenical resources even if not nearly as big or as visible as the mainline.

12

The Assimilation of Southern Presbyterians

The southern Presbyterian Church began on a note that was at once both separatist and ecumenical. The first act of the first General Assembly of the Presbyterian Church of the Confederate States was the preparation and publication of its "Address to All the Churches of Jesus Christ throughout the Earth."

The paper contained its rationale for withdrawing from the northern Old School assembly, outlining the ecclesiastical indiscretions that required the exodus. At the same time, by addressing all true churches of Christ, the Assembly convened with a consciousness of being part of and in dialogue with the church catholic. This is not to suggest that the southern Presbyterians had a heightened ecumenical consciousness in 1861. Rather, both in their interchurch relations and the development of their theological identity, their eyes were constantly fixed to the North, and the separated brethren of the PCUSA.

When the war ended in 1865, Presbyterians in the South made clear that they were in no ecumenical mood to reunite with the North. Still, they were confronted with a question of no small ecumenical significance: with the death of the Confederacy, the church needed a new name. The 1865 General Assembly at Macon, Georgia, gave consideration to the name, "Presbyterian Church in the South," but rejected it in favor of "The Presbyterian Church in the United States." Its close similarity to the "Presbyterian Church in the United States of America" was perhaps intentional as the church challenged the northern claim to represent the entire country.

In opting for a national Presbyterian name, however, the church was not abandoning its regional identity. The task before the church was to help rebuild the South, which commissioners vowed to do. A pastoral letter to the churches read: "our desolation shall be repaired, until 'streams shall break out in the desert, and the wilderness shall blossom as the rose.' " The devastation of the war that destroyed many church buildings was enough to provoke anti-northern sentiment. The tyranny of Reconstruction added insult to injury, especially when the northern church dispatched workers to the South to establish black churches.

The testing of the boundaries of confessional orthodoxy in the North both scandalized Presbyterians in the South and served to strengthen southern attachment to Old School ways. Southerners were eager to defend these convictions and to highlight their devotion to them in order to underscore the decline of the North. Thus Old School Presbyterianism enjoyed a longer shelf life south of the Mason-Dixon line, as it assumed certain distinctive characteristics.

Among the most significant features of the southern version of the Old School was its emphasis on the spirituality of the church. Championed by James H. Thornwell, the doctrine would long outlive his death in 1862. Southern Presbyterians saw the church's task as preaching the gospel, trusting that the Holy Spirit would regenerate sinners by His Word and build them up in Christ. The church was not commissioned to make the world a better place in which to live. It had no business telling the government how to rule the body politic. It was not to feed the hungry, or provide houses for the homeless, or protest social injustice. These political and social temptations only distracted the church from its spiritual calling.

A closely connected principle that southerners equally cherished was *jure divino* (or "divine right") Presbyterianism. According to divine

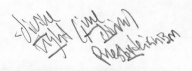

right Presbyterians, God had plainly set forth his law for his church in Scripture. The only pronouncements the church could make about its theology, polity, or worship were ones to which it could append the words, "Thus says the Lord." Since God speaks to his church only through his Word, scriptural warrant must undergird every aspect of its faith and practice. John L. Girardeau put the matter plainly when he stated before the 1875 General Assembly that the church "can utter no new doctrine, make no new laws, ordain no new forms of government, and invent no new modes of worship."

This doctrine reinforced the southern Presbyterian preference for church committees rather than boards. Since the 1838 division, Old Schoolers agreed that only the church and its official agencies were commissioned to do the work of the church. Southerners went further and argued that even those official agencies required biblical warrant. As southern Presbyterians watched the growth of the bureaucracy of the northern church, it prided itself in its modest administrative structure, and the greater accountability of its General Assembly committees in contrast to the autonomy of northern boards.

Jure divino Presbyterianism also helped to perpetuate the Puritan austerity of southern Presbyterian worship, guarding it against the innovations of ritualism and the idolatries of Rome. Emphasis fell on the exposition of the Word, which ministers were trained to deliver three times a week (Sunday morning and evening worship and Wednesday evening prayer meeting).

Above all, southern Presbyterians maintained and defended the doctrine of the inspiration and authority of Scripture. About the time of the Briggs trial in the North, Professor William M. McPheeters of Columbia Seminary eagerly reassured the church that the southern seminaries were protecting this vital doctrine. In 1891, he wrote in the *Presbyterian Quarterly*: "It is upon this foundation—the integrity, authenticity, genuineness, supernatural origin and divine authority of the Bible—that the church needs to center her most serious attention."

The southern Presbyterians also experienced a reunion with their New School counterpart. This in fact antedated the 1869 northern reunion when the United Synod of the South (New School) joined with the PCCS in 1864. However, the southern merger was not a precarious union of Old School and New School, as the North experienced in 1869. Rather, the southern Presbyterians swallowed up the much smaller United Synod under terms that resulted in a self-consciously Old School denomination. The PCUS dismissed the northern merger as a very different settlement:

> The union now consummated between the Old and New School Assemblies was accomplished by methods which, in our judgment, involve a total surrender of all the great testimonies of the Church for the fundamental doctrines of grace, at a time when the victory of truth over error hung in the balance. The united Assembly stands of necessity upon an allowed latitude of interpretation of the Standards and must come at length to embrace nearly all shades of doctrinal belief. Of those unfailing testimonies we are now the sole surviving heir, which we must lift from the dust and bear to the generations after us. It would be a serious compromise of this sacred trust to enter into public and official fellowship with those repudiating these testimonies.

This analysis contained standard southern Presbyterian rhetoric in its insistence that it was the true Presbyterian Church in America, zealous to maintain and defend the Reformed faith. Yet another northern Presbyterian departure from Calvinistic orthodoxy was its momentum for confessional revision, which southern Presbyterian writers eagerly pounced on as another way to underscore southern faithfulness. Not only was the church unwilling to countenance revision; it would guard against confessional decline by a heightened sense of confessional subscription. Contrary to northern Old School versions of system subscription, southerners formulated tighter vows. In Girardeau's words, "the [Westminster] Standards were the impregnable ramparts against error; . . . to teach what is contrary to any statement of the doctrinal standards was to teach what is contrary to some statement of doctrine in the Scriptures."

Indeed, as progressive Presbyterians in the North lobbied for a modified Calvinism better fit for modern times, southerners returned with rhetoric about their "jealous loyalty" to the "undiluted Calvinism" of the Westminster Standards. By southern reckoning there was no need for a restatement of timeless truth.

"Dead Hand of the Past"

Southern Presbyterian convictions were put to the test in the case of Professor James Woodrow (1828–1907). The uncle of President Woodrow Wilson, James Woodrow was a professor of natural science at Columbia Theological Seminary. An early opponent of evolution, Woodrow came to embrace the theory, although he preferred to call it "mediate creation." According to Woodrow, science and Scripture presented no conflicts, since the Bible was silent on evolution. Furthermore, that very silence freed both the scientist and the theologian from the task of artificial harmonization; non-contradiction was enough for both to conduct their work. Though Woodrow was never convicted of heresy, Robert L. Dabney and others considered his views "mischievous" because evolution tended toward atheism. Although the Columbia board exonerated him in 1884, it yielded to outside pressure and released him from his post in 1886 after the General Assembly resolved, by a vote of 137 to 13, that "Adam's body was directly fashioned by Almighty God, without any natural animal parentage." Woodrow remained a minister in good standing in the church and went on to serve as president of the University of South Carolina.

Throughout the course of the investigation of his views, many of the charges against Woodrow entailed ecclesiastical pronouncements about scientific theory. That those pronouncements themselves violated the spirituality of the church was an inconsistency not lost among Woodrow's supporters. Nor for that matter did observers in the North overlook the irony of a chair of natural science at a southern Presbyterian seminary.

Woodrow's ouster from Columbia marked the defeat of evolution in the church. The 1886 General Assembly deliverance condemning evolution was reiterated in 1888, 1889, and 1924, and the PCUS waited until 1968 to reverse its position.

The effects of the case reached far beyond evolution. According to historian Ernest Trice Thompson of Union Seminary in Virginia, the church's hostility to free and open theological inquiry marked its descent into a theological dark age, ruled by an "unyielding Calvinism" that was symbolized by the rigid "doubtlessness" of Robert L. Dabney. For at least a generation, the PCUS would be governed and directed, in

Thompson's words, by the "dead hand of the past." The Woodrow case silenced the work of biblical exegesis. By Thompson's reckoning, southern Presbyterians made no significant contributions to biblical scholarship for over fifty years. (Their schools did manage to produce idiosyncratic exegesis in defense of southern causes, locating, for example, a rationale for racial segregation in the Old Testament precedent of the Israelites' separation from the Canaanites.)

As Thompson summed up this period, "At the close of the nineteenth century the southern Presbyterian Church seemed solidly conservative, strongly Calvinistic, distinctly sectarian, and remarkably homogenous in outlook and belief." The theological consensus was defined around four key affirmations: the inerrancy of Scripture, strict subscription to the Westminster Standards, divine right Presbyterianism, and the spirituality of the church.

Southern Ecumenicity

Another shared value, of course, was southern animosity toward the North, although southern Presbyterians were unsettled about how that should find expression. Benjamin Morgan Palmer (1818–1902), long-time pastor of First Presbyterian Church in New Orleans, relentlessly pointed the church in the direction of ecclesiastical separation. There could be no reconciliation without northern repentance.

On the other hand, Stuart Robinson (1814–81) of Louisville, even though he led the Kentucky Synod out of the northern church and into the PCUS, argued that the church had nothing to fear from interchurch relations, least of all any contamination from the North. "In proportion to our numbers, we have more brains and more orthodoxy than any, and can better defend ourselves in any common scrimmage." And Moses Hoge (1819–99), a minister in Richmond, Virginia, reminded the church of its obligation to recognize other churches of like faith and practice: "Is there no genuine Presbyterianism but ours? If the only pure church is the Presbyterian Church of these Southern States . . . then may God have mercy on the world and on His Church."

By 1876 the southern church was cosmopolitan enough to join the World Presbyterian Alliance. Ecumenical interest also generated discussions with the Associate Reformed Presbyterians (though they would never overcome the obstacle of the latter's exclusive psalmody). But reunion with the North was another matter. When fraternal delegates from the North (fresh from the Old School-New School reunion) conveyed greetings before the 1870 General Assembly in Louisville, they did not catch the church in a reconciling mood. As Dabney thundered from the floor, "I hear brethren saying it is time to forgive. Mr. Chairman, I do not forgive. I do not try to forgive. What! Forgive these people, who have invaded our country, burned our cities, destroyed our homes, slain our young men, and spread desolation and ruin over our land!" Dabney's fiery rhetoric left the northern envoys in shock. Said Henry J. Van Dyke, "they have stripped every leaf from the olive branch and made a rod of it to beat us with."

Gradually, southern Presbyterian anger cooled off at least to the point where, by 1882, the two bodies established formal fraternal relations and began regularly to exchange delegates. Even so, southern Presbyterians regarded with dismay the northern enthusiasm for confessional revision. In 1884, they took steps to prevent revision in the South by tightening the constitutional procedure for amending the Westminster Confession. Rather than requiring approval of two-thirds of the presbyteries (a threshold that mainstream American Presbyterians established in 1789), the southern church adopted a three-fourths requirement. This action served not only to stabilize the church's confessional standard (no confessional changes would take place in the PCUS until 1942); it also delayed the prospect of church union, especially after 1903 when the interchurch dialogue involved different confessional versions.

Still skittish about organic union, the southern church made another constitutional adjustment in 1914, when it required a three-fourths super majority of the presbyteries in order to approve a union with any denomination. At the same time, southern Presbyterians proposed an alternative to organic union with the North. A federation of Presbyterian churches, they argued, would establish the unity of the visible church while preserving regional Presbyterian identity, both North and South. Not surprisingly, the model failed to interest northern ecumenicists, who pressed on for organic union.

Southern ecumenical ambivalence also found expression in the church's relationship to the Federal Council of Churches. Southerners declined an invitation to join in 1911, and then accepted in 1912. By

1931, wearied of the social-gospel tone of FCC pronouncements, the church withdrew, only to rejoin a decade later.

Southern ecumenical ties were most effectively established on the mission field. Where northern and southern Presbyterians found themselves laboring together in foreign fields, they sought ways to cooperate. After the 1906 union of northern Presbyterians and the Cumberland Presbyterian Church brought the PCUSA below the Mason-Dixon line, domestic missionaries found it necessary to establish comity agreements in border states and even in parts of the Deep South.

These opportunities for unity and fellowship had to overcome deep-seated suspicions that lasted for decades, especially when modernism began to infiltrate the northern church. The first third of the twentieth century witnessed southern schizophrenia on the subject of ecumenicity in general and especially union with the North. It may have seemed inevitable to some churchmen, but everyone agreed it would take more time.

A New Church for the New South

By this point the southern Presbyterian Church was still a conservative denomination in a rural and agrarian culture, and its identity was tied to preserving its heritage. Dr. R. C. Reed, of Columbia Seminary, in his *History of the Presbyterian Churches of the World,* argued that the southern church sought to preserve two historic Presbyterian affirmations that the northern church abandoned: belief that Scripture sanctioned the institution of slavery and that it forbade the ordination of women. Yet another distinguishing southern characteristic was its preference for separate churches for African-Americans. Reed's rationale was that the Bible did not condemn segregation, and a separation protected both races from the "social embarrassments which might arise from ecclesiastical mixture." He also relied on the spirituality argument: it was not the duty of the church to meddle in deeply established patterns of social life.

Other southern Presbyterians, especially in the border states, began to come to different assessments about the church's calling and its culture. When Harris A. Kirk of the Franklin Street Presbyterian Church of Baltimore preached before the General Assembly as its retiring moderator in 1929, his sermon, titled, "The Presbyterian Mind," sought to awaken the church to the challenges of its age. "The weakness of the church at the close of the nineteenth century," he said, "was its acceptance of the ideal of comfortableness. . . . But the age of comfortableness is gone, for this generation, gone forever." Southern Presbyterians needed to step out of their undisturbed middle-class enclaves to serve the world. The church, Kirk continued, "must not be afraid of living thought; it must be generous in accepting truth from any quarter; it must never retreat towards any kind of shelter in the interest of living safely. It must wholeheartedly determine to live dangerously; keep in close contact with living generations, and advance with the moving tide."

Kirk's sermon was an early call to recognize the emergence of the new South. The South was experiencing immense social change. Its population was exploding, its cities were growing, and its economy was industrializing. As it became part of the national economy, its isolation drawing to an end, so must it be with the Presbyterian Church.

Kirk's call was put in more explicit terms two decades later in Ernest Trice Thompson's book, *The Changing South and the Presbyterian Church in the United States*. Thompson identified two key moments in southern history: the colonial period, whose challenges were best met by the Baptists, and the nineteenth century, which was won by the Methodists. In his assessment, the latter half of the twentieth century could be the Presbyterian moment if the church could adapt its mission to changing times. Industrialization, urbanization, and especially the race question all required southern Presbyterians to rethink their mission. In a later book, *Tomorrow's Church, Tomorrow's World*, Thompson posed the problem more pointedly:

> The question which now confronts Southern Presbyterianism is this: Shall we increasingly become a Church of the comfortable middle class, appealing to businessmen, professional men, and independent farmers in a few restricted areas, to executives and engineers, and white collar workers, or shall we seek to win also those in the lower income brackets, sharecroppers as well as independent farmers, laborers as well as industrialists, the less privileged as well as the more privileged, those who labor with their hands as well as those who labor with their minds?

In Thompson's judgment, that question divided the church into two wings, "both equally sincere, one protecting an older way of life as essential to the faith, and the other lobbying for changes necessary for the church to minister in the modern world." Thompson did not disguise where his sentiments lay, and as longtime professor of church history at Union Seminary in Virginia (where by the end of his career he had educated at least half of the ministers of the southern church), Thompson wielded enormous influence on the church.

If conservatives in the church managed to fend off earlier theological innovations, they were less successful by mid-century. By the 1940s, changing southern sentiments began to take root in the theological seminaries (Union, Columbia, Louisville, and Austin), which began to expose students to perspectives beyond Old School Calvinism, including the neo-orthodoxy of Karl Barth.

At roughly the same time the church engaged in two landmark cases of church discipline. Hay Watson Smith was a minister in Little Rock, Arkansas, who was received by the Presbytery of Arkansas as a minister in good standing, despite his belief in evolution and his denial of biblical inerrancy. When the General Assembly received complaints from other presbyteries, it remanded the matter back to the presbytery, which declined to re-examine him.

A few years later, Ernest Trice Thompson himself became the subject of controversy when an elder in the church, Tom Glasgow, publicly accused him of denying the spirituality of the church. Glasgow declined to press charges in Thompson's presbytery, surmising that Thompson would likely be exonerated. Instead, several presbyteries petitioned that General Assembly examine Thompson's teaching. The Assembly refused and directed the complainants to Thompson's presbytery as the proper court of original jurisdiction.

Both progressives and conservatives agreed that these were watershed cases in the church but for different reasons. Conservatives feared that the General Assembly was procedurally protecting deviant views from prosecution while the church was losing its confessional identity.

Liberals welcomed signs of a maturing church that manifested a more theologically tolerant spirit and a greater respect for dissent from the standards. Moreover, they were gladdened at the way in which the Thompson case in particular was a reversal of the Woodrow episode. Woodrow was

231

ousted from Columbia when its board yielded to the pressures of public opinion. In the Thompson case, the General Assembly refused Glasgow's efforts to pursue Thompson outside the courts of the church.

The trials of Smith and Thompson yielded two ironies. First, the refusal of the General Assembly to take up conservative complaints was arguably in keeping with the conservative principle of regionalism. Second, the principle of original jurisdiction would come to protect conservatives in subsequent conflicts in the southern church.

The failure of conservatives to drive progressives out of the church was a clear sign that the southern church was changing. As with northern Presbyterians, this took shape early with confessional revision. In 1939, southern Presbyterians approved minor linguistic changes to the confession in order to improve its readability. In 1942, two new chapters were added, "Of the Gospel" and "Of the Holy Spirit," which modified the Calvinism in ways similar to the 1903 changes in the North. And in 1959, the General Assembly rewrote the chapter on "Of Marriage and Divorce."

On other occasions the Westminster Confession survived initiatives to alter it, but these did not bring solace to conservatives. In 1961 the General Assembly turned down an overture to revise the confession's teaching on predestination on grounds that the original wording's "historic" character was worth preserving, even if it was an "inadequate statement" and "not essential to Reformed theology." Moreover, conservatives lamented that even while the South may have preserved the confession far longer than did the North, the practice of the church was falling increasingly out of step with its standards. Southerners began to speak of Calvinism in modified terms. "The so-called five points of Calvinism were seldom proclaimed from the pulpits," according to Ernest Trice Thompson. By mid-century it was common to refer to the theology of the southern church as "low Calvinism," as the teachings of Barth, Brunner, and Tillich replaced the rigid and dogmatic Calvinism of the past.

A modified Calvinism meant a reexamination of the spirituality of the church. In 1935 the General Assembly redefined the doctrine to expand the church's social witness. The Assembly reasoned that the church could not fulfill its "spiritual function" unless it "deals with those actual evils in the individual life, and in the social order, which threaten man's moral and spiritual development." A socially active church in the South, in turn, could not ignore the problem of race. Progressives in the church rallied for greater support for the cause of integration. In 1954 the denomination's Division on Christian Relations reported that "enforced segregation of the races is discrimination which is out of harmony with Christian theology and ethics." [handwritten: 1954]

In that same year the church's Committee on Co-operation and Union culminated its seventeen-year effort when southern Presbyterians voted to merge with the North. In the churches along the borders and among the leaders of the church—former moderators, seminary faculty, committee secretaries, and synod officials—there was overwhelming support for union. Opposition came from the Deep South and especially among its ruling elders. The General Assembly vote to send the proposal to the presbyteries, 283 to 169, gave supporters slight hope that it could garner a three-fourths approval of the presbyteries. But the union cause then encountered the unanticipated timing of the Supreme Court decision, *Brown v. Board of Education*, that mandated school desegregation. Southern Presbyteries proceeded to reject the proposal by a vote of 43 to 42, in what was widely interpreted to be an emotional reaction to the high court's decision. Conservatives insisted that the vote showed there still existed theological differences between the North and the South that could not be overlooked.

The supporters of union did secure the General Assembly's authorization for the committees of the denomination to pursue as much joint activity and cooperation as possible. That included the production of a joint hymnal in 1955, further united efforts in foreign missions, and the establishment of union churches and presbyteries in 1968. Conservatives in the church viewed the latter as blatantly unconstitutional.

The PCUS also followed the northern church in permitting the ordination of women in 1964. General Assembly pronouncements took [handwritten: 1964] on increasingly liberal causes, including support for the legalization of abortion and the condemnation of capital punishment. Conservatives saw these as liberal tactics to bring the southern church into greater alignment with the northern Church, in anticipation of union.

All of these theological changes, as significant as they were, may have paled in comparison with the managerial revolution in the southern Presbyterian Church. As they slowly abandoned their regional and grassroots mentality, southerners moved toward greater effectiveness and coordination. Committees of the church expanded dramatically.

If the church continued to pay lip service to the Thornwellian ideal of decentralization and accountability, its preference for committees instead of boards became a distinction without a difference. By mid-century the modernization of the PCUS was virtually complete. The church may have caught up with the theological developments in the UPCUSA, but more important, it also bore striking organizational resemblance.

Voices of Dissent

Meanwhile, changes were taking shape within the conservative opposition to these progressive developments. Two influential dispensationalist schools had begun in the South, Columbia Bible College (1923) and Dallas Theological Seminary (1924), and both began with Presbyterians as their inaugural presidents. As dispensationalist teaching infiltrated conservative circles in the southern Presbyterian Church, opposition to liberalism took on fundamentalist and nonconfessional forms of expression.

Second, as the seminaries embraced new theological perspectives and progressive causes, the conservative leadership would fall into the hands of laypeople. A suspicion toward higher education would give the conservative cause a vaguely anti-intellectual spirit, and arguments against liberalism became more expedient and less dependent on older principles of southern Presbyterianism.

Conservative opposition to the liberal trends in the church began to organize in 1942. In that year the *Southern Presbyterian Journal* was launched, largely through the energy of Dr. L. Nelson Bell, a longtime medical missionary to China (and the father-in-law of Billy Graham). The magazine's purpose was "to call our Southern Presbyterian Church back to her original position, a position unequivocally loyal to the Word of God and the Standards of our Church." As a weekly, it served to counter the influence of its progressive counterpart, the *Presbyterian Outlook*. In 1954, the *Southern Presbyterian Journal* joined with the Association for the Preservation of the Southern Presbyterian Church, and together they launched a successful campaign to thwart merger with the north.

In 1964, Concerned Presbyterians became a vehicle to mobilize laypeople, and it was joined by a similar group for clergy, Presbyterian Churchmen United. In that same year, Rev. William Hill organized the

Presbyterian Evangelistic Fellowship with the purpose of supporting evangelism that was devoid of the social gospel. In 1971 the leadership of PEF formed the Executive Committee on Overseas Missions (ECOE), which sought to protect the spirituality of the church in the conduct of foreign missions.

As in the Presbyterian controversy in the North, these groups represented a mixture of theological commitments, ranging from Old School Presbyterians to fundamentalists who feared social change. There were divisions also between those who sought to reform the church from within and others who thought that a split in the church was inevitable. Where these disparate parties agreed was in affirming the importance of a seminary to provide ministers for the conservative cause. So a final component to the movement was the formation of Reformed Theological Seminary in Jackson, Mississippi, in 1966, an independent school whose charter established its identity in explicitly Old School terms.

In these developments the crisis in the South bore remarkable resemblance to the events in northern Presbyterianism in the first half of the century. Both narratives involved controversies in foreign missions that led to the establishment of parachurch mission agencies. Yet the continuing church movement of the South also revealed significant differences from the covenant union of the North. For one, the heresies that triggered the fight—liberalism of the North and neo-orthodoxy of the South—were not the same. The latter was subtler and less overtly hostile to confessional orthodoxy. Independent missionary work could proceed in the South without the threat of church discipline. Moreover, unlike Westminster Seminary, Reformed Theological Seminary strove to stay neutral in the ecclesiastical struggle (and several of its faculty would remain in the PCUS). All of these differences allowed the southern continuing church movement to slow cook over several decades and not explode the way it did in the North, thus allowing for the formation of a greater, if more diverse, constituency.

In 1969 representatives of these renewal groups composed a *Declaration of Commitment* in order "to preserve a confessional Church, thoroughly Reformed and Presbyterian." If the polity of the church was altered or diluted, the statement vowed to take "such actions as may be necessary to fulfill the obligations imposed by our ordination vows to maintain our Presbyterian faith."

[handwritten margin notes: "-PCA B formed in the faith. First Great awakening", "OPC - North", "PCA - South", "12/4/73 National Presbyterian Church ↓ PCA"]

Conservatives waited for the moment to move as the mainline Presbyterian churches inched closer to reunion. What finally pushed conservatives over the edge was a report that the Plan of Union would not contain a promised escape clause. The escape clause provided an amicable means for congregations to decline the union and to leave the denomination while maintaining their property. Although the Plan of Union committee then announced a two-year delay in the completion of its report, conservatives feared that the plan, when finally released, would provide no means of escape. In 1973 the steering committee organized from these renewal groups called on member churches to practice what it called "discipline in reverse" and leave the PCUS to establish a continuing Presbyterian Church.

Southern Church's Thirty Years' War Ends

On December 4, 1973, the thirty years' war in the southern church came to an end when delegates from 260 churches (representing a membership of forty-one thousand) gathered in Birmingham, Alabama, to form the National Presbyterian Church (the name soon changed to the Presbyterian Church in America).

The symmetry between the founding of the Presbyterian Church of the Confederate States of America and the Presbyterian Church in America have led some to call the PCA to its Old School heritage, citing especially its return to the 1861 version of the confession. But the PCA was a theologically diverse collection of often-conflicting agendas. Many of its founders, eager to escape from theological liberalism, were not committed to the high Calvinism of the southern Presbyterian past. The well-established practice of supporting parachurch organizations prompted an impulse toward independency that proved difficult for some churches to outgrow.

As in the Orthodox Presbyterian Church before it, theological controversies marked the General Assemblies of its early years, as commissioners debated continuing revelation and the charismatic movement, the nature and extent of confessional subscription, and the doctrine of creation. "The real unity of the Church was remarkably unrealized in the PCA's early years," observed Paul Settle, one of its founding ministers.

After the exodus of conservatives to the PCA, the PCUS found itself on the verge of completing its nearly century-long process of reunion with the North. In an effort to align themselves even more closely, southern Presbyterians drafted a "Declaration of Faith" along an activist theological agenda that paralleled the Confession of 1967. The General Assembly approved it in 1976, but the presbyteries rejected it, after which the 1977 GA approved it for study purposes. Though an unofficial statement, it laid to rest any doubt about its rejection of its theological past. The declaration confessed that "antagonisms between races, nations, and neighbors are manifestations of our sin against God," and that the calling of the church, beyond the preaching of the gospel, was to advance justice, compassion, and peace. This included a willingness "to make such amends as we can for centuries of injustice which the church condoned."

The PCUS had become a national church, and it relinquished its southern distinctives, so carefully guarded at its founding, in the interests of an expanded mission and the pursuit of union. When the PCA was founded, its "Message to All Churches of Jesus Christ throughout the World" (which intentionally paralleled the 1861 statement) declared: "we have called ourselves 'Continuing' Presbyterians because we seek to continue the faith of the founding fathers" of the PCUS. It remained to be negotiated in the theology and practice of the young church precisely what that founding faith was, and what southern Presbyterian principles the church would preserve.

13

Vanishing Presbyterianism

The departure of thousands of conservatives from the PCUS drew the church even closer to reunion with the North. Union presbyteries in the border states, begun in 1969, continued to spread: there were ten by 1978 and seventeen by 1983. The South, now liberated from the doctrine of the spirituality of the church, generally kept pace with the North in its left-wing social and political resolutions. Both churches had sanctioned abortion on demand and called for a freeze on America's nuclear arsenal.

Still, reunion was by no one's reckoning a *fait accompli*. After all, the South had already declined the union, and it constitutionally held a high bar of approval by three-fourths of its presbyteries for passage. For all the rhetoric about peacemaking coming from General Assemblies in the 1970s, there were few signs of tranquility in the UPCUSA. The northern Presbyterian contribution to the defense fund of Black Panther Angela Davis provoked protests both in the North and the South, and two judicial cases in the 1970s added to the turmoil and strife.

The 1958 merger between the United Presbyterians and the northern Presbyterians went through after a compromise that permitted but

238

did not require that ministers and congregations commit themselves to women in church office. The agreement eventually gave way to feminist demands for complete compliance. The church could not rest, feminists argued, on its mere endorsement of women's ordination. It would provide true opportunities for women in ministry only when women and men served together on every level of the church, including all of its sessions.

When Walter Wynn Kenyon, a student at Pittsburgh Theological Seminary, was examined for ordination in 1974, he informed the Pittsburgh Presbytery that he could not participate in services of ordination for women, though he would neither impede their ordination nor refuse to work with women ministers. After the presbytery authorized his ordination by a narrow margin, a complaint came before the Permanent Judicial Commission of the General Assembly. The commission overturned the presbytery in 1975, ruling that "it is the responsibility of our Church to deny ordination to one who has refused the ordination of women," because the General Assembly had no power "to allow a presbytery to grant an exception to an explicit constitutional provision."

What the Assembly demanded of ministers it required of churches as well. By 1979 the General Assembly ruled that all congregations must elect men and women to the office of ruling elder. A church that did not elect women officers could apply for a waiver from its presbytery, which could be granted for three years, if the congregation demonstrated that it was taking sufficient steps toward compliance.

The Kenyon ruling generated howls of protest within the church and prompted the exodus of forty congregations by the end of the decade. Among them was the historic, 150-year-old Tenth Presbyterian Church in Philadelphia. Its minister, James M. Boice, explained to the congregation that the Kenyon case brought to an end its "reform from within" efforts, a strategy championed by Boice's predecessor, Donald Grey Barnhouse. Now was the time for "peaceable withdrawal." That compliance to women's ordination, and not the Confession of 1967, provoked the crisis of conscience for churches such as Tenth Presbyterian and revealed the extent to which the church had become functionally independent from its denominational connection. That spirit of independence might also explain why Tenth realigned with the evangelical-friendly Reformed Presbyterian Church, Evangelical Synod, rather than the more confessionally conscious Orthodox Presbyterians.

The second controversy took place when the National Capital Union Presbytery determined to receive a minister, Mansfield Kaseman, who denied the deity of Christ, along with his sinless nature and bodily resurrection. Ordained in the United Church of Christ, Kaseman had been called to co-pastor a church in Rockville, Maryland, that was affiliated both with the UCC and the UPCUSA.

Once again, complaints against the presbytery's action reached the General Assembly's Permanent Judicial Commission. This time the PJC sustained the presbytery in 1981 by affirming that Kaseman's beliefs were within the "acceptable range of interpretation" of the church's confessions. The landmark ruling was the first significant test of the new theological boundaries drawn by the Confession of 1967 and the Book of Confessions. While the ruling correctly understood Kaseman's obligation as limited to seeking guidance from the church's standards, the failure of those standards to uphold a doctrine so basic as the deity of Christ confirmed the worst fears of evangelicals. So they found little comfort when the Commission further affirmed the church's belief in the "full deity and full humanity of Christ."

Another wave of departures from the church followed the Kaseman verdict. Among them was John Gerstner, a longtime professor at Pittsburgh Seminary and a holdover from its UPCNA days. Gerstner, who struggled to stay in the church after the passage of the Confession of 1967, described the Kaseman decision as apostasy. Although he backed away from his threat to lead a walkout from the 1981 General Assembly meeting in Houston, he soon left the denomination for the Presbyterian Church in America.

The Kaseman ruling also distressed a group of renewal-minded evangelicals in the North and the South who had previously resisted efforts to leave the church. Convinced now that this was the time to leave, they struggled to find a suitable denomination to join, especially because they were open to the ordination of women and to the practice of charismatic gifts.

In 1981, seventy-five ministers representing twelve churches announced the formation of the Evangelical Presbyterian Church. The new church adopted a modern-language version of the Westminster

240

Confession as its standard, in the interest of greater evangelistic zeal and effectiveness. It also approved an intentionally brief list of the "Essentials of Our Faith." The eight-point summary contained boilerplate affirmations about evangelical theology in language that was mildly Calvinistic. Congregations of the church were free to determine worship style, to elect women elders, to exercise charismatic gifts, and to maintain control of their property. The church has experienced modest growth as it continues to debate the constitutional status of the Essentials statement and the nature of Presbyterian connectedness.

While the Kenyon and Kaseman controversies challenged the courtship between the North and the South, union advocates were worried about a far more volatile issue that threatened to give reluctant southerners another reason to remain separate. In 1976, the New York Presbytery petitioned the General Assembly for guidance on whether to ordain a "person who is an avowed homosexual, and is well qualified in every other part of the trials for ordination. The General Assembly assigned the question to a task force that reported to the 1978 General Assembly. This sparked a heated debate throughout the denomination, rivaling the rhetoric that accompanied the Angela Davis controversy of the previous decade.

The task force majority recommended to the 1978 General Assembly that the ordination of practicing homosexuals should be properly left to the presbyteries. This argument was in keeping with a venerable Presbyterian tradition that dated back to Old Side-New Side settlement in colonial times. But it was also shrewd politics. Acknowledging the authority of the presbyteries was the ecclesiastical equivalent to states' rights, and so the proposal seemed an accommodation to southern Presbyterian grassroots sensibilities at the same time. The pro-gay majority of the task force was not only seeking to serve the interests of regionalism. Promoting the power of the presbyteries was also a common tactic for any Presbyterian cause—on the left or the right—that lacked the confidence of prevailing in a General Assembly showdown. Four years earlier, in the Kenyon case, it was conservatives who pushed, unsuccessfully, for the principle of presbytery autonomy.

After vigorous lobbying by the Presbyterians United for Biblical Concerns, the General Assembly rejected the majority proposal and voted overwhelmingly that "unrepentant homosexual practice does not accord with the requirements of ordination as set forth in the *Book of Order.*" Many southern Presbyterians welcomed the decision as a hopeful sign of evangelical renewal in the church. At the same time, it galvanized the pro-gay lobbyists in the church, such as the Presbyterians for Lesbian and Gay Concerns and More Light Presbyterians.

A final hurdle for both denominations regarded church property rights. Until 1979, the UPCUSA and the PCUS claimed that congregations held church buildings in trust for the denomination, and that this was implicit in their church order. A Supreme Court decision in that year, however, determined that the courts could intervene in property disputes where that trust was not explicitly specified in the church order. The northern church quickly amended its church order to meet the requirement of the Supreme Court decision. In 1982, the southern church changed its constitution in a similar way. For the traditionally grassroots-oriented denomination, this controversial procedure invoked ironic arguments. The stated clerk dusted off the Westminster Confession to argue that the "oneness of the church" implied that individual congregations were part of a larger whole, and that congregational independency had no place in the Presbyterian tradition. Opponents may have been on equally unfamiliar terrain by objecting on the basis of their civil rights.

Presbyterians Unite

The Plan of Union first drafted in 1970 finally came to a vote in 1983. That all 151 northern Presbyteries approved the plan came as little surprise. Conservative renewal groups enthusiastically embraced the plan as the best hope for northern renewal. The strongest objection from the North came from feminists who feared the merger as regressive for women's causes. Particularly offensive was a fifteen-year window granted for southern congregations to elect women elders. The decision to forgo immediate compliance for gentle persuasion was, in their judgment, a sacrifice of justice for expedience, and feminists made a symbolic witness of their dissent by voting against the plan.

In the South, the departures of conservatives into the Presbyterian Church in America and the Evangelical Presbyterian Church left little organized resistance to the union. Southern presbyteries voted for the

Plan of Union by a comfortable margin of 53 to 8. The Covenant Fellow-ship of Presbyterians, a broadly evangelical renewal group, had opposed merger since its founding in 1970, but it abruptly changed its position on the eve of the vote. Heartened by the show of strength by northern conservatives in the 1978 General Assembly ruling against homosexual clergy, the Covenant Fellowship joined renewal groups in the North in endorsing the union as an opportunity to revive the church.

For mainline American Presbyterians, the Civil War finally ended on June 10, 1983. The reunion was held in Georgia, where the division began in 1861. Atlanta was a fitting site, because northern atrocities were a distant memory, and the city was now a gleaming model of the new South. The first Assembly affirmed the rights of minorities and women in the church, and, as a foreshadow of conflicts on the horizon, the modera-tor, Jay Randolph Taylor, a Charlotte, North Carolina, minister, stressed the need for the united church to be "affirming" homosexuals.

The reunion was the third and greatest achievement for the ecu-menical ambitions of the Presbyterians in the twentieth century. The four major Presbyterian church denominations at the beginning of the century—Cumberland Presbyterians, Northern Presbyterians, Southern Presbyterians, and United Presbyterians—were one Church by century's end (even if those mergers produced splinter groups of the disaffected). With a combined membership of 3.2 million, Presbyterians were the fourth largest American denomination, behind Catholics, Southern Baptists, and United Methodists. According to Presbyterian pollster George Gallup, they were also geographically the most widely distributed denomination in the nation.

Though the mainline Presbyterians claimed to heal a 122-year divi-sion amid great fanfare (climaxing in a communion service with thirteen thousand in attendance), they were actually beaten to that distinction when the Reformed Presbyterian Church, Evangelical Synod joined the younger but larger Presbyterian Church in America in the previ-ous year. This was a noteworthy marriage because it not only marked a North-South reunion, but it also brought together descendents of the Old and New Schools.

While the RPCES was not lobbying for temperance more than the southerners were demanding segregated churches, there remained features in each tradition that tested the Reformed and Presbyterian identity of

very
old
school
heritage

the PCA (which retained its name). For southern Presbyterian traditional-ists within the PCA, the terms of the union explicitly required that the RPCES accept the historic theological positions of the PCA, including its embrace of the southern Presbyterian practice of strict confessional subscription. When RPCES-influenced changes were eventually incorporated in the Book of Church Order that established looser terms of subscription, there were fears among southern Old Schoolers that the church was broadening in a more diverse and evangelical direction, at the expense of its southern heritage.

The 1982 Plan of Union originally included the Orthodox Presbyterian Church as well. But the PCA presbyteries declined to receive the OPC, fearing the narrowness of its militant Calvinism. When the invitation was reissued in 1986, it was the OPC's turn to reject the plan, amid concerns that its Reformed identity might be swallowed up in the more broadly evangelical denomination. Though the OPC itself was never a fully self-conscious Old School denomination, its refusal to merge in 1986 frustrated some of its larger and more evangelical churches, which then joined the PCA through a process described as voluntary realignment.

Presbyterian Decline

After the 1983 merger, mainline Presbyterians dropped the word "united" from their name in favor of the more streamlined designation, Presbyterian Church (USA). Although it was the most organizationally united that mainstream Presbyterians had been since 1837, that was a fitting decision because it was difficult to describe the new denomination as genuinely united.

The spirit of the reunion bore a striking contrast to the sentiment of 1869, when reunited northerners saw themselves strengthened for new opportunities to conquer the western frontier and to provide moral leadership to the nation. Jonathan F. Stearns expressed that ambition in the *Presbyterian Reunion* memorial volume (1870):

> The church expects of us—the world with all its sorrows and sins, well aware that the true church is by its vocation the salt of the earth and the light of the world, expects from us—more than all, the Master

himself expects of us—that we, thus favored in the happy healing of our long-broken unity, should now reunite our force in one harmonious, resolute, persevering effort for the salvation of our race and the spread of the benign principles of our holy religion.

Presbyterian rhetoric in 1983 employed less-hopeful terms such as malaise, fragmentation, division, and even balkanization to describe the state of the church. Administrative streamlining and retrenchment accompanied the relocation of denominational offices from New York and Atlanta to Louisville. The eleven mainline Presbyterian seminaries fought for institutional survival. Presbyterian colleges pursued greater autonomy from denominational control and oversight.

Above all, Presbyterians sought an end to decades of declining membership. The numbers were staggering: from 1967 to the merger in 1983, American mainline Presbyterians plummeted from 4.2 million members to 3.2 million. In twenty years since the merger, the membership has further declined to 2.45 million, a loss of another 750,000 members, representing a total decline of 42 percent over a thirty-five-year period. The demise had reached a point where practitioners of the Hindu method of transcendental meditation in America outnumbered Presbyterians. Cynics predicted that if the rate of decline continued, the mainline Presbyterian Church would disappear before its 350th anniversary.

Evangelicals in the church were quick to analyze the crisis by citing the work of Dean Kelley in his 1972 book, *Why Conservative Churches Are Growing.* Kelley argued that strong churches (with well-defined systems of belief, clear behavioral expectations, and discipline to enforce both) are churches that grow, and weak churches (characterized by relativism, permissiveness, and toleration of deviant behavior) do not. For critics of the church bureaucracy, the lessons from Kelley's study were obvious: the general state of the PC(USA) matched his weak church description, while the agenda of evangelical renewal groups matched his strong church profile.

But studies of Presbyterian membership patterns indicated that the causes for decline were more complicated than Kelley suggested. Presbyterians took some comfort that the membership decline had not been matched by a comparable loss of giving to the church (except for a slight dip in offerings in the late 1960s, triggered by the Presbyterian contribution to the Angela Davis defense fund). Presbyterian giving, adjusted for inflation, remained steady for the same period, so if the church had fewer members it may have had more committed members.

Exit interviews revealed that members were not leaving the PC(USA) for more conservative churches; the trend was to abandon the institutional church altogether. Rather than find a home in more conservative (or "stronger") churches, ex-Presbyterians were searching for highly individualistic and personalized spirituality that resisted submission to external authority, much less traditional doctrine and practice.

Other studies blamed demographic factors, such as the decline in Presbyterian birth rates and the effects of higher education, which tended to secularize Presbyterian college students or invite intermarriage with members of other faiths. Still others pointed to the 1960s, a decade of social activism and religious experimentation, where Presbyterian young people left a denomination that seemed too staid and tradition-bound.

Denominational number crunching was not getting at the deeper problem, according to sociologist Robert Wuthnow, which was not the decline in Presbyterian numbers but the disappearance of Presbyterian identity. The tendency toward confessional mobility in American culture eroded the "ascriptive boundaries" that all denominations formerly possessed. Wade Clark Roof and William Mackinney argued that American denominations formerly served as quasi-ethnic groups that bound membership across generations. But that binding address weakened through the process of cultural assimilation and church mergers that made religious, ethnic, and regional distinctions disappear.

Presbyterians have stirred this melting pot through their advocacy of pan-Protestant causes such as the Consultation on Church Union. The theological and cultural tolerance generated by the ecumenical movement has made harder the task of boundary maintenance. Moreover, the weakening of confessional standards, culminating in a Book of Confessions, has made those boundaries all the harder to identify.

In these ways Presbyterians have been their own gravediggers, and the disappearance of denominational distinctives has been the fulfillment of their ecumenical and progressive agenda. By Presbyterian design, denominational boundaries have become fluid and permeable. When Presbyterians acknowledge their "full communion" with mainline Protestantism, denominations become brands of little or no significance to their membership. And without a compelling tradition to inherit and maintain, Americans are now shopping for faith as religious consumers.

In this sense, denominations are not disappearing but are being reinvented as networks that deliver goods and services. Congregations use denominations as one of several means of establishing strategic networks. PC(USA) congregations may align themselves with liberal or conservative interest groups. It is also common to find mainline and separate Presbyterian congregations becoming members of Willow Creek or Saddleback associations of churches. Denominational membership is but one of several connections for congregations that have become hyphenated or accidental Presbyterians.

Yet another cause for the recession of denominational identity is the tendency for American Protestants, along with Catholics and Jews, to define themselves more broadly in terms of orthodox or progressive. Cross-denominational engagement in the culture war in America, in the battlefronts over abortion, education, politics, family policy, and the like, has bifurcated American religion into liberal and conservative camps. American Presbyterians discovered themselves fighting other Presbyterians on public policy issues where they are joined by Catholics and Jews as co-belligerents.

As divisive as these issues have become within the PC(USA), Presbyterian cultural warriors share the assumption that the role of the church is to maintain and defend American civil religion (of either a conservative or a liberal expression). Presbyterian special interest groups have proliferated as Presbyterians have embraced the task of being the moral custodians of American values. The granddaddy of these groups is the conservative Presbyterian Lay Committee. Formed in 1965 to combat the passage of the Confession of 1967, it has consistently exposed the theological and political drift of the denomination to the theological and political left. Its magazine, the *Presbyterian Layman,* is distributed to a mailing list of 630,000.

As many other special interest groups, on the left and the right, joined the Presbyterian Lay Committee, pluralism increasingly characterized mainline Presbyterian life. While some Presbyterians applauded this development as a healthy sign of the diversity that has always marked the denomination, most feared that this was a pluralism of a different sort. Where Presbyterians in the past saw diversity as a challenge to be overcome as the church pursued its peace, purity, and unity, contemporary advocates were embracing pluralism itself as its identity.

Proposals to overcome divisiveness offered little hope for a coherent Presbyterian witness. One plan suggested that presbyteries be ideologically and not geographically drawn. That would present its own difficulties: thwarting ministers from moving from one presbytery to another and straining the relationships between one presbytery that ordained a minister and another presbytery that denied the call.

Separatist Presbyterians joined the culture war as well, often at the expense of their theological identity. At an address on the occasion of the merger between the RPCES and the PCA in 1982, Francis Schaeffer surveyed the devastating departure from a Christian consensus in America, and he urged the new church not to find contentment in its Presbyterian and Reformed identity. He reminded commissioners of their responsibility to serve the whole church and to transform the nation's political and cultural life. This calling required the church to accept "the privilege and duty of confrontation rather than accommodation," and that confrontation was most effective in co-belligerency with non-Presbyterian Christians.

Schaeffer's impassioned call to arms in the culture wars has been echoed by other separatist Presbyterian voices, most notably in PCA pastor D. James Kennedy's coalition to recover Christian America. The rise of Christian Reconstruction (or theonomy) in the PCA and OPC circles is a further sign of the social agenda of conservative Presbyterians who forged General Assembly declarations against homosexual marriage and women in the military. For mainline and separatists alike, the call to cultural warfare underscored the dilemma of being American and Reformed and the struggle of pursuing a social agenda while maintaining a confessional identity. Silenced in the noise of the debate was the voice of Presbyterian restraint that opted for conscientious objection from enlistment in the culture wars.

Defining Human Sexuality

The most acrimonious front of the Presbyterian culture wars involved issues of human sexuality. The 1978 General Assembly decision against homosexual clergy withstood several subsequent challenges, as pro-gay

248

advocacy groups have raised the issue before every subsequent General Assembly. In 1993, the General Assembly declared the decision against "unrepentant homosexual practice" among church officers as "authoritative." The 2004 General Assembly retained the prohibition by a close vote of 259 to 255.

Meanwhile, Presbyterian progressives pushed their agenda in other ways. The PC(USA) was a chief sponsor of the 1993 Re-Imaging Conference of the World Council of Churches in Minneapolis, Minnesota, which introduced goddess worship and Wicca practices, amid feminist skepticism that salvation is possible for women from a male redeemer.

In 1991 a special Committee on Human Sexuality released a two-hundred-page report that called for a radical change in Presbyterian attitudes toward sexual behavior. It recommended the endorsement of any sexual relationship, including extramarital and homosexual, where "justice-love" was present.

Exasperated conservatives in the church found an unlikely spokesperson for their frustration in Camille Paglia, a radical feminist who savaged the authors of the report in the pages of the *New Republic* for their liberal sentimentality and oppressive unwillingness to claim full responsibility for their sexual behavior.

> The report is so eager to ignore away the inconvenient facts of Christian morality about sex that one has to ask the committee members, Why remain Christian at all? . . . As a lapsed Catholic of wavering sexual orientation, I have never understood the pressure for ordination of gay clergy or even the creation of gay Catholic groups. They seem to me to indicate a need for parental approval, an inability to take personal responsibility for one's own identity. The institutional religions, Catholic and Protestant, carry with them the majesty of history. Their theology is impressive and coherent. Efforts to revise or dilute that theology for present convenience seem to me misguided.

Paglia, a pagan, could see what many Presbyterians failed to grasp, that the report was a desperate effort to maintain the church's credibility by abandoning its creeds. Far from a prophetic witness, this accommodation rendered the church indistinguishable from culture.

As gay rights advocates pushed the legalization of same-sex unions and other legal changes, Presbyterian renewal groups continued lobbying for traditional morality. In 1997, a majority of the Presbyteries approved an amendment to the Book of Order requiring church officers to live "in fidelity within the covenant of marriage between man and a woman or chastity in singleness." Fearing the reversal of the openness established by the Confession of 1967, fifty pastors, theologians, and seminary presidents wrote an open letter to the denomination against the language of fidelity and chastity: "We believe that an amendment such as this . . . transforms the confessions from great teaching documents which provide *guidance* into standards which require *compliance*." A pro-gay effort to change the language to "fidelity and integrity in marriage or singleness, and in all relationships of life" failed in the following year.

There was irony in the open letter's concern about compliance, because if traditionalists in the church managed to protect the letter of church law on sexuality, they were far less successful in policing Presbyterian practice. Pro-gay Presbyterians openly defied these General Assembly directives, and most of the courts of the church refused to bring discipline. In the case of one that did, the Permanent Judicial Commission in 2004 incoherently overturned a synod's discipline of a minister for performing a same-sex marriage. While identifying a tension in the Book of Church Order between the spirit and the letter of the law, the PJC determined that homosexual marriages were "impermissible" yet not prohibited.

The double standard employed by Presbyterian courts regarding compliance to Presbyterian law prompted great indignation among evangelicals, when the principle established by the 1974 Kenyon case met with open defiance from presbyteries that ordained practicing homosexuals. In the minds of liberals, however, selective enforcement of compliance was consistent with the Presbyterian commitment to progress. Church law cracked down on congregations not ordaining women, but not on those ordaining gays and lesbians, because the former impeded Presbyterian progress and the latter served Presbyterian evolution into higher truth and greater justice.

The ever-expanding notions of Presbyterian inclusiveness, especially on matters of human sexuality, raised the question of how broad could a broadening church become. Lefferts Loetscher himself prophesied in the conclusion to his study of the broadening resulting from the Presbyterian controversy that the church was "seriously hindered for the future from preventing more radical theological innovations." As if to prove his point, gay advocates plotted another strategy by taking a page from the Presbyterian past. On the seventy-fifth anniversary of the Auburn Affirmation in 1999, Auburn Theological Seminary President Barbara Wheeler suggested that the conditions that gave rise to the Affirmation bore resemblance to the current standoff in the church on sexual ethics. In both instances Presbyterians adopted ordination policies that excluded minorities in the church. The Auburn Affirmation taught Presbyterians to "take the offensive" through a proactive strategy to win the moderates of the church, reclaiming the church from fundamentalists who forced a non-Reformed standard upon the ministers of the denomination.

While a new Auburn Affirmation has yet to be composed, no compromise seemed in sight on the long debates over human sexuality. If the twenty-year reunion of northern and southern Presbyterians has not produced schism, that is only because heresy trials and break-away denominations have given way to advocacy groups and special interest caucuses. Trials and divisions at least give closure to the conflicts in the church's past, and Presbyterians today are regretting the endless debate of human sexuality. One denominational official was led to observe that "Presbyterians now engage sexuality issues with the same vehemence and deadly seriousness that their Calvinist forebears brought to discussions of predestination."

The Search for Presbyterian Identity

Presbyterian sex talk may itself be a coping device in that it distracts them from reckoning with the theological bankruptcy of the denomination. Perhaps the greatest indication of the disappearance of theological reflection in the denomination was the rise of the Confessing Church Movement. Sponsored by the Presbyterian Lay Committee, the Confessing Church Movement was founded in 2001 in response to the leftward drift of the General Assembly and its increasing accommodation to American culture. Confessing Presbyterians patterned their movement after the protest in Germany in 1933 against the Nazi-sponsored state church. Within a few years it grew to more than thirteen hundred member congregations that are committed to three affirmations:

251

1. That Jesus Christ alone is the Lord of all and the way of salvation.
2. That holy Scripture is the Triune God's revealed Word, the Church's only infallible rule of faith and practice.
3. That God's people are called to holiness in all aspects of life. This includes honoring the sanctity of marriage between a man and a woman, the only relationship within which sexual activity is appropriate.

By drawing a line in the sand on Jesus, the Bible, and heterosexual fidelity and chastity, renewal-minded Presbyterians lowered the confessional bar to a standard that contained nothing distinctively Reformed. At the same time, the movement's analogy with the church under Nazi Germany raised the stakes by invoking the language of *status confessionis*: this was no mere difference in theological perspective, but a crisis where the gospel itself was at stake.

Status confessionis recalled the Barmen Declaration against Hitler and the declaration of the World Alliance of Reformed Churches against apartheid in the 1980s. These comparisons meant that Confessing Presbyterians were claiming nothing less than that the PC(USA) had ceased to be the church, and that a breach in fellowship was necessary and imminent. Yet confessing congregations have not left the denomination, and do not plan to leave until the debate over church property can be resolved to their satisfaction. This casts doubt over the urgency of the crisis, while it raises the question of cultural accommodation. The Confessing Church Movement itself demonstrates the confessional bankruptcy of the church. While it laments the divisiveness in the church, it undermines the Presbyterian means to establish genuine terms of unity and diversity, which is the maintenance of a confessional tradition.

The quandary of identity is not limited to the mainline. The exodus that created the Presbyterian Church in America was frustrated with the cold, organizational bureaucracy of the mainline as much as its theological decline. The PCA's grassroots intimacy is what many of its members miss most about its founding, as the PCA increasingly resembles the organizational machine that its founders fled. Assessment centers find experts subjecting ministerial candidates to intense psychological profiling, bureaucratic caucusing has replaced Assembly deliberation, and ministries of mercy trump the spirituality of the church.

Of course, the PCA is not in numerical decline, but rather it claims to be among the fastest growing denominations in America. In twenty years it has grown to more than fifteen hundred congregations and more than three hundred thousand members. The denomination supports five hundred full-time career missionaries and over one hundred chaplains in the military, hospitals, and prisons. Still those numbers, impressive though they are, beg the question of whether the PCA is contributing to the growth of Presbyterianism in America. The PCA is more concerned with being on the cutting edge of "culture-formation" than fostering Presbyterian consciousness, and its growth often requires the disguise of its Presbyterian identity. The same may be said of the Evangelical Presbyterian Church.

Orthodox Presbyterians may bear the closest resemblance to the Presbyterian Old School. Yet while the OPC has grown very steadily in its seventy-year history from five thousand to thirty thousand members, it has watched several younger Presbyterian denominations leap ahead of it in size. Its struggle to maintain the identity has produced confusion over what is confessional and extra-confessional Presbyterianism. Some in the church have expressed frustration over the rise of a new fundamentalism that is departing from the Old School.

As different as the PC(USA) seems from the sideline Presbyterians, all have struggled in some way with the dilemma of maintaining confessional boundaries under the conditions of intense cultural pluralism and secularization. If an assimilationist impulse prompts an accommodation to prevailing cultural trends, a confrontational cultural agenda can also yield a secularization of the work of the church.

Vanishing Presbyterianism is a subset of vanishing denominational boundaries. Members today make little sense of denominational identity. As Hoge, Johnson, and Luidens put it in their book, *Vanishing Boundaries,* "The children have asked over and over what is distinctive about Presbyterianism—or even about Protestantism—and why they should believe and cherish it. The answers have apparently not been very clear."

There are no answers because there is no well-defined and coherent system of belief and conduct. If the Bible taught "what man is to believe concerning God and what duties God requires of man," Presbyterians in the past were more readily willing to pour Presbyterian content into those categories of faith and practice, establishing a Presbyterian ecology of Reformed worship, expository preaching, catechetical instruction, Sabbath observance, and a confession that defines and provides an identity for the church. All of these features of robust Presbyterianism have given way to a worldly cultural agenda. If Presbyterians in America are vanishing, then, conclude Hoge, Johnson, and Luidens, "they have no one to blame but themselves."

A worldly cultural agenda

Conclusion:
No Abiding City

The Bible is not the best model for writing history. This is not meant to denigrate Scripture but rather to point to an important difference between the writers of the sacred page and contemporary historians. While the former have divine authority and inspiration of the Holy Spirit, the latter are blessed at best to render a plausible interpretation of the past. Having conceded as much, the authors are reminded of a passage from Scripture that might lend perspective on the three hundred years of Presbyterian history summarized in the preceding pages.

The writer of the epistle to the Hebrews engages in a pre-modern form of religious history when in chapter 11 he recounts the "heroes" of the Old Testament. The stories of those saints were recorded to inspire the first Christians to new levels of faith and obedience.

Roughly midway through the chapter, the writer of the epistle pauses from the list of the faithful to make sure that Christians knew the Old Testament saints were much more similar to the church than the followers of Christ might have imagined. After all, Israel had the glories of Jerusalem, the Temple, and the promised land, but what did the early church have that might compare? And so the author of Hebrews wrote that the Old Testament saints died, "not having received the things promised, but having seen them and greeted them from afar, and having acknowledged that they were strangers and exiles on the earth. For people who speak thus make it clear that they are seeking a homeland," he continued, and the particular homeland that these saints sought was "a better country, that is, a heavenly one" (Heb. 11:13–14, 16).

If the authors of this book tried to assert, not midway but in the conclusion of their narrative, that the Presbyterians we think most faithful were seeking a heavenly city, not an earthly church of prominence and influence, we would justly open ourselves up to criticism. Again, the author of Hebrews possessed religious auspices that we obviously lack. Nevertheless, a point that a reader could plausibly draw from both the eleventh chapter of Hebrews and the history of American Presbyterianism told here is that there is no golden age in the history of the church. To expect such an age of wisdom for fallen creatures is to demand too much.

Students of the history of American Presbyterianism, at least as recounted here, should not be tempted to such expectations, because the history of this body of Protestant believers is one that perplexes more than it inspires. Some of the accomplishments were indeed notable, maybe even bordering on noble. But just as often, American Presbyterians left a mixed legacy, one from which their denominational heirs need to separate the precious metal from the dross.

As such, and as we tried to warn at the outset, the history of American Presbyterianism that recognizes warts and all is not the kind of historical writing that inspires or celebrates the past. Neither has this story been one that tells all in an effort to demean the American church. The Presbyterians surveyed here, like the saints of Hebrews 11, were people of faith. And their theology taught them, whether they always practiced it or not, that they were exiles and strangers, as much here in the United States as in Scotland or Northern Ireland. For that reason, readers should keep in mind the author of Hebrews' idea about seeking "a better country, a heavenly city." The real rewards of Presbyterian faith and practice are not to be found in a golden age of American Presbyterianism but in an expression of Reformed Christianity that sustains pilgrims longing for a better country, a heavenly city.

Silver Linings

Having first mentioned a significant factor that prevents the authors from celebrating a golden age of Presbyterianism's past, the authors believe it may still be useful to reflect on three types of readers who might try to discern through this book the better, if not golden, period of American Presbyterianism, the time when the church came into its own, showed itself to be a vibrant and intelligent communion, and made a difference in American Christianity.

The three types of readers who come most readily to mind are confessional, evangelical, and mainline Presbyterians. The former two, the one more theological, the other more activist, generally exist in the sideline Presbyterian denominations such as the Orthodox Presbyterian Church and the Presbyterian Church in America. The third group of readers is, as the name suggests, in the Presbyterian Church (USA) and likely still holds on to many of the conventions of the old Protestant establishment in the United States. As each group of readers looks to the American Presbyterian past, they are liable to find one period that best exhibited the strengths of their theological and ecclesiastical heritage as they have come to practice it.

For confessional Presbyterians, including the authors, who tend to put a premium on the teachings of the Westminster Standards, highly prize the Presbyterian form of church government, and esteem the reverence and simplicity of historic Presbyterian worship, the era of Old School Presbyterianism is the most appealing. The theologians of the Old School church brought unparalleled insight on the singularity of Presbyterianism—not simply for the fine points of Calvinist theology, but also for church polity and even for worship, a topic that seldom gained the interest of Presbyterians that it should have. And unlike the "heroes" of the other Presbyterian readers, Old School theologians continue to be assigned in seminary classrooms, studied by church officers, and read by church members for edification. But as impressive as those learned divines were, they were a minority within the Old School church and could not replicate their arguments in the next generation to avert the politicization of their denomination and reunion with the New School. What is more, they seldom commented on the damage that Presbyterian

257

respectability and cultural status could do to their Calvinistic faith, a possible source of their demise in the 1860s.

For evangelical Presbyterians, the awakenings of the colonial era, along with the evangelistically inspired reforms of the Second Great Awakening, are a source of inspiration and appropriate pride. Here the Calvinism of a Tennent, or a Dickinson, and their revivalistic ties to Jonathan Edwards reflect genuine affirmation of the system of doctrine taught in the Westminster Standards. That Calvinist theology may account for some discomfort with the revivals of the nineteenth century. But evangelical Presbyterians can likely take comfort in the Second Great Awakening's moderate representatives, such as Lyman Beecher or George Duffield. They may also regard the moral earnestness of antebellum Presbyterians as a vindication of the positive role that their tradition played in the Christianization of America, and as a model for contemporary participation in public life. But evangelical Presbyterians will likely concede that their heritage's revivalism was never as doctrinally precise as it should have been, and the even more critical will admit that the patriotism of the New School was excessive to the point of illegitimately ascribing redemptive meaning to the United States.

For mainline Presbyterians, the era that generates the most nostalgia is that of the mid-twentieth century when the Presbyterian Church in the U.S.A. was firmly part of the so-called Protestant establishment. This was a time when presidents and statesmen were glad to be seen worshiping in the oldest Protestant denominations and when a high number of those worshipers were Presbyterians. But the appeal of this period is not merely the access to the corridors of power. It was also a period of theological seriousness, when through the lead of neo-orthodox theologians including Karl Barth and Reinhold Niebuhr, Presbyterian seminaries recovered from the excesses of Protestant liberalism and restored a measure of dedication to the historic teachings of the Reformed churches. Likewise, it was an era when Presbyterians led America's Protestant mainline churches in reinvigorating the study of Christianity at the nation's university and college campuses. But these Presbyterian resources also ran dry or, at least like the Old School before them, could not mount sufficient resilience to withstand the cultural revolution of the 1960s. That was when the Protestant establishment's support for the American way of life looked especially preposterous to American minorities and their supporters, who felt excluded by that way of life.

Of course, these are not the only options in the search for a usable and inspiring Presbyterian past. But no matter where contemporary Presbyterians might turn in their history for inspiration and validation, they are also going to find impermanence if not also folly, weakness, and cowardice. To be sure, some of this is simply the function of being human, even if sanctified persons at that. But Presbyterianism in America is a repeated cycle of accomplishment and failure, insight and ignorance, faithfulness and disloyalty. There is no golden age of American Presbyterianism (or of any nation's Presbyterianism for that matter).

The Present Presbyterian Predicament

Evaluations of the present invite similar assessments. If the past teaches humility about Presbyterian accomplishments, the present may invite despair about the future of Presbyterianism. On the one hand, membership statistics for Presbyterian denominations in the United States do not reveal a tradition in the peak of health. For instance, Presbyterians in 2001 accounted for close to 5.6 million adherents in the United States, a figure that included all persons who identified themselves as Presbyterian, as well as all Presbyterian denominations, not simply those whose institutional roots are in the 1706 founding of American Presbyterianism. This made Presbyterianism the sixth largest religious affiliation in the United States, behind Roman Catholics, Baptists, Methodists, Lutherans, and Pentecostals, and accounting for only 2.7 percent of the entire population. (To put this figure in perspective, only forty-nine percent of these self-identified Presbyterians attend church weekly.) The mainline denomination, the Presbyterian Church (USA), has 2.1 million church members, which makes it the tenth largest denomination in the United States. But trends in that denomination, like those for the mainline more generally are not good. Between 1970 and 2000, according to the World Christian Database, the Presbyterian Church (USA) lost 1.1 million communicant and non-communicant members.

Some of this loss owed to the founding of new denominations, such as the Presbyterian Church in America and the Evangelical Pres-

[handwritten margin note: 2.7% of the pop.]

259

byterian Church. But these denominations have not shown remarkable growth themselves. The PCA has hovered around three hundred thousand members for the past ten years, and the EPC ranged between fifty thousand and sixty thousand during the 1990s. Meanwhile, the Orthodox Presbyterian Church remains the runt of the litter, holding steady in the mid-twenty thousands. That Presbyterians (2.7 percent of the population), who were part of the Anglo-American culture that founded the United States, are almost half the size of Lutherans (4.6 percent) who generally arrived later and came from German- and Scandinavian-speaking countries, may support Charles Hodge's observation from the 1830s about the inability of Presbyterians to hold on to their own. Considering that in 1776 Presbyterians were 25 percent of the American population, Hodge had a point.

To be sure, immigration and a host of other demographic factors made it impossible for Presbyterians to maintain their numerical share of American church membership. But even taking those circumstances into account, the health of American Presbyterianism since World War II has been in serious condition. Arguably, one of the gravest factors has been the decline of denominationalism and the rise of parachurch organizations. These religious endeavors that exist independently of any church oversight, from magazines and publishers, to Christian electronic media and celebrities, have been a large component in the decline of Presbyterianism defining a person's religious affiliation or identity. When the average American Protestant can listen to James Dobson nightly on the radio, follow the advance of Billy Graham's crusades through *Decision* magazine, meet with local Christians to study a book of the Bible organized around a study published by Zondervan, and listen to any number of Christian recording artists during his or her commute to and from work, it is easy to see how the efforts of a Presbyterian denomination, let alone the meager resources of the average Presbyterian congregation, can hardly keep up.

Equally important to this decline of denominationalism and rising popularity of parachurch Christianity are the journalistic and academic explanations of American Protestantism that divide the population between its mainline and evangelical halves. Presbyterians on both sides of the division, accordingly, tend to consider themselves first either liberal or conservative, and so adopt the moniker either mainline or evangelical accordingly. Which raises the question afresh whether being Presbyterian means anything, and specifically what it means to be a member of a Presbyterian denomination. These questions are even more pressing in the light of recent books such as the one by Mark A. Noll and Carolyn Nystrom, which asks, *Is the Reformation Over?* Christianity in the United States has reached a stage when a denominational identity like Presbyterian is up for grabs, and when it is uncertain whether the division between Protestants and Roman Catholics even matters.

These are indeed sober times for American Presbyterians. And that is why this book has avoided celebration and inspiration. The times demand self-awareness, discernment, and wisdom, and these are virtues that a critical history of American Presbyterianism may yield.

Of course, contemporary Presbyterians need to know a lot more than their history. The Bible, their confessional heritage, their reasons for restraint in worship, and the scriptural basis for their form of church government are likely more important for the health of Presbyterianism than historical knowledge. But without some awareness of how American Presbyterianism has come to its present state, biblical, theological and ecclesiological insights may not be as insightful as they need to be.

Still, such a solemn account of the American Presbyterian past need not lead to disillusionment, nor is that the authors' intent. Here is where the author of Hebrews may serve again as a model for church historians. What appears to be defeat in the history of redemption turns out ultimately to be victory. The example of Old Testament saints in Hebrews 11 is usually one of outward defeat. Yes, Moses led Israel across the Red Sea into the promised land, but the writer's account of Moses is not far from the stories of those saints who were mocked, stoned, tortured, and destitute (vv. 35–37). Even so, the martyrs were as "successful" as the victors in the contest with Pharaoh because none had received what God ultimately promised, namely, "a better country," "a heavenly one."

The same lesson applies to American Presbyterianism. The apparent lack of success that Presbyterians have experienced, and now face perhaps to an unprecedented degree, should not necessarily be any more disheartening compared with those times when Presbyterianism in the United States flourished, since adversity is what the church should expect. Christ and the apostles regularly warned New Testament believers that the church's pilgrimage to glory would be rocky, that opposition would be constant, that faithlessness would be an ongoing dilemma for officers and members.

The history of American Presbyterianism clearly proves why Christians have referred to God's people between the advents of Christ as the "church militant." This is not an excuse for indifference to those ways in which Presbyterians can and should seek self-correction and reform. But it does mean that the history of American Presbyterianism should not disillusion, that the church has faced constant adversity, and that God has blessed men and women to endure the opposition both from within and outside the Presbyterian fold.

As the apostle Paul informed the church in Corinth, through such earthen vessels as the Presbyterian ministry, God shows that "the surpassing power" to save belongs to him. And so, like Paul and the early church, American Presbyterians should "not lose heart." We may be "afflicted in every way, but not crushed; perplexed, but not driven to despair; persecuted, but not forsaken; struck down, but not destroyed" (2 Cor. 4:1, 7–9). Ultimately, the hope for American Presbyterians rests not in their own accomplishments but in the God whose glory, as the Shorter Catechism has it, is their "chief end" and source of eternal joy.

Notes

Introduction: Of Sobriety and Legends

5. "extended through time in which certain fundamental agreements." Alasdair McIntyre, *Whose Justice? Which Rationality?* (Notre Dame: University of Notre Dame Press, 1988), 12.

Chapter 1: Scotland to America

25. "the Puritan type of Presbyterianism." Charles Briggs, *American Presbyterianism: Its Origin and Early History* (Edinburgh: T. & T. Clark, 1885), 99.
26. "Towns and cohabitation would highly." Francis Makemie, *Plain and Friendly Persuasive to the Inhabitants of Virginia and Maryland . . .* (1705), quoted in Briggs, *American Presbyterianism*, 139.
28. "pernicious doctrines." E. H. Gillett, *History of the Presbyterian Church in the United States of America*, vol. 1 (Philadelphia: Presbyterian Publication Committee, 1864), 13.
28. "to live always so as to keep a conscience." Ibid., 14.
29. "The Presbyterians have come a great way." Ibid., 21.
30. "I am afraid will draw away a great part." Ibid., 24.
30. "one of the most laborious and useful members." Charles Hodge, *Constitutional History of the Presbyterian Church in the United States of America: Part I, 1705–1741* (Philadelphia: William S. Martien, 1839), 91.

Chapter 2: In Search of Presbyterian Identity

33. "Wha ever heard o' ganging doon." Ned C. Landsman, *Scotland and Its First American Colony, 1683–1760* (Princeton: Princeton University Press, 1985), 3.
34. "one should beware of taking too much." Ibid., 4.

263

34. "was the basis for presbyterianism." Charles Hodge, *Constitutional History of the Presbyterian Church in the United States of America: Part I, 1705–1741* (Philadelphia: William S. Martien, 1839), 69.

35. "between one and two hundred thousand." Ibid., 70.

36. "to meet yearly, and oftener." Francis Makemie, quoted in Charles Briggs, *American Presbyterianism: Its Origin and Early History* (Edinburgh: T. & T. Clark, 1885), 142.

41. "for the better carrying on." Synod quoted in Briggs, *American Presbyterianism*, 208.

41. "conscientiously dissent from them." Ibid., 209.

42. "I do own the Westminster Confession." Vow quoted in Briggs, *American Presbyterianism*, 210.

42. "usurpation of Presbyterial power." Briggs, *American Presbyterianism*, 210.

42. "publicly and authoritatively." Overture quoted in Briggs, *American Presbyterianism*, 211.

42. "to entertain the truth." Synod quoted in Briggs, *American Presbyterianism*, 211.

43. "detect heresies, resist gainsayers." Dickinson quoted in Briggs, *American Presbyterianism*, 212–13.

43. "belonged to that small class." Hodge, *Constitutional History*, 171.

44–45. "All the Ministers of this Synod." Adopting Act reprinted in *Records of the Presbyterian Church in the United States of America* (Philadelphia: PCUSA, 1904), 94–95.

45–46. "Although the synod do not claim." Ibid., 94.

46. "all the Ministers of this Synod." Ibid., 94.

47. "all the Presbyteries within." Ibid., 94.

47. "none of us will traduce or use." Preamble to Adopting Act, reprinted in *Records*, 94.

48. "that they understand these clauses." Synod, quoted in Adopting Act, reprinted in *Records*, 97.

48–49. "hope and desire, that this our Synodical." Ibid., 126–27.

Chapter 3: Enthusiasm and Order

50. "a man going to be put upon a rack." Gilbert Tennent quoted in Milton J Coalter Jr., *Gilbert Tennent, Son of Thunder: A Case Study of Continental Pietism's Impact on the First Great Awakening in the Middle Colonies* (New York: Greenwood Press, 1986), 39.

51. "gave a dreadful groan and sank again." Ibid., 39–40.

53–54. "adopted & still do adhere." Synod, reprinted in *Records of the Presbyterian Church in the United States of America* (Philadelphia: PCUSA, 1904), 127.

54. "due care be taken in examining." Tennent's motion quoted in Charles Briggs, *American Presbyterianism: Its Origin and Early History* (Edinburgh: T. & T. Clark, 1885), 240–41.

56. "the several branches of philosophy." Presbytery of Lewes motion quoted in Briggs, *American Presbyterianism*, 243.

56. "in any congregation belonging to another." Ibid.

57. "prosecute the design of erecting." Synod resolution quoted in Briggs, *American Presbyterianism*, 245.

58. "false hypothesis." Tennent complaint quoted in Briggs, *American Presbyterianism*, 246.

58. "cast the Standards out of doors." Synod affirmation quoted in Briggs, *American Presbyterianism*, 247.

61. "I beseech you, my dear Brethren." Gilbert Tennent, "The Danger of an Unconverted Ministry," reprinted in Alan Heimert and Perry Miller, eds., *The Great Awakening: Documents Illustrating the Crisis and Its Consequences* (Indianapolis: Bobbs-Merrill Publishing, 1967), 98–99.

61. "unhappy violence." Charles Hodge, *Constitutional History of the Presbyterian Church in the United States of America: Part I, 1741–1788* (Philadelphia: William S. Martien, 1840), 162.

62. "private mint to put the guinea-stamp." Richard Webster, *A History of the Presbyterian Church in America from Its Origin until the Year 1760* (Philadelphia: Joseph M. Wilson, 1857), 151.

62. "as they will answer." Minutes of Synod, quoted in Webster, *History*, 152.

62. "It is difficult to conceive." Webster, *History*, 153.

62–63. "to preserve this swooning." Ibid., 166.

63. "anarchical principles." Protestation of 1741, reprinted in Webster, *History*, 166.

63. "How monstrously absurd." Ibid., 171.

64. "have called themselves members." Jedediah Andrews, reprinted in Webster, *A History*, 178.

66–67. "it is cruel and censorious Judging." Gilbert Tennent, *Irenicum Ecclesiasticum*, in Heimert and Miller, eds., *Great Awakening*, 371.

68. "experimental acquaintance." "The Plan of Union, 1758," reprinted in Briggs, *American Presbyterianism*, appendices, cviii.

68. "a blessed work of God's Holy Spirit." "The Plan of Union, 1758," reprinted in Briggs, *American Presbyterianism*, appendices, cx.

Chapter 4: From a Colonial to a National Church

74. "their experimental acquaintance." E. H. Gillett, *History of the Presbyterian Church in the United States of America*, vol. 1 (Philadelphia: Presbyterian Publication Committee, 1864), 143.

75. "temper of schismatical tendency." Protest to Synod quoted in Gillett, *History*, 144.

75. "a case study in ecclesiastical manipulation." Elizabeth Nybakken, "New Light on the Old Side: Irish Influences on Colonial Presbyterianism," *Journal of American History* 68:4 (1982) 826.

75. "could support ministers singly." Synod of 1769, quoted in Charles Briggs, *American Presbyterianism: Its Origin and Early History* (Edinburgh: T. & T. Clark, 1885), 333.

76. "disposed." Letter from William Marshall to Synod quoted in Briggs, *American Presbyterianism*, 340.

76. "collect accounts relating thereto." Correspondence quoted in Gillett, *History*, 164.

77. "as the first magistrate of the empire." Letter of Synod quoted in Briggs, *American Presbyterianism*, 350.

77. "Let your prayers be offered." Ibid., 351.

78. "The cause in which America." John Witherspoon, "The Dominion of Providence over the Passions of Men," in Ellis Sandoz, ed., *Political Sermons of the American Founding Era, 1730–1805*, vol. 1 (Indianapolis: Liberty Fund, 1997), 549.

78–79. "They call themselves . . . " John King quoted in Gillett, *History*, 183–84.

79. "call this war . . . " From Mark A. Noll, *A History of Christianity in the United States and Canada* (Grand Rapids: Eerdmans, 1992), 122.

80. "ringleaders of rebellion." Gillett, *History*, 189.

81–82. "We cannot help congratulating." Letter of Synod quoted in Briggs, *American Presbyterianism*, 357.

82. "Had [the war] been unsuccessful." Ibid.

82. "the ecclesiastical polity of the Presbyterian churches." Briggs, *American Presbyterianism*, 354, 356.

83. "a habit of neglect." Letter of Synod quoted in Leonard J. Trinterud, *The Forming of an American Tradition: A Re-Examination of Colonial Presbyterianism* (Philadelphia: Westminster Press, 1949), 282.

83. "constitution of the church of Scotland." Motion quoted in Leonard J. Trinterud, *Forming of an American Tradition*, 283.

Chapter 5: Presbyterianism's Ferment

92. "The nation that adheres to the laws." Ashbel Green quoted in Mark A. Noll, *Princeton and the Republic, 1768–1822: The Search for a Christian Enlightenment in the Era of Samuel Stanhope Smith* (Princeton: Princeton University Press, 1989), 137–38.

93. "deep concern and awful dread." Minutes of the General Assembly (1798), quoted in E. H. Gillett, *History of the Presbyterian Church in the United States of America*, vol. 1 (Philadelphia: Presbyterian Publication Committee, 1864), 297.

94. "strong and musical voice." Gillett, *History*, 287.

95. "There was not in the whole region." Gillett, *History*, 506.

96–97. "in the power and majesty." E. H. Gillett, *History of the Presbyterian Church in the United States of America*, vol. 2 (Philadelphia: Presbyterian Publication Committee, 1864), 58.

97. "A meagre salary was given them." Ibid., 74.

97. "his solemn and fervid manner." Ibid., 58.

95. "I saw at least five hundred." Spectator quoted in Gillett, *History*, vol. 2, 167.

99. "Numbers sank down in their distress." Gillett, *History*, vol. 1, 541.

101. "The decrees of God." Cumberland Presbyterian Catechism available at http://www.cumberland.org/hfcpc/catech.htm. See answer number seven.

101. "other denominations, not connected." Cumberland Presbyterian Church General Assembly quoted in Gillett, *History*, vol. 2, 192.

103. "strictly enjoined." "The Plan of Union" (1801), reprinted in Maurice W. Armstrong, et. al, eds., *The Presbyterian Enterprise: Sources of American Presbyterian History* (Philadelphia: Westminster Press, 1956), 128.

103. "at this crisis in the religious progress." Gillett, *History*, vol. 1, 439.

105. "the school for statesmen." Quoted in Noll, *Princeton and the Republic*, 52.

106. "Give us ministers." Minutes of the General Assembly (1805), quoted in Noll, *Princeton and the Republic*, 259.

106. "little adapted to introduce a youth." Alexander sermon, quoted in Noll, *Princeton and the Republic*, 260.

107. "a learned, orthodox, pious." Line from sermon delivered at the inauguration of Archibald Alexander as professor of theology, quoted in Noll, *Princeton and the Republic*, 265.

Chapter 6: Revivalism and Division (Again)

110. "grand defect." Charles G. Finney, *Lectures on Revivals of Religion* (1835; Oberlin, OH: E. J. Goodrich, 1868), 178–79.

110. "with any attention." Finney quoted in Charles Hambrick-Stowe, *Charles G. Finney and the Spirit of American Evangelicalism* (Grand Rapids: Eerdmans, 1996), 26.

NOTES

110–11. "the most important public figures." Mark A. Noll, *A History of Christianity in the United States and Canada* (Grand Rapids: Eerdmans, 1992), 176.

111–12. "not less than fifty thousand." E. H. Gillett, *History of the Presbyterian Church in the United States of America*, vol. 2 (Philadelphia: Presbyterian Publication Committee, 1864), 216.

113. "the human constitution." Finney quoted in Hambrick-Stowe, *Charles G. Finney*, 33.

113. "a revival is not a miracle." Charles G. Finney, *Lectures on Revivals* of Religion (1835; Oberlin, OH: E. J. Goodrich, 1868), 12.

115. "Embrace every opportunity." Minutes of the General Assembly, quoted in Gillett, *History*, vol. 2, 218.

115. "That differences of opinion." Minutes of the General Assembly, quoted in Gillett, *History*, vol. 2, 218–19.

117. "the means by which the enemy." Synod of Philadelphia, quoted in Gillett, *History*, vol. 2, 221.

117. "to promote strict conformity." Minutes of the General Assembly, quoted in Gillett, *History*, vol. 2, 222.

117. "We do not believe." Objections quoted in Gillett, *History*, vol. 2, 223–24.

118. "personally responsible for the transgressions." Albert Barnes, *The Way of Salvation*, 7th ed. (New York: Leavit Lord and Co., 1836), 15.

118–19. "was for all men." Ibid., 19.

119. "The real question is whether." *Christian Spectator*, quoted in Samuel J. Baird, *A History of the New School* (Philadelphia: Claxton, Remesen and Haffelfinger, 1868), 362.

119. "We loved the great features." Barnes quoted in Ernest Trice Thompson, *Presbyterians in the South*, vol. 1 (Richmond: John Knox Press, 1963), 397.

119. "There occurred such disorder." Ashbel Green quoted in Earl A. Pope, "New England Calvinism and the Disruption of the Presbyterian Church," (Ph.D. Dissertation, Brown University, 1962), 192.

120. "Unless in the passing year." Green quoted in George M. Marsden, *The Evangelical Mind and the New School Presbyterian Experience: A Case Study of Thought and Theology in Nineteenth-Century America* (New Haven: Yale University Press, 1970), 55.

120. "in the misdirection and inappropriate exercise." George Duffield quoted in Marsden, *Evangelical Mind*, 55.

121. "comparatively orthodox." Samuel Baird quoted in Marsden, *Evangelical Mind*, 57.

121. "No doubt there is a jubilee." Finney, *Lectures on Revivals of Religion*, ed. William G. McLoughlin (1853; Cambridge, MA: Harvard University Press, 1960), 291.

122. "doctrinal errors" and following. *The Western Memorial,* reprinted in Samuel J. Baird, *A Collection of Acts, Deliverances, and Testimonies of the Supreme Judicatory of the Presbyterian Church* (Philadelphia: Presbyterian Board of Publication, 1855), 675–79.

124. "Fathers, Brethren, Fellow-Christians." Committee quoted in Marsden, *Evangelical Mind,* 62.

125. "to retain their present organization." Auburn Convention quoted in Marsden, *Evangelical Mind,* 64.

125–26. "Sir, we do not know." Old School moderator quoted in Marsden, *Evangelical Mind,* 65.

Chapter 7: The Flowering of American Presbyterianism

129. "General Assembly of the Presbyterian Church." E. H. Gillett, *History of the Presbyterian Church in the United States of America* vol. 2 (Philadelphia: Presbyterian Publication Committee, 1864), 536.

129. "certainly constitutional and strictly just." Pennsylvania Supreme Court justice quoted in Ernest Trice Thompson, *Presbyterians in the South.,* vol. 1 (Richmond: John Knox Press, 1963), 396.

130. "seem to indicate the purpose of God." Lyman Beecher, "The Memory of Our Fathers," quoted in George M. Marsden, *The Evangelical Mind and the New School Presbyterian Experience: A Case Study of Thought and Theology in Nineteenth-Century America* (New Haven: Yale University Press, 1970), 22–23.

130. "Europe never will be qualified." Beecher, "Perils of Atheism," quoted in Marsden, *Evangelical Mind,* 23.

130. "Intemperance is the sin of our land." Beecher, "Nature and Occasions of Intemperance," quoted in Marsden, *Evangelical Mind,* 25.

131. "On all that is wrong in social life." Albert Barnes, *The Church and Slavery* (Philadelphia: Parry & McMillan, 1857), 21–22.

131. "They sought a distinct theological." Marsden, *Evangelical Mind,* 113.

132. "It contains dogmas so abhorrent." Barnes, "The Relation of Theology to Preaching," quoted in Marsden, *Evangelical Mind,* 111.

132. "we had supposed that the terms." Albert Barnes, "Our Position: A Sermon Preached before the General Assembly of the Presbyterian Church in the United States, May 20, 1852" (New York: Newman & Ivison, 1852), 20–21.

133. "the doctrines of God's absolute." New School General Assembly Minutes, quoted in Marsden, *Evangelical Mind,* 118.

133. "of vital importance." Proceedings of the Synod of New York and New Jersey, quoted in Marsden, *Evangelical Mind,* 121.

133. "more reason for censure." Duffield quoted in Marsden, *Evangelical Mind,* 122–23.

134. "command obligatory to our branch." New School General Assembly Minutes, quoted in Marsden, *Evangelical Mind*, 125.

134. "have milked our Congregational cows." Congregationalist General Convention quoted in Marsden, *Evangelical Mind*, 128.

134–35. "This from New England!" *Presbyterian Quarterly Review* quoted in Marsden, *Evangelical Mind*, 128.

135. "we wish to be more Calvinistic." Richards quoted in Marsden, *Evangelical Mind*, 138.

136. "to treat those who are." Barnes quoted in Marsden, *Evangelical Mind*, 139.

136. "every saint, without exception." Barnes quoted in Marsden, *The Evangelical Mind*, 140.

136–37. "in the doctrine of redemption." Henry B. Smith quoted in Marsden, *Evangelical Mind*, 159.

137. "It gives us a fact." Smith quoted in Marsden, *Evangelical Mind*, 173.

137. "never completely dominated." Marsden, *Evangelical Mind*, 141.

138. "the one party is in favour." Charles Hodge, *Constitutional History of the Presbyterian Church in the United States of America: Part I, 1741–1788* (Philadelphia: William S. Martien, 1840), 9.

139. "the radical principle of Pelagius's system." Charles Hodge, *Essays and Reviews* (New York: Robert Carter & Bros., 1879), 253.

139. "The doctrine of the atonement." Ibid., 162.

140. "the Church, before she can move." Thornwell, *The Collected Writings of James Henley Thornwell*, vol. 4, ed. B. M. Palmer (1875; Edinburgh: Banner of Truth Trust, 1974), 244–45.

141. "We hold that her organization." Ibid., 251.

142. "The doctrine of our church on this subject." Charles Hodge, "The General Assembly," *Biblical Repertory and Princeton Review* 33 (1861) 557.

143. "serve two distinct ends in the great scheme." Stuart M. Robinson, *The Church of God as an Essential Element of the Gospel* (Philadelphia: Joseph M. Wilson, 1858), 87.

143. "the most conservative Church." Charles Hodge quoted in Lewis G. Vander Velde, *The Presbyterian Churches and the Federal Union, 1861–1869* (Cambridge: Harvard University Press, 1932), 24.

143. "it is without distinctive meaning." Charles Hodge, *Biblical Repertory and Princeton Review, Index Volume* (1870–1871), I:11.

Chapter 8: War and Division

148. "expediency of making some expression." Spring Resolution quoted in Lewis G. Vander Velde, *The Presbyterian Churches and the Federal Union, 1861–1869* (Cambridge: Harvard University Press, 1932), 48.

148. "to do all in their power." Spring quoted in Vander Velde, *Presbyterian Churches*, 48.

148–49. "to keep unbroken the unity." Hodge quoted in Vander Velde, *Presbyterian Churches*, 60.

148–49. "to sustain the Government." Bates and Chase quoted in Vander Velde, *Presbyterian Churches*, 61.

149. "promote and perpetuate." Spring Resolution quoted in Vander Velde, *Presbyterian Churches*, 58–59.

149. "any particular administration." Ibid., 62–63.

149–50. "first taking the oath of allegiance." Editorial from *American Presbyterian* quoted in Vander Velde, *Presbyterian Churches*, 75.

152. "total abolition of slavery." General Assembly Minutes quoted in E. H. Gillett, *History of the Presbyterian Church in the United States of America*, vol. 2 (Philadelphia: Presbyterian Publication Committee, 1864), 241.

153. "from principle" and following paragraph. Presbytery of Lexington quoted in Gillett, *History*, vol. 2, 557–58.

154–55. "It is impossible to answer" and following paragraph. General Assembly Minutes quoted in Robert Livingston Stanton, *The Church and the Rebellion of the Government of the United States* (New York: Derby & Miller, 1964), 382.

155. "the action of the General Assembly." Ibid., 389.

156–57. "The Union, which our fathers designed." Thornwell quoted in Vander Velde, *Presbyterian Churches*, 29–30.

158. "The constitution of society." Thomas Smyth quoted in Ernest Trice Thompson, *Presbyterians in the South*, vol. 2 (Richmond: John Knox Press, 1963), 59–60.

158. "there is nothing in our legislation." James A. Lyon quoted in Thompson, *Presbyterians in the South*, vol. 2, 57.

159. "peculiar mission of the Southern Church." General Assembly Minutes quoted in Thompson, *Presbyterians in the South.*, vol. 2, 62.

159. "manifest our hearty agreement." Committee quoted in Thompson, *Presbyterians in the South*, vol. 2, 121.

159. "except upon a formal and distinct." John B. Adger quoted in Thompson, *Presbyterians in the South.*, vol. 2, 120–21.

160. "on the basis of our." Dabney quoted in Thompson, *Presbyterians in the South*, vol. 2, 121.

160. "all authority, human and divine." General Assembly Minutes quoted in Vander Velde, *Presbyterian Churches*, 111.

160. "use their influence, in all lawful." Synod of Buffalo quoted in Vander Velde, *Presbyterian Churches*, 116–17.

161. "the time has come, in the providence." General Assembly Minutes quoted in Vander Velde, *Presbyterian Churches*, 126–27.

161. "beyond the jurisdiction of the United States." General Assembly Minutes quoted in Vander Velde, *Presbyterian Churches*, 200.

162. "transcended its power." Hodge quoted in Vander Velde, *Presbyterian Churches*, 202.

162. "civil commonwealth." "Declaration and Testimony," quoted in Vander Velde, *Presbyterian Churches*, 204.

163. "heartfelt Christian salutations." General Assembly Minutes quoted in Vander Velde, *Presbyterian Churches*, 492.

163. "less prompt than some in reaching." New School delegate quoted in Vander Velde, *Presbyterian Churches*, 495–96.

165. "from their ecclesiastical differences." Vander Velde, *Presbyterian Churches*, 520.

Chapter 9: Ecumenism and Progress

169. "the tidal wave of wickedness" and "it was going out to the churchless." Quoted in Norman J. Bender, *Winning the World for Christ: Sheldon Jackson and Presbyterianism on the Rocky Mountain Frontier, 1869–1888* (Albuquerque: University of New Mexico Press, 1996), 21.

170. "disputes over moral depravity." George M. Marsden, *The Evangelical Mind and the New School Presbyterian Experience: A Case Study in Thought and Theology in Nineteenth Century America* (New Haven: Yale University Press, 1970), 211.

170–71. "welfare of the whole country." Minutes of the General Assembly of the Presbyterian Church in the United States of America (Old School), 1868, 5.

172. "Reflecting the spirit of the times." Lefferts A. Loetscher, *The Broadening Church: A Study of Theological Issues in the Presbyterian Church Since 1869* (Philadelphia: University of Pennsylvania Press, 1954), 8.

172. "combine the scattered energies." Quoted in J. David Hoeveler Jr., "Evangelical Ecumenism: James McCosh and the Intellectual Origins of the World Alliance of Reformed Churches," *Journal of Presbyterian History* 55 (1977), 47.

173. "efficient and good." Samuel Haber, *Efficiency and Uplift: Scientific Management in the Progressive Era* (Chicago: University of Chicago Press, 1964), ix.

175. "there is little difference." Robert Lewis Dabney, "The Pan-Presbyterian Alliance" in *Discussion of Robert Lewis Dabney*, vol. 2., 537.

175–76. "the same argument." Ibid., 538.

176. "the suppression of the truth." "Broad Churchism," *Southern Presbyterian Review* 28 (1877) 259.

176. "the broader the basis of union." Ibid., 263.

178. "we cannot see how." Charles Hodge, "What is Darwinism?" in *The Princeton Theology, 1812–1921*, ed. Mark A. Noll (Grand Rapids: Baker Book House, 1983), 151.

178–79. "There is a wonderful correspondence." *The Presbyterian Enterprise: Sources of American Presbyterian History*, ed. Maurice W. Armstrong, Lefferts A. Loetscher, and Charles A. Anderson (Philadelphia: Westminster Press, 1956), 238.

179. "we have no sympathy." A. A. Hodge, quoted in Noll, *The Princeton Theology*, 233.

179. "not only evolutionism." B. B. Warfield, "Calvin's Doctrine of Creation," in Noll, *The Princeton Theology*, 297.

179. "no one can charge." Andrew C. Zenos, *Presbyterianism in America: Past, Present and Prospective* (New York: Thomas Nelson and Sons, 1937), 182.

180. "the hope of advancement." Ibid., 193.

180. "The conclusion of the matter." Ibid., 197.

181. "missionary enthusiasm and progress." *Presbyterian Enterprise*, 254.

181–82. "great barrier to the reunion." Charles A. Briggs, "The Barriers to Christian Union," *Presbyterian Review* 8 (1887), 454.

182. "progress in religion." Charles A. Briggs, *Whither? A Theological Question for the Times* (New York: Charles Scribner's Sons, 1889), 266.

182. "Orthodoxism assumes to know." Ibid., 7.

182. "to the higher knowledge." Ibid., 274–75.

183. "some time-honored rigidity." Benjamin J. Lake, *The Story of the Presbyterian Church in the U.S.A.* (Philadelphia: Westminster Press, 1956), 90–91.

183. "I shall venture to affirm." *Presbyterian Enterprise*, 251.

183. "It is an inexpressible grief." B. B. Warfield, *Revision or Reaffirmation* (Princeton: privately printed, 1900).

184. "These two truths." *The Presbyterian Enterprise*, 247.

184. "to render it." Quoted in Loetscher, *The Broadening Church*, 89.

184. "change to Arminianism." Lefferts A. Loetscher, "Some Trends and Events Since 1869," in *They Seek a Country: The American Presbyterians*, ed. Gaius Jackson Slosser (New York: Macmillan, 1955), 262.

185. "differences as to the nature." B. B. Warfield, "The Proposed Union with the Cumberland Presbyterians," *Princeton Theological Review* 2 (1904), 301.

185. "greater efficiency." William Brenton Greene Jr., "Broad Churchism and the Christian Life," *Princeton Theological Review* 4 (1906), 308, 310.

Chapter 10: The Presbyterian Conflict (North)

188–89. "Made in Germany." Quoted in George M. Marsden, *Fundamentalism and American Culture: The Shaping of Twentieth Century Evangelicalism, 1870–1925* (New York: Oxford University Press, 1980), 142.

189. "hot-bed of patriotic enthusiasm." Quoted in Ned B. Stonehouse, *J. Gresham Machen: A Biographical Memoir* (Grand Rapids: Eerdmans, 1954), 247.

189. "the great lesson of the war." John F. Piper Jr., *Robert E. Speer: Prophet of the American Church* (Louisville: Geneva Press, 2000), 298.

190. "the time has come." *Minutes of the General Assembly of the Presbyterian Church in the U.S.A.* 1918), 154.

190. "the creed on the basis of which." B. B. Warfield, *Selected Shorter Writings* (Nutley, NJ: Presbyterian and Reformed, 1970), 1:386.

191–92. "the controversy, despite the noise it made." Harry Emerson Fosdick, *The Living of These Days: An Autobiography* (New York: Harper and Brothers, 1956), 164.

192. "I am convinced." Clarence Macartney, "Shall Unbelief Win?" in William S. Barker and Samuel T. Logan, eds., *Sermons that Made America: Reformed Preaching from 1630 to 2001* (Philipsburg, NJ: P&R Publishing, 2003), 343.

194. "a separation between the two parties." J. Gresham Machen, *Christianity and Liberalism* (Grand Rapids: Eerdmans, 1956), 160.

195. "to study the present spiritual condition." *Minutes of the General Assembly of the Presbyterian Church in the U.S.A.*, part 1 (1925), 88.

195. "reducible to the one great underlying cause." J. Gresham Machen, *Selected Shorter Writings* (Phillipsburg, NJ: P&R, 2004), 291.

196. "plunge the church into calamitous litigation." Bradley Longfield, *The Presbyterian Controversy: Fundamentalists, Modernists, and Moderates* (New York: Oxford, 1991), 157.

196. "Presbyterian system admits." *Minutes of the General Assembly of the Presbyterian Church in the U.S.A.*, part 1 (1926), 78.

196. "all slander and misrepresentation." *Minutes of the General Assembly of the Presbyterian Church in the U.S.A.*, part 1 (1927), 60.

197. "fork in the road." William Ernest Hocking, ed., *Re-Thinking Missions: A Layman's Inquiry After One Hundred Years* (New York: Harper and Brothers, 1932), ix.

197. "very essence of Christianity" and "it is a profound mistake." Robert E. Speer, *"Re-Thinking Missions" Examined* (New York: Fleming H. Revell, 1933), 31, 33.

197. "have scattered the fog." Clarence E. Macartney, " 'Renouncing Missions' or 'Modernism Unmasked.' " *Christianity Today* 3 (Jan. 1933), 6.

198. "great danger that lurks." Overture reprinted in Edwin H. Rian, *The Presbyterian Conflict* (Philadelphia: Committee for the Historian of the OPC, 1992), 217.

198. "truly amazing power." Quoted in Stonehouse, *J. Gresham Machen*, 472.

198. "time when the church had to fight." Robert E. Speer, *Missionary Principles and Practice: A Discussion of Christian Missions and Some Criticisms Upon Them* (New York: Fleming H. Revell, 1902), 540.

198. "administrative functions." Quoted in D. G. Hart, *Defending the Faith: J. Gresham Machen and the Crisis of Conservative Protestantism in America* (Baltimore: Johns Hopkins University Press, 1994), 152.

199. "unscriptural and unpresbyterian." Clarence E. Macartney, "Presbyterians, Awake!" *Presbyterian* 104 (Jul. 19, 1934), 8.

199. "those who enjoy a bit of irony." William Childs Robinson, "Which is the Rule of Faith and Life: The Word of God or the Voice of the Church?" *Christianity Today* 6:1 (June 1935), 6.

199–200. "if I were the pastor." Quoted in George M. Marsden, *Reforming Fundamentalism: Fuller Seminary and the New Evangelicalism* (Grand Rapids: Eerdmans, 1987), 42–43.

200. "I value less." Clarence E. Macartney, "Warm Hearts and Steady Faith," *Christian Century* 56 (March 8, 1939), 317.

200. "all is quiet on the theological front." J. A. MacCallum, "Valediction," *The Presbyterian Tribune* 54 (March 16, 1939), 5.

200. "become members, at last" J. Gresham Machen, "A True Presbyterian Church at Last," *Presbyterian Guardian* 2:6 (June 22, 1936), 110.

201. "condemnatory spirit." Carl F. H. Henry, *Confessions of a Theologian: An Autobiography* (Waco: Word Books, 1986), 68.

202. "lost its nerve." D. Clair Davis, "Evangelicals and the Presbyterian Tradition: An Alternative Perspective," *Westminster Theological Journal* 42 (1979), 156.

203. "it appears that Machen's fears." Bradley J. Longfield, *The Presbyterian Controversy: Fundamentalists, Modernists, and Moderates* (New York: Oxford University Press, 1991), 234.

203. "largely inhibit among Presbyterians." Lefferts A. Loetscher, *The Broadening Church*, 156.

Chapter 11: Presbyterian Consolidation

206. "fundamentally sound in the faith." Ernest Trice Thompson, "Is the Northern Church Theologically Sound?" *Union Seminary Review* (1931), 134.

209. "great-heartedness [of Presbyterianism]" and "example of that great neo-Calvinist." John Mackay, *The Presbyterian Way of Life* (Englewood, NJ: Prentice-Hall, 1960), 37, 43.

209–10. "If the late J. Gresham Machen." Cornelius Van Til, *The New Modernism: An Appraisal of the Theology of Barth and Brunner* (Philadelphia: Presbyterian and Reformed, 1947), 376.

210. "putting down only a very thin sheet." Sidney Ahlstrom, *Religious History of the American People* (New Haven: Yale University Press, 1972), 947.

211. "makes no sense." Quoted in Sidney Ahlstrom. *Religious History of the American People*, 954.

211. "very fervent faith." Martin E. Marty, *The New Shape of American Religion* (New York: Harper & Row, 1959), 79.

212. "domesticated and tailored leftover." Quoted in Richard Wightman Fox, *Reinhold Niebuhr: A Biography* (New York: Pantheon, 1985), 288.

212. "blandness that befits." Ibid., 266.

212. "readily digestable form." Henry P. Van Dusen, Letter to the editor, *Christianity and Crisis* (April 2, 1956), 40.

212. "To be ecumenical." Robert McAfee Brown, "I am Presbyterian—Therefore I am Ecumenical," *Presbyterian Survey* 77 (Sept 1987), 15.

215. "we are late." Quoted in Betty Thompson, "Eugene Carson Blake: A Noble Prophet," *Christian Century* 102:26 (Aug 28, 1985), 756.

215. "never before." Eugene Carson Blake, "A Proposal Towards the Reunion of Christ's Church," reprinted in *Ecumenical Review* 38 (1986), 141–42.

216. "Any Presbyterian church." Eugene Carson Blake, "Which Way the Presbyterian Church?" *Princeton Seminary Bulletin* 43 (1949), 11.

216. "There is *no future* for a sectarian church." Quoted in R. Douglas Breckenridge, *Eugene Carson Blake: Prophet with Portfolio* (New York: Seabury Press, 1978), 188.

219. "than its avoidance of the challenge." *Is Christ Divided? Report of the Task Force on Theological Pluralism in the Presbyterian Community of Faith* (Louisville: Office of the General Assembly, PC(USA), 1988), 11.

Chapter 12: The Assimilation of Southern Presbyterians

223. "our desolation shall be repaired." T. Watson Street, *The Story of Southern Presbyterians* (Richmond: John Knox, 1961), 76.

224. "can utter no new doctrine." John L. Girardeau, "The General Assembly at St. Louis," *Southern Presbyterian Review* 26 (1875), 606.

224. "It is upon this foundation." W. M. McPheeters, Book Review of *Current Discussions in Theology, Presbyterian Quarterly* 5:15 (Jan 1891), 126.

225. "The union now consummated." *Minutes of the General Assembly of the Presbyterian Church in the United States* (1870), 529.

225. "the [Westminster] standards." Quoted in Earnest Trice Thompson, *Presbyterians in the South*, 3:210.

226. "Adam's body was directly fashioned." *Minutes of the General Assembly of the Presbyterian Church in the United States* (1886), 18.

226–27. "dead hand of the past." Ernest Trice Thompson, *Presbyterians in the South,* vol. 2 (Richmond: John Knox Press, 1973), 490.

227. "At the close of the nineteenth century." Ernest Trice Thompson, *Presbyterians in the South,* vol. 3 (Richmond: John Knox Press, 1973), 215.

227. "In proportion to our numbers." Quoted in "The General Assembly at St. Louis," *Southern Presbyterian Review* 26 (1875), 667.

227. "Is there no genuine Presbyterianism but ours?" Peyton Harrison Hoge, *Moses Drury Hoge: Life and Letters* (Richmond: Presbyterian Committee of Publication, 1899), 285.

227–28. "I hear brethren saying." Thomas Cary Johnson, *The Life and Letters of Robert Lewis Dabney* (Edinburgh: Banner of Truth Trust, 1977), 352.

227–28. "they have stripped every leaf." Ibid., 355.

229. "social embarrassments." R. C. Reed, *History of the Presbyterian Churches of the World* (Philadelphia: Westminster Press, 1922), 288.

229–30. "the weakness of the church." Harris A. Kirk, "The Presbyterian Mind," *Christian Observer* (May 22, 1929), 3.

230. "The question which now confronts." Ernest Trice Thompson, *Tomorrow's Church, Tomorrow's World* (Richmond: John Knox Press, 1960), 58.

232. "The so-called five points of Calvinism." Thompson, *Presbyterians in the South,* 3:215.

232. "deals with those actual evils." *Minutes of the General Assembly of the Presbyterian Church in the United States* (1935), 94.

232–33. "enforced segregation of the races." *Minutes of the General Assembly of the Presbyterian Church in the United States* (1954), 193.

234. "to call our Southern Presbyterian Church." Quoted in Paul Settle, *To God All Praise and Glory: The 25th Anniversary of the Presbyterian Church in America* (Atlanta: PCA Christian Education Bookstore, 1998), 27.

235. "to preserve a confessional Church." Ibid., 32.

236. "the real unity of the Church." Ibid., 55.

237. "we have called ourselves 'Continuing' Presbyterians." *Minutes of the First General Assembly of the National Presbyterian Church* (1973), 41.

Chapter 13: Vanishing Presbyterianism

239. "it is the responsibility." *Minutes of the General Assembly of the United Presbyterian Church in the United States of America,* part 1 (1975), 258–59.

240. "acceptable range" and "full deity and full humanity." Rodney Clapp, "Kaseman's Beliefs Ruled 'Within Acceptable Range.'" *Christianity Today* 25 (March 13, 1981), 358.

241–42. "unrepentance homosexual practice." *Minutes of the General Assembly of the United Presbyterian Church in the United States of America*, part 1 (1978), 265.

244–45. "The church expects of us." Jonathan F. Stearns, "Historical Review of the Church (New School Branch)" in *Presbyterian Reunion: A Memorial Volume, 1837–1871* (New York: De Witt C. Lent, 1870), 102.

248. "privilege and duty of confrontation." Francis A. Schaeffer, "A Day of Sober Rejoicing," address before the Tenth General Assembly of the PCA, June 16, 1982.

249. "The report is so eager." Camille Paglia, "The Joy of Presbyterian Sex," *The New Republic*, Dec. 2, 1991. Reprinted in *Sex, Art, and American Culture* (New York: Vintage, 1992), 36.

250. "in fidelity within the covenant of marriage." *The Constitution of the Presbyterian Church (USA): Part II, Book of Order, 1998–99* (Louisville: Office of the General Assembly, 1998), section G6.0106b.

250. "We believe that an amendment." "Letter to the Presbyterian Church," *More Light Update* 17:3 (Jan–Feb 1997).

250–51. "seriously hindered for the future." Lefferts A. Loetscher, *The Broadening Church,* 135.

251. "Presbyterians now engage sexuality issues." John P. Burgess, "Can't Stop Talking About Sex," *Christian Century* 110:22 (July 28, 1993), 733–34.

253. "the children have asked" and "they have no one to blame." Dean R. Hodge, Benton Johnson, and Donald A. Luidens, *Vanishing Boundaries: The Religion of Mainline Protestant Baby Boomers* (Louisville: Westminster/John Knox Press, 1994), 200.

Index of Subjects and Names

conversion, 68, 73, 204
Cornbury, Lord, 27–28
corporate witness of the church, 177, 186,
 194
Covenanters, 8, 18, 20–21, 24, 25
Covenant Fellowship of Presbyterians, 243
Cox, S. H., 118
Craighead, Thomas, 100
creedal subscription, 39, 41–49, 53–54,
 57–58, 60, 63, 65, 164, 182, 225
Cromwell, Oliver, 18
Cross, Robert, 63
culture war, 247–48
Cumberland Presbyterians, 5, 7, 100–101,
 164, 184–85, 193, 229, 243
Cunningham, William, 144
Cuthbertson, John, 22

Dabney, Robert L., 159–60, 175–77, 226,
 228
Dallas Theological Seminary, 234
"Danger of an Unconverted Ministry"
 (Tennent), 60–61, 66
Danville Theological Seminary, 107, 142
Darwin, Charles, 178–79
Darwinism, 193
Davies, Samuel, 66, 71
Davis, Angela, 220, 238, 241, 246
Davis, Clair, 202
Declaration and Testimony (1866), 162
Declaration of Commitment (1969), 235
"Declaration of Faith" (PCUS), 237
Declaration of Independence, 70
"Declaratory Statement," 184
Delaware, 13, 29
Democrats, 156
denominations, 246–47, 253–54, 260
Dickinson College, 105
Dickinson, Jonathan, 39–40, 41, 43–44, 45,
 48, 53, 54, 58, 64–65, 68, 258
Directory for Public Worship, 78, 85
dispensationalism, 234
diversity, 219, 247–48
"divine right" Presbyterianism. *See jure
 divino* Presbyterianism
Dobson, James, 260
doctrinal indifference, 176, 186, 194

Dodge, William E., Sr., 172
"Dominion of Providence Over the Passions
 of Men" (Witherspoon), 78
Doughty, Francis, 25
Duffield, George, 75, 120, 122, 125, 133,
 164, 258
Dulles, John Foster, 211
Duncan, John, 144
Dutch Reformed, 14, 24, 27
Dwight, Theodore, 152

ecumenism, 9, 172–78, 185–87, 198,
 212–16
 of Southern Presbyterians, 228–29
Edinburgh, 37, 38
Edwards, Jonathan, 40, 110, 111, 116, 121,
 133, 258
Edwards, Jonathan, Jr., 102
Edward VI, 1, 6
Eighteenth Amendment, 193
Eisenhower, Dwight D., 1, 210–11
elders, 3, 140–41
Ellsworth, Elmer Ephraim, 147
Ely, Ezra Stiles, 117
Emancipation Proclamation, 159
English Civil War, 15, 17
English Puritans, 6–7
episcopalian polity, 3
Erdman, Charles, 191, 195, 203, 204
Erskine, Ebenezer, 23
Erskine, Ralph, 23
"essential and necessary articles", 46–48
Evangelical Alliance, 170–71, 176, 185, 212
Evangelical Presbyterian Church (1956–
 1965), 221
Evangelical Presbyterian Church (1981–), 7,
 9, 240–41, 242, 253
evangelical Presbyterians, 257, 258
evolution, 178–79, 193, 226
exclusive psalmody, 206, 207–8, 228
Executive Committee on Overseas Missions,
 235

Federal Council of Churches, 173, 185,
 211, 212, 228–29
federal government, 160, 165
feminism, 219, 239, 242, 249

theological education, 55–57, 60, 104–8, 235
theonomy, 248
Thirty-Nine Articles, 28
Thompson, Ernest Trice, 226–27, 230–32
Thomson, John, 39, 40, 44, 42–43, 48, 53, 65
Thornwell, James Henley, 140–42, 157, 159, 223, 234
Tillich, Paul, 209
tobacco, 221
toleration, 196
Toleration Act (1689), 19, 28
tradition, 5, 246–47
transcendentalism, 131
Turretin, Francis, 110

Ulster, 17, 19, 20, 34
Union, preserving of, 151, 156–57, 165
Union College, 102
Union Theological Seminary (New York), 107, 136, 183, 209, 212
Union Theological Seminary (Virginia), 107, 175, 205, 231
Unitarians, 106, 132
United Church of Christ, 215, 240
United Methodists, 215, 243
United Nations, 213
United Presbyterian Church in the U.S.A., 213–14
United Presbyterian Church of North America, 164, 206, 213, 238, 240
United Reformed Presbyterian Church of North America, 24
United States Constitution, 91–92, 149
United Synod of the South, 150, 153, 159–60, 224–25
University of South Carolina, 226
urbanization, 171

Vander Velde, Lewis G., 163, 165
Van Dusen, Henry P., 192, 212
Van Dyke, Henry, 184, 188
Van Dyke, Henry J., 228
Van Til, Cornelius, 209–10, 218
Veto Act, 144
virgin birth, 192

voluntary church, 88
voluntary societies, 114

warfare, 219, 238
Warfield, Benjamin B.
   on church union, 185, 190
   on evolution, 179
   on inerrancy, 175, 182
   on revision of Westminster Confession, 183
Watts, Isaac, 86
"Way of Salvation" (Barnes), 119–20
Webster, Richard, 62
Weld, Theodore Dwight, 114, 152
Welsh Calvinistic Methodists, 164
Wesley, John and Charles, 59
Western Theological Seminary (Pittsburgh), 107
Westminster Assembly, 15, 17
Westminster Confession of Faith, 63, 67, 217. *See also* Adopting Act (1729); creedal subscription
   on biblical inerrancy, 181
   on Christian liberty, 79
   Cumberland Presbyterians on, 100–101
   Finney on, 110
   obsolescence of, 187
   revision of 1789, 84, 86–87, 147
   revision of 1903, 181–85, 206, 225, 228
   revision by southern Presbyterians, 232
   on spirituality of the church, 142
Westminster Larger Catechism, 15, 217
Westminster Shorter Catechism, 15, 101, 217, 262
Westminster Theological Seminary, 196, 200–201, 235
Wheeler, Barbara, 251
Whigs, 156
Whitefield, George, 51, 59–60, 62, 112–13
Wicca practice, 249
William of Orange, 19, 20
Willow Creek Church, 247
Wilson, John, 31
Wilson, Woodrow, 1, 189, 193, 226
Witherspoon, John, 1, 2, 70–72, 78–79, 81, 82, 105

Index of Subjects and Names

D. G. Hart studied American history at the Johns Hopkins University and has served as director of the Institute for the Study of American Evangelicals at Wheaton College and academic dean and professor of church history at Westminster Seminary California. He is currently the director for partnered projects at the Intercollegiate Studies Institute. His books include *Defending the Faith: J. Gresham Machen and the Crisis of Conservative Protestantism in America* (1994); *The Lost Soul of American Protestantism* (2002); *John Williamson Nevin: High Church Calvinist* (2005); and *A Secular Faith: Why Christianity Favors the Separation of Church and State* (2006).

John R. Muether (M.A.R., Westminster Theological Seminary) is librarian and associate professor of church history at Reformed Theological Seminary in Orlando. The coauthor of four volumes, Muether has served on the Harvard Divinity School library staff and has been librarian at Western Theological Seminary and Westminster Theological Seminary. He has served on the editorial board of Regeneration Quarterly and on the board of directors of Mars Hill Audio. He is historian of the Orthodox Presbyterian Church and serves on that denomination's Christian Education Committee.